S0-ASY-704

PELICAN BOOKS

A377

CHRISTIAN FAITH TO-DAY

STEPHEN NEILL

DATE DUE

GAYLORD 234			PRINTED IN U. S. A.

L.I.F.E. College Library
1100 Glendale Blvd.
Los Angeles, Calif. 90026

STEPHEN NEILL

CHRISTIAN FAITH
TO-DAY

1150

PENGUIN BOOKS

L.I.F.E. College Library
1100 Glendale Blvd.
Los Angeles, Calif. 90026

Pengui Books Ltd, Harmondsworth, Middlesex

U.S.A.: Penguin Books Inc., 3300 Clipper Mill Road, Baltimore 11, Md

CANADA: Penguin Books (Canada) Ltd, 47 Green Street,
Saint Lambert, Montreal, P.Q.

AUSTRALIA: Penguin Books Pty Ltd, 762 Whitehorse Road,
Mitcham, Victoria

SOUTH AFRICA: Penguin Books (S.A.) Pty Ltd, Gibraltar House,
Regents Road, Sea Point, Cape Town

—

First published in Penguin Books 1955

Made and printed in Great Britain
by The Whitefriars Press, Tonbridge

230
N317c

CONTENTS

The poem by Francis Thompson on pp. 148–9
is taken by kind permission of
Burns Oates & Washbourne Ltd
from
The Collected Poems of Francis Thompson

*

INTRODUCTION

THE faith of Jesus Christ is a faith for reasonable men.

This is not to say that it has anything to do with that 'religion of all reasonable men', which was one of the favoured inventions of the eighteenth century. In that age of reason, it was widely supposed that all men of honesty and culture could agree in the acceptance of a Supreme Being as the author of the Universe, of human immortality, and of some scheme of rewards and punishments for virtue and vice respectively, and that everything which went beyond these general convictions belonged to the realm of dogma and superstition. In a surprising number of the first constitutions of the States of what later became the United States of America, these three basic beliefs are laid down as the limits of religious toleration; one who does not accept them is an atheist – not to be tolerated, or at least not to be given civic equality or responsibility in the virtuous communities of the New World. Those who held such views had not observed that, in point of fact, it is not the general idea but the particular application which most readily engages the attention and the affections of men. Experience shows that, in a time of conflict, men are more generally swayed by local patriotism and loyalties than by a general sense of responsibility for the welfare of the human race. Nor had they taken account of the narrow limits within which the actions of men are really determined by reason. By the end of the century, men were beginning to realize the inadequacy of these ideas; in the early years of the nineteenth, some at least were willing to give ear to Coleridge's protest against purely intellectual process and in favour of understanding derived from other and deeper levels of human nature.[1]

Nor does the affirmation of the reasonableness of the

1. For an admirable exposition of the nature and significance of Coleridge's protest, see B. Willey, *Nineteenth Century Studies* (London, 1949), pp. 27-31.

Christian faith imply that its tenets can be arrived at by a process of logical deduction from first principles. The attempt to establish first principles and to carry logical deduction from them as far as it will go is a legitimate activity of philosophers. But the greatest exponents of this method have never supposed that religious concepts could either be derived from a process of intellectual reasoning or established by it. Beyond the world of the intellect lies the realm of faith. If religious truth could be established by logical argument, acceptance of it would be of the nature of intellectual assent and not of faith; each of these in its own sphere is admirable; but they are not the same thing, and without faith religion would no more be religion. Intellectual conviction cannot, by any process of accumulation, transform itself into the experience of faith in God. The passage from one to the other is, to use the phrase made popular by Kierkegaard, not a quantitative aggregation but a qualitative leap. Reason and faith may revolve about the same centre – Truth, or God, or what you will – but the transition from one to the other involves a leap from one orbit to another, such as is accomplished, as the scientists tell us, in certain conditions by the electron. The two are related to the same object, yet each is incommensurable with the other.

Still less should our initial affirmation be taken to imply that everything in Christian faith can be made quite clear and lucid, like a sunlit landscape, without mystery or paradox. Human nature itself is paradoxical and has its dark unillumined areas. As to the nature of mind and its relationship with body, philosophers still dispute merrily; it cannot be said that knowledge in that realm is much further forward than it was 2,000 years ago. If, in a world of experience which we know so intimately from within, we cannot go far without encountering mystery, it may readily be expected that, in trying to penetrate that world of ultimate reality which is the concern of religion, we shall soon come up against the mysterious and the paradoxical. But, if the recognition that we cannot know all about ourselves is not held to imply that we can have no reasonable knowledge of ourselves at all, the admission that, with the limitations imposed upon us by our present condition, we cannot know all about ultimate reality should not be taken to imply that we are debarred all reasonable knowledge of it.

The claim that Christianity is a faith for reasonable men is based on the conviction that religion, and in particular the religion of Jesus, is concerned with the whole of man's being. Man has discourse of reason, and this is the gift which principally distinguishes him from the beasts. How precious a gift this is can be learned only by the experience of serving those in whom the light of reason has been by ill-chance diminished or altogether extinguished. But, if reason is one of the best parts of man's equipment, it is impossible that religion should be related only to emotion; or interpreted solely in terms of ritual or devotional action, without reference to the judgement of man's mind; it is impossible that any religion should long survive, except through the conviction of its adherents as to its *truth*, or that any religion should affirm itself as fully adequate to man's needs, unless it can increasingly validate itself as an answer, such as man is at present able to receive, to his questions concerning the *truth* about ultimate reality.

From the very beginning the Christian Gospel has made its appeal to the consent of man's understanding as well as to the surrender of his will. This appeal is everywhere present in the words and teaching of Jesus Himself. It is remarkable that, in the Authorized Version of the New Testament, no less than nine Greek verbs are, in one context or another, translated by the word 'understand', and no less than four nouns are translated 'understanding'. With our present limited knowledge of Greek, it is difficult to distinguish precisely the connotation of these four words; yet they seem to cover between them the whole field of what in English we might define as the capacity for reasoned thought, ratiocination, discernment, and spiritual penetration. The demand for understanding is one of the most characteristic features of the teaching of Jesus: 'Do not ye yet understand?'[1] 'How is it that ye do not understand?'[2] Again and again, when men put questions to Him, the burden of His answer is, 'You know the answer already, if only you will use your own common sense'. What else is the significance of such a parable as that concerning the Good Samaritan? Willingness to reflect on ordinary experience and to make reasonable inferences from it seems almost to be, in His judgement, an indispensable condition for entering into the Kingdom of Heaven.

It must readily be admitted, of course, that there is a great deal more in the Gospel than this appeal to reason. It must be admitted also that many, perhaps the majority of religious people, do not feel any great need for reasoned explanations. The faith has come to them as an inheritance, accepted almost without question on the authority of revered elders and teachers; its behests are carried out as the expression of simple and humble obedience. There is always the danger that such obedience may become merely mechanical, and that a faith uncriticized may degenerate into superstition; but, since religion is more a matter of the will than of the mind, of obedience than of speculation, to deny the reality of such religion would be sheer intellectual arrogance. The apostolic succession of simple people, no less than the acumen of the theologians, makes possible the continued existence of a religion as a living faith.

Nevertheless, there are also those to whom religion can mean nothing, unless it shows respect for them as reasonable creatures, and finds a link between the processes of faith and those of the understanding.

There are those who, having sincerely accepted the Gospel as a way of life, and having committed themselves to follow and to serve Jesus Christ, find that they can make no further progress, unless the intellectual content of what they have been led to accept in faith is worked out in a more or less systematic way; unless the different parts of the faith are seen in some relationship to one another as parts of an at least in some measure intelligible whole; and unless some

1. Matthew xv: 17. 2. Matthew xvi: 11.

light is thrown on the relationship between their new-found faith and their other intellectual activities. Such have found themselves called, in the phrase of the second Epistle of Peter, to add to their faith virtue, and to their virtue knowledge.[1]

Others, while attracted by the Christian faith, know well that a certain intellectual scrupulousness will make it impossible for them ever to commit themselves to it, unless doubts and questionings have first been faced with absolute honesty. The clearing away of intellectual questionings cannot of itself lead on to faith. But such seekers desire to be assured that, if faith goes beyond reason, it is not irrational in the sense of being nonsensical. They wish to see the congruity of the affirmations of faith with those things that they believe, or know, to be true in other fields of knowledge and other aspects of life. They may go so far as to hope that, though Christianity cannot conclusively be demonstrated to be true, it may at least be possible to establish, in Bishop Butler's phrase, a reasonable probability, on which a man may act without prejudice to his honesty.

Such a demand is not evidence of resistance to truth or of unwillingness to learn. It is legitimate and honourable; to satisfy it, as far as it can be satisfied, is the specific task of Christian apologetics.

The apologist desires to produce conviction; but it is his aim to produce it under strictly observed conditions of academic integrity. His task is to set out the facts in the plainest possible way, and to submit them to the unfettered judgement of the reader. It is impossible to dispense entirely with presuppositions: thought must start somewhere. But the presuppositions should be as few as possible; they should be such as are likely to command general acceptance, and such as are common to the intellectual approach to all subjects of academic study. Above all, the honest apologist must make perfectly plain to the reader what his presuppositions are. He may suggest the desirability of provisionally accepting certain hypotheses or making certain assumptions, on the

1. 2 Peter i: 5.

clear understanding that the validity of these hypotheses and assumptions will be tested according to the ordinary rules of evidence and inference. Such provisional or tentative acceptance involves no intellectual dishonesty; indeed there is hardly any other known method by which thought or science can make progress. What the apologist must be on his guard against is the use of presuppositions, which have been tacitly introduced without explication, and which, if they had been made explicit, the reader would have found unacceptable.

Any exposition of the Christian faith by a convinced Christian must be of the nature of a *Confessio Fidei*. The apologist sets out his case because he passionately believes it to be true, and because he regards it as desirable that others also should come to see that it is true. But the apologist is an evangelist in chains. He has accepted from the start the exclusion of emotion from the presentation of his case; it is not within his province to make a definite appeal for decision. Yet all the time his aim is to produce the kind of conviction which leads on to action.

The reader cannot but be aware that, however moderate the exposition, and however scrupulous the regard for his intellectual integrity may be, any statement of the Christian faith is bound to present him with a great many questions, on which he will have to make up his mind. 'Under which King, Bezonian?'[1] The answer cannot be indefinitely postponed; indeed, the attempt to postpone decision is itself a decision of a particular kind. The greater part of the material contained in this book was originally given as a series of 'open lectures' sponsored by the Faculty of Divinity of the University of Cambridge. The last lecture ended in a silence that could be felt; evidently the hearers realized that any statement of the Christian Gospel involves a challenge, and that it was no longer open to them to be strictly neutral. If any reader is prepared to pursue the argument of this book to its conclusion, he may find that he too is faced by a challenge, and he will be in no doubt as to the sense in which the writer wishes him to make up his mind. It may be hoped

1. *Henry IV, Pt. II*, Act V, Sc. 3, line 116.

that he will feel that the argument has been honest through-out, that no hidden presuppositions have been illegitimately slipped in, and that the decision he is asked to make is not to be swayed by any extraneous or irrelevant considerations. If he is a true student, he is pledged in advance to follow the argument whithersoever it may lead, and to yield his allegiance to anything that, in the course of his voyage of intel-lectual discovery, may have commended itself to him as the truth.

I

MAN AND HIS WORLD

THE Christian missionary 'to the heathen', living surrounded by and in intimate contact with adherents of other
and non-Christian faiths, is very well situated for getting his
mind clear as to the nature of the religion which he professes
and teaches. What is the faith by which he really lives?
What is it that makes it different from these other faiths, of
the truth of which their adherents are as firmly convinced
as he is of the truth of the Christian revelation?

The missionary living among Hindus very soon realizes
that Christianity is a historical religion, and that Hinduism
is not.

The history of India is as a whole not very interesting.
Invasions take place. Dynasties rise and fall. But there is no
clear and continuous development of political ideas and
experiments. What gives its dignity and stability to Indian
history is the continuity and the evolution of religious and
philosophical ideas. Long before the beginning of the
Christian era the main ideas had already shaped themselves
– the unity of all real existence; the unity of the spirit in man
with the unchanging and invisible reality behind the universe;
the iron law of *Karma*, the principle that a man must 'eat
the fruit' of his own doings and pay the price of sin; rein-
carnation as the means by which this payment is made
possible; salvation as final deliverance from rebirth into this
changing world of unreality. In varying forms these great
ideas recur, and their determinative influence is felt through
the whole subsequent period of more than 2,000 years.

Of course in this long history Hinduism has had its outstanding personalities. There are the great figures of the
epics, legendary, yet perhaps in part historical – Rama and
Sita, Draupadi and the Pandava brothers. There are the
interlocutors in the fascinating discussions of the early

Upanishads, some of whom at least must have been real people, as real as the characters in the equally fascinating dialogues of Plato. There are famous philosophers, Sankara, Ramanuja, and the rest. Yet it is possible for a man never to have heard even the names of these leaders of thought and action, and still to be a perfectly good Hindu. If he accepts some or all of the dominant religious ideas, and adheres to the law and custom of that caste into which he happens to have been born, he is a Hindu, and nothing can invalidate his claim to this title.

As against this religion of timeless ideas, Christianity takes its place with, for example, Buddhism and Islam, among the historical religions of the world.

Both Buddhism and Islam, like Christianity, look back to founders, the location of whose careers in time and space is verifiable and well known. Historical criticism has established that Gautama the Buddha was born in North India, not far from the frontier of what is now Nepal, in the first half of the sixth century B.C., and that he died just about the time at which the Greeks were fighting their epic battles against the Persians. Of Muhammad we can say with certainty that he was born in Medina and that he died in Mecca; and the dates of his birth and death have been determined, with almost perfect accuracy, as having fallen respectively in 578 and 633 A.D. The career of Jesus is known to have taken place in an easily identifiable region, and at a period, the first century of the Roman Empire, about which we have a great deal of contemporary information.

Yet these similarities may mislead, unless certain differences are also noted.

Gautama was one of the noblest of the sons of men. The early stories of classical Buddhism are irradiated with a peculiar charm, a strangely moving Eastern parallel, perhaps, to the *Little Flowers* of St Francis, in which also an exquisite literary setting and a certain admixture of legend cannot conceal that peculiar grace and gaiety which Francis introduced into a troubled world. But the Buddha is first and foremost a teacher, the herald of a doctrine. He is venerated by all true Buddhists as the Enlightened One and the Enlightener. Paradoxically in a religion which strictly speaking has no place for the idea of God, in certain regions the Buddha has become the object of adoration such as in other religions is accorded to God alone. Yet the truth or otherwise of his doctrine does not depend intrinsically on any connexion with the Founder. If it is true that desire is the origin of all men's ills, and that salvation comes through the elimination of desire and the following of the noble Eightfold Path, this would remain true, even if Gautama had never been born, and even if the revelation had come in some entirely different fashion.

The position of Muhammad in Islam is even more central than that of Gautama in Buddhism. The brief Moslem creed affirms that there is no God but Allah, and that Muhammad is the prophet of Allah. Other prophets have come and gone and had their day; but now the final word of God to men has been spoken. To have had the honour of being the recipient of that revelation raises Muhammad far above any other man among the sons of men. But the uncompromising monotheism of Islam had made it impossible that any Moslem should ever think of Muhammad as other than a man among men. He may be the intercessor for the faithful at the last day. But he is not to the Moslem what Jesus is to the Christian. The difference may be briefly indicated in the fact that from a very early date it has been the habit of Christians to end their prayers 'through Jesus Christ our Lord'. In Islam there is no corresponding formula.

Jesus also was a teacher. But Christianity is not the acceptance of certain ideas. It is a personal attitude of trust and devotion to a person. That person is believed to be alive and accessible to all. The nature of the relation of the Christian to Him is described in such phrases as 'whom not having seen ye love', 'that Christ may dwell in your hearts by faith', 'Christ in you the hope of glory' – phrases which recur on page after page of the New Testament, and make clear that it is this intimate and personal relationship of

17

trust, devotion, and communion, which is the very heart of Christian faith.

It is, of course, possible to construct a Christian philosophy. The sayings of Jesus are so rich in content and so profound in penetration as to afford the basis for a total view of God, the world and man. Indeed, the working out of such a philosophy may be held to be one of the tasks necessarily laid on the faithful. But, if such a doctrine or set of ideas is separated from the history in which they are rooted, the situation is falsified and truth becomes something other than Christian truth. Some years ago, an able philosopher endeavoured to separate the pure gold of Christian truth from the historical alloy with which it has been compounded, and to show that, even if it could be proved that Jesus Christ had never existed, these ideas being timeless would still be true and valid for us; on which a great New Testament scholar, Dr F. C. Burkitt, remarked, 'God may not be in time; *but I am*'.

In Christian faith, the event and the meaning of the event cannot be separated. The Creed is mainly an enumeration of things which happened; Jesus was born, He died, He rose again. It is unalterably tied to time and place in history by the note that these things happened 'under Pontius Pilate'. Christianity is the affirmation, not of certain things which Jesus said, but of certain things which God did. God accepted history as the medium in which He would work. And if God was specially active in those events which concerned Jesus of Nazareth, this can only be, from the Christian point of view, because He is always active in the affairs of men. All history is His concern, and it is there, if anywhere, that He is to be found.

It may be well to emphasize a little at this point the radical difference between idea and event, and so to indicate in advance the divergence that is likely to arise between systems centred on one or other of these two poles. History is that which flows in one direction only. Pure thought, like much scientific experiment, can move freely in either direction. We may begin with first principles or hypotheses, and develop them logically to their furthest possible conclusions; or we may begin at the end and work backwards to the first principles implicit in any conclusion. Both these are legitimate and useful methods of thought. But in history processes are not reversible. The future is full of an indefinite range of possibilities. 'Now' is the indeterminate moment, in which all is fluid and yet to be. But as soon as it is past, it is frozen solid; only one of the many possible things has come to pass, and all the other possibilities are for ever excluded. If an event has happened, even God cannot make it not to have happened, though He may open up another vast range of possibilities consequent upon it. But that event is now a permanent part of the structure of the universe. It *was* as event; it *is* for ever as consequence. If Christianity is true, it is in this irreversible flow that God has been pleased to act; it is through this partly refractory material that He has been pleased to bring to effect His great designs.

This means that the Christian faith, though it is a message of eternal life, is committed to taking time very seriously. It is concerned with men and women as beings existing in time and space. It cannot accept that dichotomy which regards the body as an inferior substance, of its nature perishable and therefore insignificant, and the soul as a separable entity, belonging by its nature to another and more enduring world. It is here, in the ebb and flow of human experience that man, body and soul, if he is redeemable at all, must be redeemed.

The Christian view of history can be thrown into relief by contrasting Christian faith at this point with two other great areas of human thought.

It is not surprising that India has produced no great school of historical writing. At first sight it may appear strange that in these great literatures, so rich in epic and drama, in lyric and in philosophy, history should be represented by a blank. Yet so it is. The history of India has to be reconstructed slowly and painfully from archaeological data, and from chance allusions in works on other subjects. Long periods are still almost dark. The establishment of chronology depends on the contact of India with other races, and in particular on the invasion by Alexander the Great in the fourth century B.C. But, if we take into account one constant characteristic of Indian thought, this lack of historical interest and record is just what we might expect. The concentration of the Indian mind on the unchanging unity which lies beyond the changing surface of events has been so intense as to discourage attention to the passing phenomenon. The visible world is *māyā*, illusion, unreality; it has no more stability than the changing panoramas of the clouds. What profit then to spend time and energy on rendering permanent in writing that which of its very nature is impermanent?

The Greeks did write history, and were indeed the pioneers in historical writing in the West. Yet even in this great achievement there is perhaps an element of scepticism. Plato, dependent in part on older sources, had set forth the view that *being* can be predicated only of that which does not change, and that, since evidently this phenomenal world is always in process of *becoming*, nothing that can be correctly called knowledge can be obtained concerning it, but only right opinion. Later, Stoicism made popular the view of the grand return, in which all things in the end come back exactly to what they were before. The movement of history is cyclic. There is an unending process of expansion and withdrawal, but no true development. In this sphere nothing is ever permanently gained or finally lost. If this is so, history can have no final significance; this is not a world in which eternal significance can attach to acts and events in time.

To the Christian, all history presents itself as a unity. It is the sphere of the unfolding, of the development, and finally of the consummation, of a single divine and all-embracing purpose. That purpose began to be manifest when God first said 'Let us make man in our own image'. Its full significance will be evident only when human history reaches its end, and in the light of that fulfilment all the earlier stages will at last be fully understood. The significance of history is not to be found in itself, but in relation to God, and in the conviction that actions and decisions in time can and do have eternal consequences.

Since the purpose is literally all-embracing, it is concerned with all men and all nations. But it is not concerned equally and in the same way with all at all times. In fact it shows a discernible pattern, first of concentration, and then of expansion. The shape is that of the hour-glass, broad at both ends, but narrowing down to an orifice through which only a single grain of sand can pass.

The Bible opens with a section in which the subject is the dealings of God with the whole human race. But this universality is soon exchanged for concentration on the fortunes of a single chosen people, through whom for a period the main development of the purpose is to go forward. Other nations are not forgotten, but for the time being they are marginal. It is in the life and destiny of Israel that the maturing of the purpose is to be seen. But this first narrowing of interest is not the last. At a given point, at least four-fifths of the nation disappears into captivity, and thereafter plays no significant part in the unrolling of the future. The centre of interest is now the tiny kingdom of Judaea, no bigger than an English county, and with a population of little more than 100,000 people. A small enough stage, if what happens there is really of universal significance to mankind. But thereafter even that people is carried away into captivity, from which after the best part of a century only a small impoverished remnant returns to carry on the old tradition. As we approach the central point of history, with the birth of Jesus of Nazareth, the greater part even of that remnant is found to have become unfaithful; only a minority, within which are to be found Jesus and His disciples, is faithful to the sense of vocation and is looking for 'the redemption of Israel'. At the crisis, even that small group disintegrates. Jesus is deserted even by His friends; He dies forsaken and absolutely alone. At this point, the great purpose depends utterly and solely on Jesus – on His faithfulness and His obedience and on nothing else. At that moment, He is Israel; He is the people

21

of God; He is the incarnation of the purpose of God with His world.

But from that turning-point all is changed. From now on the purpose is a message to be proclaimed to all men everywhere to the very ends of the earth. The ministry of Jesus was confined to the soil of Palestine; His work was done within a Jewish setting. Now the Gospel has emerged from the cerements of the past; all limitations of geography, race, and tradition are to be broken through, and it is to stand forth in its universality as the word of God for all mankind. From that time on the history of the world has been, from the Christian point of view, simply, to borrow the title of a now famous work, the History of the Expansion of Christianity. Nation after nation has been brought within sound of the Gospel, as those who were far off have been brought near, and those who were on the margin have been brought back into the central stream of the purpose.

In the twentieth century the purpose has reached a new and remarkable phase of its development, since for the first time history has to take account of a hitherto unknown phenomenon, a universal religion. Of course Christianity is not universal in the sense that all nations or all men have accepted it. It is nevertheless true that it is to be found in every quarter of the globe, and in almost every country. Every considerable language in the world now has its complete Bible. There is no racial stock, no tradition of culture, no form of social organization, which has not yielded at least some adherents to the Christian message. The word has been able to make its appeal to every level of human intelligence, from the scholar learned in the most esoteric mysteries of the Brahmans down to the pigmy in his impenetrable forest. Quite apart from the question of the truth of the Gospel, with which we are not at the moment concerned, this world-wide spread of the Christian Church is at least a most remarkable phenomenon, and one worthy of far more attention than has been directed to it by the majority of secular historians.

Let it be noted that we are not at this point demanding

assent to the Christian view as to the meaning of history. We are simply setting out, as objectively as possible, the convictions and concerns of a number of religious systems; and, as this book is to be mainly concerned with the Christian religion, it has been necessary to state the Christian view as well as others. However odd it may appear, these are the things which Christians believe. The reader may reach the same conclusion as Browning's *Cleon*, that

> (as I gathered from a bystander)
> Their doctrine could be held by no sane man.

In any case, he will not be asked to exercise a judgement as to truth or falsehood until the end of our long course of investigation has been reached.

Since the whole of this investigation will be carried on within the framework of history, and largely in historical terms, it is necessary to remind ourselves as forcefully as possible at the outset of the pitfalls which always lie in the path of the historian. History can be perverted to become one of the more ingenious and baser forms of propaganda. We know now that the Victorian dream of purely objective history is a myth; it is impossible to separate fact and interpretation, and the historian always contributes a full measure of his own experience and his own understanding of life to the material which he handles. It is his besetting danger to read into history what is not there, and to find patterns which are discernible only because they first existed in his own imagination, and were thence projected on to the pages of history.

It will be sobering to set down the warning issued, in relation to his own work, by an eminent historian of modern times. Dr H. A. L. Fisher, in the Preface to his admirable *History of Europe*, informs us that:

One intellectual excitement has been denied me. Men, however, wiser and more learned than I, have discerned in history a plot, a rhythm, a predetermined pattern. These harmonies are concealed from me. I can see only one emergency following upon another as wave follows upon wave, only one great fact with respect to which, since it is unique, there can be no generalizations, only one safe rule for the historian: that he should recognize in the development of human destinies the play of the contingent and the unforeseen.[1]

The reader of this deservedly popular *History* might remark that, in spite of this disclaimer, there is in it some evidence of a predetermined pattern, since the book is in fact the history of the rise, the slow development, the triumph, and the temporary eclipse of the liberal idea. If this is so, and if, in spite of his own caution, Dr Fisher has in fact written history to a pattern, this simply adds emphasis to the warning he himself has given against facile generalization and the premature drawing of morals.

A similar warning may perhaps be drawn from another source. No historical work in modern times has attracted greater attention or more intensive study than Arnold Toynbee's *Study of History*. The six volumes which were first to appear are packed with interesting and recondite information, and no one, however erudite, can read them without learning a great many things that he did not know before. And yet one reader had not reached the end of the first volume before he began to feel twinges of anxiety. Does history fall into patterns as neatly as this? Is it so simple a matter to classify and arrange all the civilizations that have appeared since the beginning of recorded time? Has Mr Toynbee established a little too quickly his categories or pigeon-holes, and then fitted facts and phenomena into them, without sufficiently regarding the strangeness and infinite variety of human experience? Have all the facts been considered, or are there elements of special pleading in this versatile and brilliant presentation of so much that is of interest to the human race? Is what we find in these volumes history as it really happened?

The warning is needed by both writer and readers. But to say that it is difficult to approach history with complete objectivity is not the same as to say that the study of it is valueless for our purpose; it reminds us only of the danger of confusing certainty and probability, and of building struc-

1. H. A. L. Fisher: *A History of Europe* (London 1936), p. v.

tures on hypotheses which have not been adequately tested against the facts.

Certainties in this world are very much fewer than is generally supposed. One of the difficulties of the apologist for religion is that many hearers come to him, asking him for something that he cannot give and ought not to offer. He cannot provide such certainties as are available in simple mathematics; he cannot even provide the relative certainty of the physical sciences. He can offer only a series of converging possibilities and probabilities; in the end what transforms probabilities into assurance is not intellectual reasoning, but the experimental verification provided by the adventurous action called faith.

Our study will begin, therefore, very cautiously with possibilities, some of which may in course of time develop themselves into probabilities. And since the theme with which religion is concerned is so vast – nothing less in fact than the ultimate reality which lies behind the changing phenomena of the visible universe – we must start by asking ourselves some apparently peripheral but really central questions. These can perhaps be reduced to three:

What kind of a universe is this?

What kind of things happen in it?

What kind of purposes can be formed and carried out in it?

If we find reason to suppose from the start that the kind of things that religion claims, and the Christian religion in particular affirms, are in the strict sense of the term impossible in this universe, of which we have after all some experimental knowledge, then our quest ends before it has begun. Religion is not worth the attention of serious men and women, and we may profitably turn to the differential calculus and other gayer themes.

Let us start, then, with the general question as to what kind of a world this is in which we live.

Our first answer must be that it is a *dangerous* world.

When I was an undergraduate, Miss Rose Macaulay delighted us with a book entitled *Dangerous Ages*. The dangerous ages in that entertaining work were twenty-three, forty-three, sixty-three, and eighty-three. If that be true, it is hard to imagine what ages are not dangerous for the human species. What has been so wittily described by the novelist in relation to the individual may well be extended to the race. For the race of men upon this planet, all ages are dangerous ages, our own no less than any other. Three centuries ago the philosopher Thomas Hobbes expressed the view that the life of man was nasty, brutish, and short. We may take exception to one or other of his epithets; we can hardly doubt that man's tenure upon earth is, always has been, and as far as we can judge always will be, *precarious*.

On 2 May 1902 Mont Pelée in the island of Martinique blew up. One moment the inhabitants of the pleasant town of Saint Pierre were going about their business as on any other day; the next they had ceased to be. In a few minutes the town of 28,000 inhabitants had been blasted out of existence. There were only two survivors of the disaster.

On 30 June 1908 a large meteorite fell in the Siberian waste. It has been calculated that it must have weighed about 40,000 tons. The shock of the impact, the intense heat and the tempestuous wind generated by it, spread desolation over an area of 2,000 square miles, and laid flat 80,000,000 trees. By good luck that area was uninhabited; but there was no particular reason why the meteorite should not have fallen in the middle of Moscow; if it had, it would at once have been evident that, though man is not inept as the pupil of nature, the very worst that he has yet been able to achieve in the way of destruction is trivial when compared with the destructive potentialities that lie about us all the time in nature.

On 30 October 1937 the asteroid Hermes moved some distance out of its regular orbit, and drew considerably nearer to the earth than was normally to be expected. Hermes is one of the smaller bodies in the solar system, and its erratic conduct caused no particular damage. But, if its irregular journey towards us had been continued, it is large enough to have exercised considerable effect by its gravitational pull on the stable regularity of the movement of the earth about the sun. What happened unexpectedly in one year might well happen, less harmlessly, in another.

On that stable regularity of the earth's behaviour we are dependent for our existence. Apart from the possibility of sudden destruction, such as might arise through collision with some other heavenly body, we need only consider the effects which would follow upon a slight alteration of the mean temperature over the planet. A general rise of 20°F would reduce much of the surface of the earth to uninhabitable desert; a fall of 20°F would bring back the ice-age to many now rich and smiling areas. Science and inventiveness have done much to reduce the perils of man's existence; but there are forces all about us against which the wit of man is completely helpless. And, as soon as one danger is averted or brought under control, it appears that another grows, like the seed of dragon's teeth, to take its place. For the first time in history, the general birth-rate has come through medical skill greatly to exceed the death-rate. As a result the population of the earth has quadrupled itself in the last 300 years. The rate of increase is likely to become even more rapid in the future. For the first time, pressure of population upon soil is no more a local but a world-wide problem; the experts are not agreed as to whether better exploitation of natural resources will make possible an increase in the production of food commensurate with the increase of population.

Disasters and perplexities such as I have mentioned are sometimes felt to present a grave problem to those who would justify the ways of God to man. Were the people of Saint Pierre sinners above all others that the wrath of God should suddenly descend upon them out of heaven? Why should one suffer, when another is spared? The perplexity arises from a wrong formulation of the problem, a mistaken conjecture as to the purpose for which the world was made. If that purpose was that all men should at all times be happy and comfortable and prosperous, and that the affairs of men should be ruled by such even-handed justice that all would obtain exactly what their deserts required – then I hope I shall not be judged irreverent if I say that I think I could have managed things a great deal better myself.

If there is any purpose in the universe at all, it cannot be that which men so often and so wistfully imagine it to be. If there is any such purpose, it can only be a purpose relevant to the situation of a race of men, living always precariously on an ageing planet with a crinkling, contracting crust; surrounded perpetually by the perils of earthquake, eruption, typhoon, and tidal wave; their little life rounded by a sleep; faced at all times with the possibility of instant precipitation into the unknown, and vowed irremediably to final and total destruction.

If this were the whole story, history could be nothing but the record of man's fruitless and indignant striving against a foe who in the end is always bound to win. But there is another aspect to the situation. The universe is friendly as well as hostile. It is a universe with which a man can enter into relationship and in which he can make himself a home. It presents itself to him under the aspects of beauty and wealth as well as under the aspect of danger.

And even danger and difficulty are not necessarily destructive features in the human situation. Arnold Toynbee has summarized the origin of civilizations under the formula *challenge* and *response*; the challenge of a difficulty, and man's response, through self-adaptation such as is required for mastery, and through mastery to new possibilities of living. If one purpose of life in such a universe is the education of man through having to fend for himself in the face of difficulty, it is hard to imagine how a better educational instrument could possibly have been devised.

In point of fact, man's power of self-adaptation and his inventiveness in the face of new situations are almost unlimited. He manages to hold on where everything in the situation seems to work against him. The Esquimaux have survived for centuries under conditions which to those unused to their way of life might appear as intolerable hardship; through centuries of adaptation they have developed skills in the use of limited and unpromising materials such as have made it possible for them to maintain a way of life which, if always perilous, is at least endurable and at times even pleasant.

The oddest thing about man is that, where difficulties do not exist, he delights to create them for himself. Even the most primitive races delight in puzzles, and carry them to a very high level of elaboration. Where civilization has eliminated the physical difficulties of living, it is man's pleasure to recreate them for himself. If one asks the young men who will cheerfully spend a winter on the ice-cap of Greenland, or set themselves to scale a yet virgin peak, why they do these foolish things, they may make reply in terms of the value of scientific discovery; but that is merely rationalization; the fact is that man likes to pit his wits and his strength against some formidable obstacle, and in some strange way finds the fulfilment of his being in triumph against heavy odds. No account of man's nature is complete which does not include this odd and unexpected trait. Apparently man thrives on difficulty; and, if that be true, a universe which swarms with difficulties may not be such a bad universe for man to live in as might at first appear.

To hold his own against nature, to win round after round in the ceaseless battle against circumstance, man has two main instruments – understanding and experiment. It is idle to ask in any given situation which came first. In one field, man may have begun with the search for truth, for an answer to the questions that his ranging mind had presented to him, and subsequently discovered the usefulness of the discovered answer for the handling of some pressing problem of practical life. Or man may have begun with experiment, and gradually seen that various experiments all pointed in one direction, thus finding his way to a principle through which all the experiments could be held together in a unity. Whichever be the order of his seeking, each bears witness to man's search as always a search for *unity*. It is through an understanding of the relatedness of things that mastery over them can be achieved.

It might be thought that such a search for unities came at a very late stage of human development, and it is certainly probable that the formulation of the search in such terms demands much greater capacity for abstract thought than is within the range of primitive man. Yet an expert in the psychology of primitive peoples may be called on to testify that this element is present in the search from the very beginning; Mr Murphy has written:

An avenue of approach to the psychology of primitive man may be found in the principle of the Quest for Unity, which it appears to us is fundamental in human nature. It is a tendency traceable and profoundly influential through all Man's thinking and practical life, as soon as, and wherever, he is recognisably human. Its presence in the life of civilized Man needs no demonstration. Mr Bosanquet defined reason as 'the Spirit of Totality', and again as 'the nisus towards the whole'. Certainly the characteristic activity of the mind, from the formation of a general idea to the great system of Philosophy, from the humblest perception of nature to the laws of science and the uniformity of nature itself, from the vaguest conception of Spirit to the majestic unity of the Supreme Personality of Religion, is the endeavour to create wholes in thought, to organize experience into some form or other of coherent totality. . . . A larger range of phenomena and activity is opened to man than before; and for a time they elude the grasp of his mind and of his practical endeavour to reduce them to some unity of mental comprehension or some form of unified life. He wanders about in the wide new field, trying many wrong paths and culs-de-sac, making many false integrations, before his unifying power is sufficiently developed to form the new and higher integration.[1]

Man thrives on difficulty. He accepts the challenge of his surroundings. He seeks to find a unity in his world, and so to render it friendly and manageable. His first contact naturally is with the physical and visible world about him; it is there that he makes his first stumbling and hesitating efforts to find the unity behind the bewildering variety of phenomena.

We may suppose that at first nature presented itself to

1. J. Murphy: *Primitive Man: His Essential Quest* (London, 1927), pp. 24–5, 29.

primitive man, as it still presents itself to the child, as a series of unrelated and unpredictable happenings. The first step forward is not so much a discovery of unity – that would be far too grand a title for such elementary lessons – as the observation of certain uniformities. Most of these observations were made so long ago that we have no certainty as to where or by whom they were first made. One of the greatest revolutions in man's life took place, perhaps towards the end of the Neolithic age, when it was realized by man, or more probably by woman, that upon the planting of certain seeds certain plants would grow, and that this would always be so, one seed being related to one particular kind of plant and to no other. This knowledge is certainly not innate in the mind of man. Each one of us must have learned it at some time or another in our childhood; it is said that some tribes among the Australian aborigines have not yet acquired this knowledge. We have no means of saying with certainty (though archaeology has afforded certain indications) when this great discovery was made; once it was made, man had potentially within his hands the whole of the science of agriculture. The observation of uniformities led on to understanding, and understanding rendered possible that measure of mastery over the world, without which a settled life for man the hunter might have remained for ever impossible.

As observation extends, man generalizes his understanding and eventually reaches that idea of the unity and regularity of the world, which is expressed in popular speech in terms of 'the laws of nature'. At once the question arises whether these uniformities are really there in nature, or whether man has simply imposed upon nature his own unifying tendencies, and discovered what he is pleased to call laws, by the simple process of having himself first inserted them into places where they do not in reality exist.

It may be at once conceded that there is no such thing, even in the physical sciences, as absolutely objective knowledge. In all study there are two factors, the 'thing as it really is', and the mind of the student. The mind is creative;

it inevitably projects something of itself into the subject that it studies. But to admit that there is a subjective element in all knowledge does not commit us to the view that knowledge is purely subjective, and that exact knowledge of external reality must remain unattainable by man. To admit the subjective element is to recognize the possibility of error and even of delusion. But we must start by affirming vigorously the principle that the existence of error does not exclude the possibility of truth; error may be pure illusion, but it may also be the distortion of an existing reality, and progress from error to truth is often arrived at by way of the progressive elimination of the factors of distortion.

The scientist can give good ground for his conviction that in discovery he is not merely imposing the pattern of his own ideas on a more or less passive nature. He can point to the uniformity of his results, and the uniformity of the results obtained by many workers in similar spheres. He can point to the possibility, within limits, of true prediction from his results. Some time before the planet Neptune was observed by the telescope, the presence of another planet beyond Uranus had been inferred from calculations based on the failure of Uranus to follow the orbit which had been charted for it; from these irregularities, the distance, size, and mass of the hypothetical planet had been established to a considerable degree of accuracy, and the path that it should follow had been traced on the map of the heavens. The empirical observations merely confirmed, and in some degree modified, what had in principle already become known. This is a good illustration, also, of the way in which some unexpected factor at first seems to disturb the principles which had been deduced from observation, but then in the light of further study is seen actually to confirm them. Finally there is the way in which research in one direction arrives helpfully to confirm investigation in some other sphere. The physical scientists were in process of reaching certain conclusions about the inner structure of matter and the atomic world which is the basic material of our visible world. The discovery by the great telescopes of the dwarf stars, and the analysis of them by the spectroscope, un-expectedly gave physicists the opportunity to study the behaviour of matter at far higher temperatures than their laboratories could possibly achieve, and so came in, as it were, by the back door to confirm the provisional results of terrestrial experiment.

What the scientist does not always observe is the element of faith which underlies even his most rigidly scientific work. The uniformity of nature cannot be logically demonstrated. The fact that a piece of matter behaves in one way to-day in no way guarantees that it will behave in the same way to-morrow. In fact we all assume that it will, and the practical usefulness of this assumption is established by the success of the scientific work which without it would be impossible. But the assumption is an act of faith; an act of faith very much like that which the religious man makes concerning the stability of the universe under another of its aspects, though different in the range of its application and in the use which is made of it. If the scientist, challenged to stand and deliver, affirms that his faith in the essential oneness of the universe and its regularity is a faith for all reasonable men, the man of religion, since in his own sphere he asks no more for himself, may well be prepared cheerfully to assent to this claim.

If the scientist starts with the assumption of a unity, the whole aim of his purpose is to establish and extend a unity of understanding. When a multitude of separate phenomena have been brought together under a small number of easily expressible principles, and the relationships between them are understood, to that extent unity of understanding has come to correspond to that unity of existence which the scientist believes himself to be discovering as already present in the world. There is still very much to be discovered; the unknown beckons the observer forward as challenge and inspiration. And each truth, as it is discovered and verified, serves not as ultimate satisfaction, but as the platform on which the observer can penetrate still further into that which is as yet unknown. Many scientists to-day would accept as a true statement of their own position, and of their humility in relation to that totality of truth which in its oneness far transcends their own particular field of studies, the remarkable utterance of Isaac Pennington in the seventeenth century:

All truth is a shadow except the last. But every truth is substance in its own place, though it be but shadow in another place. And the shadow is a true shadow, as the substance is a true substance.

Yet one more point remains to be emphasized. Progress in knowledge is never in a straight line. There is always the possibility of error and of aberration, of hasty deduction from accurate observations, or of misleading deduction from imperfect observation. But the presence of error does not invalidate truth; and the possibility of error, or even its prevalence over long periods, does not invalidate the claim of the physical sciences to be means which man may use in the confident hope of arriving at certain kinds of truth. For centuries astrology was as reputable a study as astronomy, and still holds a fascination for certain kinds of mind. If astronomy, i.e. science, was to increase, it was necessary that astrology, i.e. pseudo-science, should decrease. But it was only slowly and with infinite labour that the mind of man disengaged itself from a confusion which could only have the most harmful consequences. This is how Sir Charles Sherrington depicts the conflict, in terms of the experience of one particular man:

Wholly against the current of his time [Fernel] grew more and more sceptical of astrology as any true reading of the meaning either of the heavens or of disease. ... Fernel's defection from astrology seemed to many of his contemporaries a strange and lamentable backsliding for a man of liberal view and learned culture. His distrust seemed a reaction against perhaps the most wonderful chapter in the whole of science. We know it now as a chastening of knowledge in the interest of truth. ... When he had tested astrology and found it to be untrue, he eschewed it as a guide. If it were not true, it could not contribute to his system of Nature. His system of Nature had to coalesce with his religion. If astrology were not true it could not be consistent with his Christian convictions. It and his religion then could not harmonize. Fernel could not suffer two versions of the world.[1]

The prevalence of pseudo-science over a long period must not be allowed to create prejudice against the claims of genuine science to respectability. It will be important to bear this in mind, when we proceed to argue that the existence of superstition or pseudo-religion must not be allowed to prejudice in advance the claims of certain forms of religion to be true or to be the truth.

1. Sir Charles Sherrington: *Man on his Nature* (Cambridge 1946), pp. 60–61. The whole section pp. 51–66 is intensely interesting and valuable. Also published in Pelican Books, 1955; see pp. 63–4.

2

DISCOVERY AND REVELATION

MAN's relationship to the physical world does not exhaust his experiences with his environment. As soon as he begins to think at all, he becomes aware of another world, that surrounds him. This is sometimes called the moral world; but for the moment, to avoid using a word which at the moment may seem to claim too much, we will call it simply the world of personal relations, the world in which men meet men as men. The contact of man with man is generically different from the contact of man with things, or even of man with animals. In this world too we shall find man constantly at work in a search for unity. Are there any universal principles which govern this world of human experience? Can we here find anything which in its way corresponds to what in another sphere we have called the laws of nature?

What does it mean to be a man? We are not concerned here with scientific definitions, but simply with the observable fact that there is a wide range of experience which is common to all races, and to almost all adult specimens of the human race, unless they happen to be idiots or morons. Folk of different races can become aware of this common universe of discourse, even when difference of language excludes the ordinary medium of communication – articulate speech.

The discovery of this common humanity has again and again come as a surprise to men who ordinarily live shut up in the complacency of their own insularity. In the second book of Virgil's Aeneid, Aeneas tells the tale of Troy and of his own sufferings to the barbarian queen Dido, and she weeps; and the amazed Aeneas exclaims in one of the most famous lines of Latin literature: *Sunt lacrimae rerum, et mentem mortalia tangunt*. 'Even here, in uncouth Carthage, men and women can weep; they feel things just as we do.' This naïve discovery was put to useful service by the practical Romans in the development of what was known as the *ius gentium*, the law of the non-Roman peoples. Peoples may be strange; but the relations between them, or between them and Romans, must alike be governed by justice; and this is impossible, unless there is some substratum of a common human nature underlying the varying forms of men's ideas and the differences in the customs of their race or civilization.

It is perhaps in the development of law that we shall see most clearly evidence of man's striving after unity in this world of human relationships.

Tribal law is usually no more than case-law; a number of decisions are handed down from the chieftains of the past, guarded in the memory of the elders of the tribe, and applied, with greater or less success, to any new cases that may happen to come up. Ordinarily, this body of traditional law or lore (it is sometimes hard to make the distinction) is quite unsystematized; it covers certain areas related to what the Western world regards as moral codes of behaviour; but also others which are much more nearly allied to traditional taboos or mere prejudices. All these things co-exist. Something of this ancient tradition is represented in the curious jumble of the ancient Israelitish codes, as we find them in the books of Moses, where precepts of the highest ethical majesty are found close alongside sanitary regulations and precepts which seem to belong to the primitive world of magic, indeed almost of fetishism.

The greatest service rendered to after ages by the Romans was in the field of law. The great Roman lawyers tried to pierce through the multiplicity of cases, decisions, and traditions to the simple and permanent principles underlying each. Many of their discoveries were set forth in those pithy, epigrammatic phrases – *cui bono*, *caveat emptor* – which have become proverbial just because of their truth and the range of their application. To this day, the young student of law begins his training by wrestling with the Romans and their ancient wisdom.

Two more modern developments indicate further stages in the efforts of man to find within his world a unity of moral experience. The first is the development in modern times of international law, the earliest exponent of which was the versatile Dutchman Hugo Grotius in the seventeenth century. The second is the attempt, under the auspices of the United Nations, to arrive at a universal declaration of human rights. It has to be admitted that the progress so far made has been disappointingly small, and we may be led eventually to conclude that agreement on such matters must depend on prior agreement on some of the deeper problems which belong to the sphere of religion. For the moment we are concerned with nothing more than the fact that the effort has been made, as evidence of man's unappeasable striving towards a unity of understanding and action as yet unattained.

If the progress seems negligible, as compared with that achieved by the physical scientists, we may point in the first place to the immensely more complicated character of the material which has to be dealt with. The moment that human character and personality enter in, purely statistical methods to a very large extent lose their value. No one man is exactly like any other man, and any general statement which robs him of his particularity so far fails to include him, as himself, in the generalization. And phenomena of *relationships*, being to a large degree invisible, though to some extent susceptible of being inferred from gesture, speech, or action, do not lend themselves readily to investigation under the microscope of the scientist. Techniques of investigation which are relevant elsewhere are useless here, and quite new techniques have to be devised.

Further, account has to be taken of exceptions and aberrations. When I was a theological teacher in India, my students tended to assume that the ten commandments had fallen down from heaven in exactly their present form, and were, in principle, universally acceptable throughout the human race. I found it very useful to perplex them by pointing to the existence in our midst of wandering tribes, criminal in tendency, whose ostensible way of earning their living was basket-making, but who lived far more by stealing than by work, and among whom, as among the ancient Spartans and in certain spheres not unknown in England, the only crime was that of being found out. Where is the eighth commandment in such surroundings? It does not take long to see that aberration on one point may well arise, without totally excluding those who suffer from it from the general fellowship of mankind. The question to ask in relation to such peoples is, 'Are they totally devoid of a sense of right and wrong, of justice and injustice, even if such sense as they have works differently from that of their more numerous neighbours?' There can be hardly a doubt as to the answer that has to be returned to this question.

A more serious difficulty is presented by the phenomenon of retrogression. It appears that a whole community, or the whole of its leadership, may arrive at a pathological condition, in which all the generally accepted principles of justice go by the board, and everything is interpreted in categories which bear no relationship at all to the common convictions of the larger society of which that community is a part. It does seem that Germany, during the Hitler time, came very near to such a pathological condition of a whole nation. What is interesting, however, is that so many other nations, and not only from motives of self-interest, did condemn this situation as pathological, and as a betrayal of all that had been so laboriously learned in this area of human discovery.

Codes and moral convictions vary bewilderingly in different ages and in the several areas of the world. It might seem difficult to find any basis for common judgement or understanding. Yet there are certain indications that the confusion is no more than superficial, and that underneath it there are possibilities of genuine understanding.

Many people would find it extremely hard to define what they mean by justice; but anyone who has ever suffered *injustice* knows perfectly well what it is; the feeling is as unmistakable as that of being scorched with fire, even when the one who has suffered has no words adequate to describe his experience. The interesting thing is that, even among the most primitive peoples, the man who has suffered what he regards as injustice will say of the one who has wronged him, 'He *ought* not to have done it'. By this he unquestionably means, though he may not have words to define what he means, that the one who has done the wrong has offended against some permanent standard external to them both, by which he is judged and condemned, even though the weakness of the one whom he has wronged makes it impossible for condign vengeance to be carried out against him. Far back in the beginnings of Indo-Aryan thought is the principle of *ṛta*, the order of the world which must at all costs be maintained; and this order is concerned with what a more developed consciousness recognizes as moral principles.

The counterpart of the sense of injustice is the sense of ultimate obligation. Nothing is more certain, and nothing more irritating to a certain type of historian or moralist, than the willingness of men to die for a cause. It is indeed possible that the cause for which a man will die is trivial, or would not commend itself to the general conscience of mankind. The Communists have their martyrs no less than the Christians; but this does not commend Communism to every observer. But again, we are concerned only with the phenomenon that men do so act. Life is the most precious thing that a man has. If he is prepared to throw it away, it can only be because he recognizes something outside himself as more precious than the most precious thing that he has, as having on him an ultimate and inescapable claim for loyalty and devotion. And it has further to be noted that on the whole this perhaps futile sacrifice wins the approbation of mankind in general. It is only in periods of extreme degeneracy that folk in general scoff at the principle anciently laid down as *dulce et decorum est pro patria mori*. And this approval of the sacrifice is wholly distinct from approval of the cause in which the sacrifice has been offered.

No attempt to explain such action in terms of anything

other than a sense of ultimate obligation has really been successful. In a great many recorded instances the acceptance of death has been unaccompanied by any inner glow of heroism or triumph. Often the man who sells his life is haunted by uncertainty as to whether the sacrifice is really worth while or will lead to any notable result; it is just that he cannot act in any other way. Readers of Col. Fergusson's notable book *Beyond the Chindwin* will remember the fine passage in which he comments on the greater sacrifice made by those who had no belief in resurrection, and therefore could not be moved by any hope of ultimate compensation for themselves, or any assurance of the ultimate triumph of goodness over badness in the world; it was just that they could not act in any other way. An earlier generation, in the pre-debunking age, might even have hazarded the observation that *noblesse oblige*.

It is this sense of absolute obligation which lies behind the absolutes of ethical injunction. Certain schools of ethical interpretation have attempted to show that 'thou shalt not' really means no more than 'I rather wish you wouldn't'. In the jargon, it is semi-jussive. That may be cleverly argued, but it really is not so. An ethical affirmation cannot be made, except with the underlying conviction that that is the way the world is made, and you act against the universe at your peril. That is what it means to be a man; and, if you would be a man, you must needs recognize that manhood is a privilege which at times must be purchased by giving and losing the most precious thing that you have. To accept and to affirm the world may involve you in denying yourself.

Is there any reason to believe that there is a moral, as well as a physical, constitution of the universe? As we have already remarked, when considering the scientist's faith in the uniformity of nature, this is something that cannot be logically demonstrated; but there is much that points towards it, and it can be accepted provisionally as a working faith for reasonable men. Since the moral world, if it exists at all, is immaterial, it is even less susceptible of either experimental or logical demonstration than the kind of material with which the physicist is dealing. Yet here once again there are certain things which can be affirmed. Man knows that he can never be at home in a universe which is made up merely of things, and in which values have no place. The world of human relationships is a world of values. Many things point towards the conclusion that some attitudes and actions run along the grain of the universe, and others run contrary to it; this is really what is meant by describing some attitudes and actions as moral and others as immoral. To define this grain of the universe, to state exactly in what it consists, is most difficult; it is not therefore surprising that mankind as a whole has not made very much progress towards certain and universally acceptable definitions of it. Yet such failure need not be taken as too discouraging, since the desire to know and to understand seems still unquenchable in a large part of the race; man wants to know what is his status as a responsible being, in a universe which at least appears to be not wholly unresponsive to responsible action.

The two aspects of the universe that we have considered do not exhaust man's possible relations to it. Beyond the world of things and that of persons, there is a possible world of ultimate reality. Beside the attitudes of curiosity and of responsibility, there is the third possible attitude, that of awe, which may run all the way from sheer superstitious terror up to the rapt and mystical contemplation of the saint. There is no doubt that this is a peculiarly human characteristic and almost universal. No race, however savage, has yet been found and brought under scientific investigation, which has not the capacity to worship and to pray. Man is conscious of something that we may call, for convenience and without at present defining it, a spiritual world and of himself as a spiritual being. And here, as in our other two fields, we shall find a constant yearning of man after unity: unity of understanding and apprehension; a sense of stability through contact with one single, unchanging spiritual principle of being and of value.

We have noted that the law and custom of a primitive tribe present themselves to our systematic Western minds as disorderly and chaotic. Exactly the same is true of the tribe in its relation to whatever it believes to exist in the way of unseen powers; indeed it could not be otherwise, since so large a part of the law and custom of the tribe is concerned with what, for the moment and again without defining the word, we may call its religious ideas and observances. Over a large part of the world's surface men are still living in the animistic stage. The world is peopled with active spirits, mostly malevolent, more active by night than by day; and much of the activity of the tribe must be directed to placating these spirits, at least averting evil, if the acquisition of positive good is too much to be hoped for. It is impossible to systematize these beliefs and practices. They are not related to any moral principle – as in Homer, the best of men are often more virtuous than the gods. If a spirit is offended, this is far more often unaccountable than attributable to the violation of some moral canon. For the most evident characteristic of the spirits is that they are capricious; no one knows what they are likely to do next, or why they will do it. It is for this reason that the animist lives almost continuously in a state of fear. As a Balinese Christian once remarked to the writer, no Balinese much likes to go out of doors after dark – a point that is not generally noted by the tourists who rhapsodize over the natural and artistic beauty of that fantastically beautiful island.

But man cannot rest in a chaotic world. He pines for order and stability. And even among the animists this is not the whole story. There is evidence from many parts of the world of another, deeper, and perhaps older, stratum of primitive conviction about the universe, in which the figure of one great God is more or less dimly discerned. Pater W. Schmidt of Vienna became convinced that this conviction, so widespread, and found often amongst the most primitive races of the world, was a part of an original revelation of God to man; that this was the truly primitive, and that the other stages of the religion of primitive man were an overlay and a corruption. He wrote nine large volumes to prove his case. Anthropologists as a whole are not convinced that the evidence really bears out the whole of Pater Schmidt's conclusions. But the evidence that he has collected is impressive; it suggests that this instinct for unity, this sense that the world cannot be understood or really lived in without belief in some simple spiritual principle, is not an idea intellectually reached by Western man at a high stage of his development, but that it is something deeply present in man as man; a thirst which is part of him from the beginning and cries out for satisfaction.

A study of the religions of mankind makes evident the presence in almost all of them of this quest for unity.

This is the whole underlying theme of Greek philosophy – to find that One at the heart of things through which the existence of the many can be explained. The Greek approach is so intellectual that one can hardly speak in this connexion of religion. Yet when Plato comes to speak of the One as he has discerned it, the great unconditioned Idea which at times he seems to identify with the Good, his approach to it appears to be marked by what one can only call reverential awe. And by the neo-Platonist Plotinus the experience of mystical self-identification with the One is described in terms of passionate exaltation that have inspired mystics down the ages ever since.

Classical Hinduism is monistic. It affirms the absolute oneness of all true being. Differentiation is mere illusion. The *Ātman*, the principle of life in man, is the same as *Brahman*, the principle of being in the universe. To know this is liberation; *tat tvam asi*; 'that art thou'; live in this conviction of the oneness of all things, and you attain to deliverance from the curse of separate existence and from imprisonment in the world of illusion.

Three great religions, Judaism, Christianity, and Islam, are monotheistic, in the sense that all believe in one God, who is above the universe and above mankind, and yet is concerned with them; who is the master and ruler of the universe and of men.

The one apparent exception is in the dualistic religions, which have had a great history, but at the present time have few adherents. Such religions understand the whole universe as the scene of an unending conflict between two powers, usually identified as light and darkness, to which terms the moral significance of good and evil is sometimes also attached. Yet at least in certain cases the difference is less absolute than it seems. The two powers are not regarded as absolutely equal. Man is called to stand on the side of the light, to choose. There is a hope, if not of the final destruction of the dark power, at least of the total separation of the two, so that the light may dwell self-contented within itself, and with all that of right belongs to it.

Here, more urgently than in our consideration of the two previously considered aspects of the world, we must ask frankly the question whether there is any reality corresponding to our thoughts, or whether the whole thing is merely imagination. Just because the objects, real or supposed, with which man's religious search is dealing present themselves as being of their very nature immaterial and intangible, the question, while it presents itself as one which demands an answer, is at the same time extremely difficult to answer. Many people at the present time are prepared to dismiss the whole realm of religious faith and experience as no more than wish fulfilment. It would be pleasant for men if there were such a spiritual principle behind the world, binding it into a spiritual unity, and providing an explanation of much that else remains perplexing. And therefore man has been only too ready to project his own fears and desires upon the sky, and to call into existence a better, though quite unreal, world, to redress the injustices and to console the disappointments of this all too real and ever-present world. The Freudian explanation of religion as simply the projection upon the sky of infantile fears and hopes has spread down through popularizations and penny manuals, until it has become widely known and almost unquestioningly accepted by a great many simple folk who know little or nothing of the career of Sigmund Freud.

In answer to all this we may answer, in the first place, that the Christian is perfectly well aware that there is no conclusive demonstration of the truth of the things that he believes. It is quite possible that he is wholly wrong; if indeed he is so, he will be manifestly the fool of all the world. This is no more than to say that the principle 'Who chooses me must give and hazard all he hath' is relevant in a great many more contexts than the fanciful scene in the *Merchant of Venice* in which the words occur. That there is no final certainty, in religion any more than in science, does not mean that either of these fields is unworthy of the attention of a serious man.

Secondly, we shall remark, in this field as in others, that the presence of error or aberration need not lead to a universal scepticism, any more than the sturdy existence of astrology over so many centuries leads us to doubt the better authenticated conclusions of astronomy. We may, and should, frankly admit the existence of a great deal of bad religion; religion that is based on evidently false ideas of the nature of the world; religion that degrades or corrupts those who practise it; religion that enslaves the minds and wills of its devotees at a primitive level of experience or intelligence. But in such a connexion we cannot admit the principle that bad money drives out good. The presence of so much counterfeit money will teach us that it is wise to scrutinize carefully every coin that comes our way; it will only enhance the value of every coin that can work up for itself a respectable case as being the genuine thing.

Thirdly, we will excuse ourselves from going further into the matter now, on the ground that, if the general argument of this book has any value, that value lies in the fact that it is cumulative, and to attempt to answer now questions to which the whole of the book is an attempt to find an answer would be premature and proleptic. It is only at the very end that the reader, who is also judge, will be asked to give his summing up and to pronounce his verdict.

There is, however, one important matter, relevant to all our three worlds of discourse, to which attention must be directed at this point. We have tended all through to speak as though the objects of these various fields of study remained inert and passive under the hands of man, who had nothing to do but examine. We have now to take up the question whether this way of thinking and speaking of things is just and adequate. We may find reason to think that the so-called objects of our thought and of our search are themselves active in the process, and that it is only the abstractions of our thought that remain inert and wholly subject to our manipulation of them.

It has been customary in the past to speak of inert matter, as though the world was on the whole made of lumps of stuff just lying patiently about, until man comes along and puts them where he wants them to be. The development of modern physics has put all that for ever out of our minds. Men of my age still recall the pleasure with which they read long ago Sir Arthur Eddington's delightful development, in his Gifford Lectures on *The Nature of the Physical Universe*, of an answer to the question why we do not just fall through the floor. The common-sense answer is that we do not fall through it because it is solid, whatever that may mean. No, says Sir Arthur; the floor is very far indeed from being what you call solid; in fact only about one part in eleven hundred of it answers to that description. What supports you is the violent tattoo which the atoms and electrons, in their perpetual and unimaginably rapid dance, are beating all the time on the soles of your feet. Nature is now seen as a world of intense activity, impinging all the time violently upon our senses, and affecting us by a multitude of unseen agencies and rays. We are engaged all the time in a two-way traffic of exchange with our environment. An attitude of purely objective detachment towards it is something that we can attain to with difficulty, if at all.

This is the merely physical side of it. But there is something deeper in the experience of man as he approaches nature with the desire to know her, of which this mere physical exchange is, if I may dare to use here a religious term, sacramental. It is the experience which can be adequately described only by one word, 'revelation'. I should have hesitated myself to use this word in this connexion, were it not that I could call Professor Coulson to my aid. The evidence of the Professor of Applied Mathematics in the University of Oxford, supported by the testimony which he adduces of another distinguished scientist and former colleague of my own, encourages me to affirm something for which my own slender scientific knowledge would be a quite inadequate foundation. Professor Coulson writes:

Truth is a relationship between ourselves and some reality. . . . That suggests to me that truth, whether scientific or otherwise, has about it this quality of revelation or encounter, in which something is given. Sir Lawrence Bragg, who followed Lord Rutherford in the Chair of Physics at the Cavendish laboratory in Cambridge, gave a lecture using these words: 'When one has long sought for the clue to a secret of nature, and is rewarded by grasping some part of the answer, it comes as a blinding flash of revelation; it comes as something new, more simple and at the same time more aesthetically satisfying than anything one could have created in one's own mind. This conviction is of something revealed and not something imagined.'[1]

Ethical and legal principles present themselves to us in the form of highly developed abstractions. But that is not the starting point of experience. The moral world, as we have said, is the world of personal relationships and obligations. Experience of life in society is prior to the most elementary thought about the nature of societies. For every man it begins literally and pre-eminently with the moment of his birth, since all men are born into a family; and, where two or three are gathered together for any purpose whatsoever, there are also present at least in embryo all the law and the prophets. Problems of social living, otherwise called ethical problems, do not arise in a calm world of abstract speculation, though such speculation may be helpful in analysing and controlling them; they thrust themselves upon us every moment, because we live in a world of men moving in their own independent and largely unpredictable orbits.

We are aware of this world of human relationships only because it reveals itself to us by its activity. Men move to-

1. *Question*, Vol. VI, No. 1, pp. 37, 39.

wards us. They too reveal themselves in speech, in gesture, in activity. It is through this ceaseless activity that we become aware of others as independent selves with rights of their own. The problems of life are given to us as wholes in experience, before we begin to understand them as problems, or seek to elucidate their inner nature and connexions; here too the impression is of something revealed and not of something imagined. The nature of society, and therefore of the world of moral problems, is already present in the smallest human group, the family. Consciousness of it grows with us as we grow, though our understanding of its nature may never become very deep.

In our third world, that of religion, it is legitimate to pose exactly the same question. Is there also some activity prior to our own, which comes to meet us as we seek it? Is it possible that here too there may be a possibility of something not imagined but revealed? Is divine revelation a phrase to which some intelligible meaning can be attached?

Many great minds have affirmed the contrary. The divine, if it exists, must be conceived as so sublime as to be incapable of any activity or concern outside the sphere of its own perfection. One of the greatest minds to hold this view was that of Aristotle, and his exposition of this view is so classical that it must hold our attention for a few moments. In the eleventh book of his Metaphysics, he sets out the argument as follows: essential Being cannot be subject to change, which is a state of *becoming*; now both activity and motion involve change; therefore the Primal One must be conceived of as remaining for ever absorbed in passionless and immobile self-contemplation. The argument is summed up in the immortal phrase, κινεῖ ὡς ἐρώμενον; the One, though itself remaining unmoved, is the source and cause of motion in all other things, because it draws them as the lover is drawn by the beloved. This is a noble, though somewhat frigid, understanding of deity, and has been immensely influential in the history of thought; perhaps we may see traces of it in a well-known Christian hymn:

O strength and stay, upholding all creation,
Who ever dost thyself unmoved abide.

But we must not exclude the possibility that Aristotle may be wrong. We must not *a priori* exclude the possibility that the divine is active and self-revealing, and that here, as in our two other fields, we may hope that our encounter is with something not imagined but revealed. We are not at this point affirming that this is so; and we may yet find reason to doubt whether such revelation is possible or has actually taken place. We are merely safeguarding the place of this view as among the possibilities that must be seriously considered, and which it is not legitimate for the unprejudiced seeker after truth to discard in advance of investigation.

In point of fact, we shall find that most of the great religions of the world are familiar with the idea of revelation.

This is certainly true of classical Hinduism. In the course of its long history Hinduism has moved far away from the doctrine and practice of its sources. Yet the Veda, parts of which must be older than the oldest parts of the Old Testament, is for all sects of Hindus inspired Scripture; it is the thing seen and heard by the inspired men of old; all that comes after is commentary and explanation, and on a lower level of authority.[1]

The starting point of the life of Israel as a nation is the tremendous scene in the Book of Exodus, where God comes down in fire and terror upon the mount of God, and speaks with Moses face to face; Moses on behalf of the people receives the revelation of the covenant of God.

Muhammad, in solitude in the desert, receives the conviction that he is called to be the prophet of God, and hears the command to write; he is only the mouthpiece, through whom the word of Allah can be uttered to men. He is superbly conscious that, of all that he proclaims in the name of God the merciful, the compassionate, nothing is really his own; his is the hearing ear which is able to catch the utterance of the Unseen.

1. The writings which together make up the Veda are *Śruti*, the thing heard; all other writings are tradition, *Smṛti*, the thing remembered.

Accepting for the moment, hypothetically, the possibility that the Unknown may be active, and may desire to reveal itself to men, we must next proceed to the question how such revelation, if it is indeed a possibility, could suitably be conveyed to men.

When the word 'revelation' is used, there is an almost overwhelming tendency to think of it in terms of divine dictation, of divine communication of laws or truths set forth in the form of propositions. A good illustration of this can be found no further away than the British Museum. There the visitor can see, on the famous black stele, king Hammurabi of Babylon, the contemporary of Abraham, standing before his god to receive from him the legislation which is to be promulgated and which is written on the stele. The king cannot set forth his laws, unless he has first received them from the divine lawgiver; and, when he has received them, what he writes is to be understood as divine revelation.

It must be admitted that the account in the Book of Exodus of the giving of the law to Moses does rather closely resemble the scene pictorially represented on the black stele; it is not surprising that many Christians imagine the ten commandments to have fallen down from heaven exactly as they are written in the Bible. Indeed, one of the difficulties people have in understanding the Bible is that, unaware of the long process of development in thought and writing that lies behind it, they imagine it to have come from God all in one piece, and so are perplexed by the evident unevenness of the various parts of which the Bible is made up.

Now it is part of our agreement that we shall not exclude any possibilities, however remote; and we must recognize that revelation in the form of propositions, containing truths or moral commands, is not wholly inconceivable. We can say, however, that if revelation in this form does exist, it would be incongruous; it would not correspond with what we have found to be true of man in his relation to the other worlds, or the other aspects of the world, by which he is surrounded. We must expect the world of religion, if any

L.I.F.E. College Library
1100 Glendale Blvd.
Los Angeles, Calif. 90026

such world exists, to be different from other spheres and worlds; it would, however, be disturbing if we found that it was *wholly* different, and obeyed laws to which no parallel at all can be found in other spheres. If, on the contrary, we found that man's progress in knowledge of the divine showed at least some resemblance to his progress in other realms of knowledge, we might feel that such correspondence was more congruous to the wholeness of our experience of life; which after all, however much we analyse it into different fields and aspects, does remain in the experience of each single member of the human race one single whole.

We have already noted the view of several scholars that, in man's contact with the natural world, that world meets him as active and self-revealing. Yet nothing is made easy for him. Here are no clear and simple formulas ready to hand. Everything has had to be learned by long and painful effort, by the tedious processes of trial and error. And in this process the world has often shown itself to be dangerous. If we had made the world, doubtless we would have arranged it otherwise; as in *Alice in Wonderland*, all the nice and useful things would have borne little labels, saying 'Eat me', 'Drink me', and the dangerous and harmful things would equally have borne some warning sign. In this hard and real world it is not so. The only way by which we could ascertain the peculiar properties of the castor-oil bean was by eating it, and, as in *The Swiss Family Robinson*, observing the distressing effects of it on those in whom the sword of bold experiment was not guarded by the scabbard of prudence. It is only by slow and hard toil that man has attained to such knowledge of his environment and such mastery over it as he now possesses.

From the beginning of time man has lived in societies. But it is only very gradually that he has reached certain convictions as to the nature of society, and as to the principles on which it should be founded. The Western world has long been convinced that the best basis for society is the family, in which one man and one woman live permanently in a relation of loyalty and co-operation. (However widely denied in practice, through the prevalence of irregular sexual relations and of divorce, the principle seems not to be very widely questioned.) Over large parts of the world, as, for instance, in Islamic countries, this basic principle is not accepted. And all kinds of other experiments have been tried – polygyny; polyandry, once widely practised in India, and still surviving among the Todas; matriarchy, in which succession is not through the father but through the mother and her family, and so forth. It is only through experiment, which must include aberration, retrogression and dead ends, that a stable body of knowledge can be attained. The ancient world, even on its most civilized levels, took it for granted that society cannot exist without the institution of slavery. Over a very large part of the world to-day it is taken for granted that slavery is incompatible with human dignity and worth, and that it degrades and corrupts a society in which is exists. But how hard the struggle through which this conviction was reached; and how passionately, less than a century ago, even Christians in the southern States of America defended the naturalness and rightness of slavery. It may be that polygamy and capitalism will follow slavery into the limbo of abandoned and discredited *mores*.

To turn now to the world of religion; even if we posit the possibility of revelation, it is not necessary to suppose that the human response to revelation would be one of immediate acceptance and total understanding. The parallel with other fields would be much closer if such response were partial, hesitating and confused, and if progress towards knowledge of the truth were conditioned by much error, much uncertainty, and at times by retrogression from the level already attained. If this were so, it would not surprise us to find that revelation was from less to more, conditioned to man's capacity to receive it. This view of revelation is set forth for us with splendid eloquence in the opening verses of the Epistle to the Hebrews: 'God, having of old time spoken unto the fathers in the prophets by diverse portions and in diverse manners, hath at the end of these days spoken unto us in his Son.' If that really is the way it works, the scientist and the historian may find themselves much less uncomfortable than they had expected in the world of religion, and may find that the methods religion uses in its attempt to understand itself are much more analogous than they had supposed to the methods they are themselves accustomed to use in their respective fields.

A revelation which is conveyed by diverse portions and in diverse manners can hardly be other than a revelation given through history.

No sooner is this affirmation made than we have to face the scandal of particularity. History is concerned not with general ideas, but with particular things that happened once and only once to particular people. What right have we to attach a special significance to some events and not to others, and in particular, as Christians do, to one life, lived at one time and place and no other?

This difficulty is not really so great as at first appears. If Christ is, as Christians affirm, the central point of history, then He must be relevant to all history, and all history must be relevant to Him. But to say that all must be relevant is not to say that all must needs be equally significant. An illustration from a parallel though different aspect of history will at once make this clear.

It is generally agreed that in the development of civilization certain epochs have been marked by special fecundity and creative power; and that, through the expansive process which follows upon creative achievement, such epochs have been specially significant for the whole subsequent development of the human race. Among such epochs that of the great Athenian achievement stands supreme. Attica is hardly larger than an English county. In the great period, the total free population can hardly have been larger than that of contemporary Oxford. Yet in the 150 years which elapsed between the production of the early plays of Aeschylus and the death of Aristotle, Athens produced masterpieces in drama, in history, in oratory, in philosophy, in architecture, and in sculpture, which are still the delight and admiration of the whole civilized world. Even more remarkable than the quality of the achievement has been its power to inspire others. Captured Greece took captive its Roman conquerors, and was the inspiration of the brief and glorious period of classical Latin literature. Again and again the human spirit has returned to bathe itself in the waters of Hellas and to drink of its spirit – the spirit of wonder, of enquiry, of proportion, of self-discipline – and has found itself recreated and renewed. The poet was not exaggerating when he wrote:

> But Greece and her foundations are
> Built below the tide of war,
>
> .   .   .   .   .   .
>
> Her citizens, imperial spirits,
>   Rule the present from the past,
> On all this world of men inherits
>   Their seal is set.

For our own purpose the most important consideration is that what began as the achievement of one small people has been found to be of universal value, and has become the common property of mankind; the Greeks have brought their treasures into the city of God.

How is this sudden flowering of genius to be explained? Why was it that something of the same splendour appears in Florence on the confines of the medieval and the modern worlds? Why was it that Elizabethan England stands second only to Athens in the production of masterpieces of literature and music? Learned explanations may be given in terms of the mixture of races and cultures, of the peculiar intensity of life in the city-state, of challenge and response, and of the stimulating effects of great perils successfully endured. Yet when all this has been said, are we in reality very much nearer to an explanation? Is it not the case that genius follows its own laws, appears as it will and unpredictably, and leaves the human race for ever in its debt?

If we find that, in the realms of art and civilization, special significance attaches to certain areas in space and certain periods in time, it is not unreasonable to suppose that a similar phenomenon may manifest itself in the religious development of mankind. A true religious revelation must be intended for all mankind. But it is not necessary to infer from this that the revelation must be universal, in the sense of being given to all men or to all races equally and to all at the same time. It is at least possible that the religious experience of one race may be seen to have, in the history of religion, a central significance similar to that of Athens in the history of civilization. It is even possible that one period in the life of one country and people may come to be seen as crucial and central in the history of man's discovery of himself and in his relation to the self-disclosure of the divine.

Judaea is a small country, at its largest extension larger than Attica, but still much smaller than the whole of Greece. But the part which it has played in human thought is out of all proportion to its size. Apart from any question regarding the truth of Jewish ideas about God, or of that Christian faith which grew out of them, no one can write a history of the Western world without paying the closest attention to the religious experience of the Hebrew people. In the Western world we are all, whether we admit it or not, part Greek, part Hebrew; some of us inclining more to one pole of the ellipse, and others to the other, yet none of us able to free ourselves wholly from this ancient inheritance, whether our relation to it be one of acceptance, or of reaction and revolt. In the course of our study many religions will come before us. But since we are in the Western world, it seems not unreasonable to start with a consideration of some features in the Jewish religion, particularly in the context of that which at the moment specially interests us, the possibility of a divine revelation.

The Old Testament is not a book of general ideas about God and man; it is in the main a book of history. It is concerned with a God who reveals himself to man. But here what is offered is not simply a revelation which has occurred *in* history, as having been granted to one particular race in certain centuries of history. It is the history itself which is the revelation. History is seen as a succession of the acts of God; from these acts the nature of God and His demands upon men begin gradually to be understood. But act does not become revelation until it becomes also word; we must next ask how, to the Jew, history becomes the vehicle of the word of the Lord.

The answer, succinctly, is that revelation becomes possible only through the co-operation of three separate factors. There is first the event which merely occurred. Secondly, there is the brooding mind, which pondering the event, sees it as meaning, and, as the interpreter himself would say, under the influence of divine inspiration apprehends the event as the disclosure of a divine act and a divine purpose. Thirdly, there is the lucid and memorable speech, through which this understanding of God at work in history becomes the common possession of many men, who by their sharing in this understanding are constituted in a special sense as a people of God. The people of Israel were convinced that, when they came out of Egypt, the waters of the Red Sea divided before them to allow them to escape from the pursuing hosts of Pharaoh. The mind of the seer ponders what might be no more than a meaningless piece of wonder-working, and interprets it as divine activity related to a plan. The splendid and vivid narratives of the Book of Exodus, in which event and poetic interpretation are so closely woven together that it is hardly possible to separate them, make event and interpretation alike a permanent part of the life and experience of Israel through all the ages. All history in the Old Testament is prophetic history, history understood in the light of a divine purpose. All prophecy in the Old Testament is prophecy based on history, constantly recalling the people to the memory of the great events of their past.

The idea of the prophet as the man who foretells the future is so firmly lodged in the minds of most people that it is very hard for them to see what the characteristic of the Old Testament prophet really is. That characteristic is insight. He sees further into the nature of things than ordinary men. Where other men see only a builder's plumbline, Amos sees the implacable judgement of God going forth in righteousness against His people. Where others hear only the crash and clash of nations, the prophet hears the footsteps of God going forth into the world, holding the nations in the hollow of His hand, and guiding all things to a consummation that He has already determined.

It may be useful to consider a little more closely this concept of insight, the capacity to see beyond the phenomena to the inner construction of things. The gift is found in many connexions. It may be exercised in relation to the physical world and its structure. In relation to physical things, this gift of insight was perhaps possessed in greater measure by Sir Isaac Newton than by any other man of whom we have record. In him it was matched by a singularly calm and patient intellect. But Newton could often see things and intuitively know them to be true, though it might take him years to find the proofs by which the discoveries of his intuition could be intellectually verified. What makes a man an artist is the same gift of insight in the realm of beauty. Many men had seen sunflowers long before Vincent van Gogh was born. But no one had ever seen them or painted them before with quite that insight and affection that inspired the hand and the brush of van Gogh. His success both in seeing, and in making others see, is attested by the myriad reproductions of his pictures now to be seen in rather too many suburban drawing-rooms. What makes the peerless greatness of Shakespeare is his insight into the depths of human nature and into the way that it really works. Those who enter into his world can in their measure share his insight, and find their understanding of the world permanently enriched and deepened by participation in something that they were not qualified to discover for themselves.

What the artist is in relation to beauty, that the prophet is in relation to what is, or ought to be, the ultimate concern of every human being, the basic and deepest reality of the world in which he lives. The artist affirms that he does not invent beauty; he finds it already there. The prophet too affirms that he does not invent; he sees that which is already there, and which other men cannot see. 'This is the way the world is made; this is the truth of the world. Be willing to see and you shall see it too.' The artist tells us that he is from time to time so seized by the vision or the idea of beauty that he can do nothing but create. Often he must pass through cruel travail pangs before the idea that is striving within him comes to the birth. Sometimes the idea is so powerful that it plays upon him, as a man plays on a musical instrument; we may think of the frenzy of creative power which drove Handel to compose the whole of *The Messiah* in three weeks. Just so the prophet is so over-powered by what he has heard or seen that it is not within his power to refrain from speaking. ' The Lord GOD hath spoken; who can but prophesy? '[1] Sometimes, as in the case of the sensitive Jeremiah, his prophetic ministry is an agony to him: 'And if I say, I will not mention him, nor speak any more in his name, then there is in my heart as it were a burning fire shut up in my bones, and I am weary with forbearing, and I cannot contain.'[2]

The intensity of the prophet's experience, and of the utterance through which it is conveyed, does not of itself offer any guarantee of the truth of the prophet's teaching. But here once again the parallel with artistic creation may help us towards the formation of a judgement. What is it that makes certain works of art or literature stand out as classics? There would perhaps be general agreement in the view that a work is a classic:

If the artistic form is adequate to the content of the experience which the artist desires to convey;

If the theme is of such universal interest that, though in its original conception determined by the conditions of one time and place, it can attract the attention and sympathy of men and women living in other epochs and under wholly different conditions;

If the student finds that his experience and understanding of life is permanently deepened and enriched by his submission of himself to the influences of the masterpiece;

If the student finds that in his measure he too becomes

1. Amos iii: 8.   2. Jeremiah xx: 9.

a creator, through entering sympathetically into the experiences of the artist, as he wrestles to bring his work to birth.

If we transpose these four principles into the religious sphere, we shall find that we have sufficient criteria for judging whether a religious utterance is an authentic example of prophecy, in the true sense of the word, as a setting forth of the nature of the universe, of ' the way that the world is made'.

But it is time to turn from theoretical considerations to actual examples. Certain claims have been made on behalf of the writers of the Bible, and in particular on behalf of the prophets of Israel. Our next task must be to consider what these writers actually said and thought, and to judge whether these are self-authenticating examples of valid religious utterance, in terms of the canons of criticism which we have just laid down.

3

PROPHETIC INSIGHT AND RESPONSE

THE prophets of all religions claim to be speaking under divine inspiration. Whether men accept their utterance as true or not depends in part on a mysterious process of communication on other than purely rational levels; the prophet speaks under the power of an afflatus, and can convey to the hearer or the reader something of the same afflatus. He speaks as one who has seen a vision, and may have power to cause others also to see visions and to dream dreams. But, if we approach the prophet not as enthusiasts but in the spirit of sobriety, a certain measure of intellectual verification is possible. Is the message of the prophet consistent with what can be known of truth in other spheres? Does it conflict with moral judgements which on other grounds we judge to be reasonably well founded? Does it fulfil its function of bringing together the *disjecta membra* of experience, and at least indicating the way in which they may come together in an intelligible whole?

At the end of the second chapter, it was indicated that the next step in our study would be to consider the witness of the prophets of Israel in relation to the argument developed in that chapter.

If for the moment we concentrate our study on the Old Testament writings, we might justify our procedure simply on the grounds of the literary merit of the materials there presented to us in comparison with other religious writings.

For this there is a purely empirical test. If an intelligent audience could be persuaded to listen on four successive days to an hour's reading from the Upanishads, the Koran, the Analects of Confucius, and the Old Testament prophets – the passages should be continuous and should be chosen at random – the hearers would be in a position to judge honestly of the impression left upon their minds. For myself,

I have little doubt as to the way in which the judgement would go.

The Upanishads certainly reflect a most remarkable flowering of the human spirit. In the earlier documents we are given, in lively form, a picture of philosophic thought in the process of formation. Something of the charm of early morning rests upon those settlements in the forest, where men drew apart from the noise and cares of ordinary life to wrestle with the great problems of Being and of the Soul. In the finest passages we find high integrity and depth of philosophic vision. But also there are jungles of triviality and mere obscurity, in which the human spirit seems to have lost its way.

The early Suras of the Koran throb with a dramatic sense of the presence of a living God. But how soon this vivid sense of the divine tails off into the prolixity and tedium of the later revelations.

It may be of interest at this point to record the judgement of one who as scholar and as poet was incomparably well qualified to judge. Milton, Mr C. S. Lewis tells us,

has given his opinion that Hebrew lyrics are better than Greek 'not in their divine argument alone but in the very critical art of composition'. That is, he has told us that his preference for the Hebrew is not only moral and religious but aesthetic also. . . . If any man will read aloud on alternate mornings for a single month a page of Pindar and a page of the Psalms in any translation he chooses, I think I can guess which he will first grow tired of.[1]

I lay stress on the importance of reading in long stretches and not in brief selections. A selection may give a false impression of the whole. Some years ago Dr A. J. Appasamy, now Bishop of Coimbatore, produced an admirable little volume called *Temple Bells*, a collection of choice extracts from ancient Hindu classics. To read these chosen fragments is to be introduced to the best and highest aspirations of India over a period of more than 2,000 years. This is valuable; but the effect may be misleading, unless it is

1. *A Preface to 'Paradise Lost'* (Oxford, 1942), p. 4.

realized from how great a quantity of chaff this small amount of grain has been gathered. In the Old Testament, by contrast, it is possible to read long stretches with a sense both of aesthetic and moral satisfaction.

Macaulay once threw out the remark that there was no human composition, not even the *De Corona* of Demosthenes, which he esteemed more highly than the Seventh Book of Thucydides. I would agree with this more than with some others of Macaulay's literary judgements. The more Thucydides is read, the more he seems to stand out above other historians in his grasp of the deep springs of human action, and in his tragic sense of life. In the concluding pages of the Seventh Book, as the great Athenian tragedy of the Sicilian expedition deepens into thick darkness, he is at his incomparable best. But, if I were to read you first those pages, and then to follow them with the story of Absalom's rebellion from the second Book of Samuel, beginning with the moment when David first saw Bathsheba from the roof of his palace and ending with his heartbroken cry, 'O Absalom, my son, my son', I think you would agree that in psychological insight, in vividness of narrative writing and in dramatic power, the Hebrew writer was no whit inferior to the Greek.

Admittedly not all the Old Testament is on the same level. But consider it at its highest points. In the twenty-seven chapters which make up the second part of the Book of Isaiah there are some few things that are obscure, others that are locally and historically conditioned. But for the rest, page after page of its magnificent religious rhetoric is as intelligible and as relevant to-day as when it was first written, and, if read to a modern audience, should produce a sense of inner exaltation, with hardly a trace of spiritual or moral unease. This surely is remarkable, when it is remembered that these poems were written 2,500 years ago.

Here, however, we are concerned not so much with the literary excellence of the Old Testament as with its religious significance. It was the foundation on which Jesus Christ claimed to build His teaching. The Christian Church, with some few exceptions,[1] always read the Old Testament as sacred Scripture, because it discerned a direct historical connexion between the religious experience of Israel and its own, and believed that the God who had acted redemptively in history in Jesus Christ was the same God who had already been redemptively at work in the 2,000 years of Israel's history.

Not everyone is pleased with this exclusive idea of the dependence of the Christian Gospel on its Old Testament origins. There are Christians who would like to see in the Gospel the fulfilment, *in the same sense*, of the yearnings after God of all the other religious systems of the world. On this view these other systems are regarded rather as though they were separate and independent coral islands, growing up slowly and secretly beneath the surface of the sea, and all alike destined, given a sufficient span of time, to rise above the surface of the ocean, and to stand in all the beauty of fronded palms and dashing surf.

This evolutionary idea is plausible, but it can hardly survive the test of historical investigation.

When an Indian Christian claims that Hinduism at its highest should be regarded as a preparation for the Gospel, what exactly does he mean? Hinduism has had 3,000 years in which to experiment, and has made an immense variety of experiments. But it has never shown any tendency to change itself into anything the least like Christianity. To pretend that the two are alike or akin is impossible, unless we are prepared to abandon all objective criteria of likeness and difference, and to accept the principle of complete relativity in religion.

It is, on the contrary, the historic fact that the religious experience of Israel *did* flower in Jesus Christ. He was not ashamed to be called the Son of David; he looked back to Abraham, Isaac, and Jacob as the fathers in the faith. The words and work of Jesus may be universal in their significance, but they were historically conditioned by a relationship to a historic past which is unique. To no other system,

1. Notably the heretic Marcion in the second century A.D.

to no other process of development, does the work of Christ bear the same, or even any similar, relationship. This is a matter of plain historic fact, independent of any judgement we may later be led to pass on the teaching of Christ, or on the claims which the Christian Church has continuously made for Him.

If, however, Christ should prove to be the supreme and final manifestation of God, certain consequences may be inferred as to the probable fate of the non-Christian religions in relation to Him.

The Christian should always be as open-minded as possible in relation to other religions and their sacred books. He should delight in everything true and beautiful to be found in them. He should be prepared to believe that God has not been unresponsive to the quest of seeking souls in the ethnic religions. But he is not committed by this open-mindedness to the view that all religious systems represent parallel developments of roughly equal value. He is committed to belief in one central line of development, in which the purpose of God was going forward, a purpose into which in due course all the nations of the world should be incorporated. The ethnic religions, on this view, can be no more than provisional resting places for the human spirit, during the time of waiting for the manifestation of the fulness of the divine plan; these religions can find their fulfilment only by being incorporated into Christ; through this incorporation they must die, as separately existing systems.

Historically this is what happened to the ancient faiths of Greece and Rome. From the third century on, the Christian Church set itself to school with the Greek philosophers and poets; by the fourth, Christian writers were drawing freely on this second source of inspiration. But they could do so only because the old faiths were already dying and near to dissolution. There were pagan revivals; conservatives ascribed all the misfortunes of the Roman Empire to the treachery of Roman citizens towards the ancient gods. But history moves on. No one in the world to-day worships Zeus or Ares or Aphrodite; the altars smoke no more. Just because of this we are free to-day to learn in the same school as the great Christian fathers. Christ was not born in Hellas; yet Hellas in the end was incorporated into Him, and we are able to see that Hellas no less than Jewry, but in a wholly different way, found its fulfilment in Him. Hellas had to die in order to live; the experience of ancient Israel still lives in the life of the new Israel the Church.

At this point we must return from theory to our main purpose of empirical verification. We have made great claims for the religious experience of Israel, as specially significant in the development of a divine purpose in history. We must now consider the contents of that experience. To what kind of a spiritual world does this experience bear witness? And are its main principles such as can reasonably be regarded as permanently valid for mankind?

As we have already seen, the Old Testament does not offend against our earlier thesis that a divine self-disclosure, if made to men, is likely to come in many fragments and in diverse forms. The literature of which it is made up was composed over a period of at least 800 years, and is of the most varied character. Yet within this complex library there is a unity; there are certain central ideas, which grow and develop and are diversely expressed, and yet remain essentially unchanged throughout the whole history.

For the purpose of our study, it will suffice to take five leading ideas, each of which is assumed in the Christian Gospel, and finds fresh amplitude in that new setting.

The first of these great ideas is that God is one. 'The Lord thy God is one Lord.'

As we have seen, there has been a tendency for the human mind to work towards the principle of unity in the spiritual world, no less than in other fields of its experience. Most, though not all, of the great religious systems of the world are monotheistic, or at least monolatrous, accepting the worship of only one God.

This principle, because of its very simplicity, can be easily set forth; yet it has not been found in practice easy to arrive at or to observe.

Classical Hinduism carries to its extreme limit the doctrine of the unity of all existence. Yet India is at the same time a land of the wildest polytheism. The educated Hindu, who wishes to give as good an account as possible of the religious state of his country, has no great difficulty in reconciling these contradictory appearances. The many gods of Hinduism may be allegorized as partial representations, as broken lights of the one Supreme, like the separate colours into which pure light can be broken up by the prism. A similar process of allegorization was not unknown to the later Greeks. Or the gods can be understood as symbols, permitted for the benefit of simple people who cannot grasp the full truth. The monistic doctrine is indeed austere and difficult, only to be attained by careful training in thought and meditation, and through ascetic self-discipline; if we were to affirm that there is no way other than the *Jnāna-Mārga*, the way of wisdom, for the vast majority of mankind there would be no possibility of religious observance or devotion; and to deny to them that which is within their powers would be sheer inhumanity.

The simple worshipper would probably give his explanation in rather different terms; he knows, perhaps dimly, that there is one supreme principle of Being, but holds that so great a potentate is unapproachable by simple people like himself. If we have business with a high official of the Government, we cannot directly enter into his presence; we pay a messenger or a servant to put our business before him. So, although we know that these lesser gods are only as it were servants and inferiors, we make use of them in an approach to the God who is too high for us, and we believe that this approach will be acceptable to Him.

Primitive man peoples his world with spirits of the wood, the stream and the mountains, his nights with the injurious wraiths of those who have departed from the world angry and by violence. But much more civilized people than he have been heard to remark that 'there might be something in it after all'.

In the Old Testament itself, there are traces of various

attitudes to the one God, and to the other gods, who might possibly, or certainly, be held to exist.

There was the stage of *monolatry*, in which it was clearly understood that Israel should worship only one God, Jehovah, but also it was taken for granted that every other nation would worship each its own god. The clearest instance is in the apparently very ancient record of the controversy between Jephthah and the Ammonites, where we read: 'Wilt not thou possess that which Chemosh thy god giveth thee to possess? So whomsoever the Lord our God shall drive out from before us, them will we possess.'[1] A war between nations was regarded as a war between their gods; when a city fell, its gods might be seen forsaking it and perhaps going over to the side of the adversary. The great king Sennacherib of Assyria, boasting himself against little Judah, said: 'Where are the gods of Hamath and of Arpad? Where are the gods of Sepharvaim, Hena and Ivah? Have they delivered Samaria out of my hand?' But the peculiar arrogancy of Sennacherib was seen in his additional claim: 'Am I now come up without Jehovah against this place to destroy it? Jehovah said to me, Go up against this land and destroy it.'[2] He asserted, in fact, that even before the war had begun, the God of Israel had deserted His people, and that therefore it was certain that they could not stand before the invader.

As long as this idea of a number of gods with different spheres prevailed, no disloyalty would seem to be involved if a people, in addition to worshipping their own particular god, took pains to keep on good terms with other gods in whose area they might have occasion to do business. Jehovah was, in Israelite tradition, primarily the God of the wild places. Israelites perhaps would not have disagreed with the remark of the Syrians: 'Their god is a god of the hills. . . . Jehovah is a god of the hills, but he is not a god of the valleys.'[3] Jehovah was the wilderness God, whom they

1. Judges xi: 24.
2. 2 Kings xviii: 34, 25.
3. 1 Kings xx: 23, 28

had come to know in flame and terror and earthquake. They could still hear him, riding upon the wings of the wind in the storm-cloud and the thunder: 'Lord, when thou wentest out of Seir, when thou marchedst out of the field of Edom, the earth trembled and the heavens dropped, the clouds also dropped water. The mountains melted from before the Lord, even that Sinai, from before the Lord God of Israel.'[1] But now that Israel had left the Bedouin life of the wilderness and entered upon the settled life of agriculture, exchanged the desert for the sown, it seemed reasonable that some respect should be shown to the local lords, the Baalim – a separate Baal for each smiling valley, responsible for its fertility and for the gifts of corn and wine and oil. Why should Jehovah be jealous, when such sensible tolerance in no way derogated from the recognition of His authority in His own special sphere?

It was this attitude of confused tolerance that Hosea rebuked under the similitude of his unfaithful wife: 'She said, I will go after my lovers, that gave me my bread and my water, my wool and my flax, mine oil and my drink.' But Jehovah answers: 'Therefore, behold, I will hedge up thy way with thorns, and make a wall, that she shall not find her paths. . . . For she did not know that I gave her corn and wine and oil. . . . Therefore will I return and take away my corn in the time thereof, and my wine in the season thereof, and will recover my wool and my flax given to cover her nakedness.'[2] For the prophet, Jehovah is the God of the sown no less than of the desert; He alone is the giver of all good gifts.

A further stage is reached when the existence of other gods is not denied, but they are reduced to the status of devils. Worship of false gods is no longer simply unfaithfulness, it is degradation unspeakable. This attitude is found in many of the later books of the Old Testament, as the writers reflected on the earlier history of their people: 'Yea, they sacrificed their sons and their daughters unto demons, and shed innocent blood, even the blood of their sons and

1. Judges v: 4, 5.   2. Hosea ii: 6–9.

of their daughters, whom they sacrificed unto the idols of Canaan; and the land was polluted with blood.'[1]

This idea of the pagan gods as devils is found also in the early Christian Fathers, and persisted for centuries in popular Christian tradition.[2]

The final stage is reached when an idol is regarded, to use by anticipation a phrase of St Paul, as being 'nothing in the world'. This is not to deny the possibility that there may be evil spirits at work in the universe – St Paul undoubtedly believed that there were. But, if such beings exist, they can in no way be regarded as rivals to the one true God, and in no circumstances could worship possibly be offered to them. In the Old Testament, this absolute monotheism finds its superlative expression in the prophecies of the second Isaiah: 'Is there a God beside me? Yea, there is no Rock; I know not any. . . . I am Jehovah, and there is none else, there is no God beside me. . . . Look unto me, and be ye saved, all the ends of the earth: for I am God, and there is none else. . . . I am God, and there is none else; I am God, and there is none like me.'[3]

It may seem that this point has been excessively laboured. We in Europe tend to take it for granted that, if God exists at all, there can only be one God. Our minds are conditioned by centuries of Greek and Hebrew tradition. But we must remember that for perhaps the majority of people in the world it is not so. If the Christian convert in Asia or Africa is asked what is the specifically new thing that has come to him through his new faith, he may well answer, and

1. Psalm cvi: 37, 38.

2. Professor A. A. Bevan once explained to me on the following grounds the well-known connexion in Christian history between sanctity and dirt: The only place you could have a bath in those days was the public baths. Baths were naturally built in places where there were springs; and, as every spring had its nymph or spirit, to whom an altar would be erected and offerings made, the baths became *ipso facto* a house of devils, with whom the bather could not avoid entering into contact. Therefore the greater the piety of the Christian, the less the likelihood of his ever taking a bath!

3. Isaiah xliv: 8; xlv: 5, 22; xlvi: 9.

frequently does, that it is the immense simplification of life that Christianity has brought; instead of having to deal with an unspecified number of perhaps capricious and inconsistent powers, he is now concerned only with one majestic principle – that one God beside whom there can be no second. To the Jews of the Old Testament more than to any other people we owe the almost universal recognition of this principle in the Western world.

The second pillar of understanding is the conviction that God is active in His world. No difference could be greater than that between the deistic concept of a God who in the beginning wound up the universe like a watch and left it to run itself, and the vivid Hebrew idea of a God always present, always intensely active, whose nature can be compared to that of a devouring fire.

The characteristic phrase in which this conviction finds expression is 'the living God'. At first sight, this may appear a strange form of words: what use would a dead God be to anyone? The implications become clear, if we remember the constant contrast in Hebrew thought between the vigour of the living man and the *inertia*, the powerlessness to effect anything, of those who have gone down to Sheol, the abode of the dead, where all things are monotonously one and all earthly distinctions are blotted out.

This sense of the ever-present activity of the divine translated itself in an energetic, and at times almost reckless, anthropomorphism. There is scarcely a part of the human anatomy or character which is not at one time or another attributed to God. The eyes of the Lord are over the righteous and His ears are open to their prayer. He brought His people out of Egypt with a strong hand and stretched out arm. We even read that the Lord is a man of war. He comes down out of heaven to see what the builders of the tower of Babel are doing. He walks in the garden of Eden in the cool of the evening.

Objection is often taken to the use of this kind of language with reference to God; but is the objection really valid? We cannot think at all without the use of words, and the words we use must be drawn from those things with which we are familiar. If any pedant insists on taking this graphic and figurative language literally, he will of course reach absurd conclusions and will have only himself to blame. By this time it must have become clear that, if we are to try at all to penetrate the spiritual world, we must use our imagination; if a limit is set, as it was for the Jews, by the stern prohibition of any attempt to make a visible representation of the divine, perhaps the imagination may safely range and speculate and fashion for itself what it finds to be the appropriate forms of speech.

Greater difficulty is caused to the modern reader by the Hebrew habit, consequent on this peculiarly vivid sense of the divine activity, of eliminating all secondary causes, and attributing everything to the activity of God. 'Shall there be evil in the city, and the Lord hath not done it?'[1] The Hebrew says 'The Lord said unto Samuel' where we should more probably say 'Samuel thought'. This is in part a peculiarity of the structure of Semitic language, in part the reflection of a conviction about the way in which the world is ruled. We have a perfect right to translate Hebrew idiom into that of the languages of the West; we shall never understand the Old Testament, if we translate so freely as to eliminate both the idiomatic structure of the original and the basic convictions which are implicit in those idioms.

The Hebrew conviction is set forth with perfect clarity by a late writer, though it is implicit in every part of the Old Testament story: 'till thou know that the Most High ruleth in the kingdom of men, and giveth it to whomsoever He will'.[2]

God rules. He exercises control in every part of this visible universe, and particularly in the affairs of men. If this is true, how does it come about? What is that relation-

1. Amos iii: 6. The translators of the Authorized Version have increased the difficulty for the English reader. The word *evil*, as the context makes quite clear, does not mean *moral evil*, *wickedness*, but *trouble*, *distress*; and so in a number of other passages.
2. Daniel iv: 25.

ship between God and the world, between the spiritual and the material, which makes such control possible?

The Hebrew answer is simplicity itself. God can rule the world because He made it. 'The sea is his and he made it, and his hands prepared the dry land.' 'By the word of the Lord were the heavens made, and all the host of them by the breath of his mouth.'[1] God is not dependent on the world; the world is wholly dependent upon Him.

To this doctrine of creation there have been two main alternatives in the history of thought.

The first is pantheism, the view that all things are God, or in some way manifestations or emanations of God. The Hindu will say quite frankly or without any sense of boasting 'I am God'. There are times when we too feel a mystical sense of unity with all living things, and with whatever mysterious source of being lies behind their particular being and ours. The Wordsworthian mysticism of nature will, I suppose, never lose its power to charm and to console.

This view is attractive; it answers to that deep-rooted desire in the heart of man, to which we have alluded more than once, to find a principle of unity in all things. Its weakness is that it seems necessarily to involve a denial of the reality of the moral struggle. If all things are divine, or of the divine, why do we find so much in the world and in ourselves to condemn (and to condemn is not the same either as to dislike or aesthetically to disapprove)? Why is there so much against which, if we are to be true men, we feel that we must fight? At least, as William James has taught us, it feels as though it were a real struggle, and as though something were gained for the whole universe, when we stand fast and overcome. If this be illusion, let us give up the struggle to think seriously, and grow watercress instead.

The second view is that the divine is related to the visible world as the organizing principle, which brings a measure of order to an already existing something, different in its nature from the divine. Greek thought arrived at the belief in formless matter, unable of itself in any way to *be*, unless

1. Psalm xcv: 5; xxxiii: 6. Prayer Book Version.

form were impressed upon it from without. This matter is as far from true Being as it is possible to be without being absolutely non-existent. Matter is not non-existent; it is a permanently existing principle, in part subject to the impress of Being upon it, in part always refractory to the higher influence. But, since it can never by any possibility be changed into anything else, matter is essentially unredeemable. In some systems matter in itself is neutral, neither good nor bad; in others, more pessimistic, it becomes identified with evil; then the conclusion tends to be one of those dualistic schemes of thought, in which the whole world is seen as the permanent conflict between good and evil principles – a type of thought which seems attractive where men are deeply burdened with a sense of the evil that is in the world, but which offers escape rather than victory as the highest for which men may legitimately hope.

The Hebrew view is that God made the heavens and the earth, and that before He made them they just did not exist. Nothing was, except God; God spoke: the world was. Not being philosophically minded, the Hebrews did not express themselves in such propositions: they tended to speak in poetry; but, if we translate their poetry back into plain prose, that seems to be quite certainly what they meant.

Our human experience is limited to making use of things which already exist. Our human thinking, however abstract its conclusions, always starts from thinking about things which we have seen or touched or handled. The idea of creation out of nothing is something of which we can have no experience, and of which therefore we can form no precise idea.

But we must guard against the fallacy, often indulged in by those who argue plausibly against religion, of supposing that because we cannot understand everything about something, we cannot understand anything about it: or that, because we cannot form a precise idea of a thing, we cannot form any idea at all.

Creation out of nothing is something from which we are for ever debarred. Yet there are certain human activities in which we come remarkably near it. Where was Beethoven's Fifth Symphony before he composed it? Of course there were in the world brass and wood and catgut enough to produce the physical sounds that Beethoven had imagined. There were paper and ink, by means of which Beethoven could make certain black marks, which would convey to others the fruits of his inspiration. But obviously such things neither account for nor produce the mysterious process of musical creation. Perhaps it is not irrelevant to recall that in later life Beethoven was so deaf that he never physically heard his own greatest compositions. Such activity is not creation out of nothing; but it comes near enough to it to help us in making for ourselves some kind of picture of what creation out of nothing might be.

The first chapter of Genesis was certainly not the first part of the Old Testament to be written; but perhaps it was a special inspiration which brought it to the beginning of the Bible. 'In the beginning God created the heavens and the earth.' The statement is simple, sublime, and reasonable. All the wisdom of Greece did not attain to it. For the Old Testament believer, this doctrine is no mere philosophical abstraction, but a point of rest in a stormy and troubled world: 'Why sayest thou, O Jacob, and speakest, O Israel, My way is hid from the Lord, and my judgement is passed away from my God? Hast thou not known? hast thou not heard, that the everlasting God, the Lord, the Creator of the ends of the earth, fainteth not, neither is weary? There is no searching of his understanding.'[1]

It is only a short step from this quotation to the third of the great Old Testament convictions, that concerning the faithfulness of God – indeed the two ideas are expressly brought together in the first Epistle of Peter: 'Wherefore let them that suffer . . . commit the keeping of their souls in well-doing unto a faithful Creator.'[2]

This divine faithfulness, according to Hebrew ideas, is the guarantee of that stability of the moral order of the world without which man might easily fall into despair. To live in

1. Isaiah xl: 27, 28. 2. 1 Peter iv: 19.

a universe ruled by caprice and chance is a psychological nightmare. The all-embracing fear which we saw to be characteristic of the animistic level of man's religious experience is due just to the capriciousness of that multitude of spirits by which the life of man is believed to be surrounded; when we have appeased all the spirits that we know in all the ways we know, it is always possible that, as at Athens, there may be the unknown God, whom unwittingly we have offended or failed to propitiate, and who may take his revenge when we least expect it. To encounter a God who is reliable, and so to be delivered from this fear, is deliverance indeed.

To the Hebrew mind, with its general dislike of the abstract and preference for the concrete, it was natural to express its sense of the divine faithfulness in terms of a covenant between God and man. This man idea is present in every part of the Old Testament. The word *covenant* occurs 260 times, in almost every case in connexion with the divine covenant, though it can also be used of ordinary contracts between man and man; whereas the word generally rendered *faithfulness* is found less than fifty times, and that in a considerable variety of senses.

The divine covenant is not to be thought of as in every respect like the contracts into which men enter with one another, for mutual advantage and with mutual obligation. Between God and man there is no relationship of equality. In the making of the covenant it is always God who takes the initiative; the motive can never be anything other than His grace and favour towards the one with whom He is pleased to make the covenant. Because God is faithful and unchangeable, His covenant is always an everlasting covenant; man may break it from his side; by unfaithfulness and disobedience he may fall out of the covenant relationship and lose his inheritance. But such human failure does not affect God's part of the bargain; He always remains true and faithful to His word.

To the Israelite, the covenant *par excellence* was that which God made with Israel, when He called the people out of

Egypt, and met them in the wilderness at the Mount of God and formed them into a nation, His people. These overwhelming events left upon the mind of Israel an impress which, even in its worst days, was never wholly lost. In the narrative of the Book of Exodus there are certain poetical – we might even say mythological – elements which are perplexing to the modern mind. But he would be a dull reader who did not understand that this is a record of real happenings – as real as was the deliverance from the peril of the Armada to Elizabethan England, or the *Glorieuse Rentrée* of 1689 to the Waldensian Protestants of the Piedmontese Alps – or, we may add, the events of Dunkirk to the men of our own generation.

At times this sense of a covenant relationship with God was interpreted by Israel selfishly and arbitrarily, in terms of privilege and not of responsibility. If the God of the whole earth had entered into a special fellowship with Israel, that must mean that other peoples belonged to some lower order of creation. It does not seem unreasonable to the psalmist to pray: 'Pour out thy wrath upon the heathen that have not known thee, and upon the kingdoms that have not called upon thy name.'[1] But there is another and deeper strain of understanding. Israel's vocation is seen in the light of a divine purpose of good for all men, and as carrying with it not so much privilege as responsibility. 'In thee and in thy seed shall all the families of the earth be blessed.'[2]

In the book of Genesis, the particular experience of Israel at Sinai is carried back to an earlier stage of human experience. After the crisis of the flood God makes a covenant with Noah and his sons. Since, according to the record of Genesis, all nations are descended from those three sons of Noah, the covenant is to be understood as made with all men; the other nations do not share in the special vocation of Israel, but they are not for that reason excluded from every divinely appointed relationship to God. The sign of the covenant is the rainbow, which appears impartially in the cloud for every nation upon earth.[3]

1. Psalm lxxix: 6.   2. Genesis xii: 3.   3. Genesis ix: 1–17.

This narrative, like others in the first pages of the Bible, conveys profound spiritual insight in a mythological form. In the prophetic books we find the myth translated into more ordinary speech. The first clear instance seems to be in the prophecy of Amos in the latter part of the eighth century B.C. Amos sets forth what must have seemed to his contemporaries the paradoxical view that, because Judah enjoyed a privileged position in relation to God, the judgement of God upon His own people must be specially severe; and also the conviction that God is interested in other nations as well as in the people of His choice. 'You only have I known of all the families of the earth: therefore I will visit upon you all your iniquities. . . . Are ye not as the children of the Ethiopians unto me, O children of Israel? saith the Lord. Have not I brought up Israel out of the land of Egypt? and the Philistines from Caphtor, and the Syrians from Kir?'[1] In the second part of Isaiah, the purpose of God for the whole world is set forth repeatedly in glowing language: 'Look unto me, and be saved, all the ends of the earth: for I am God and there is none else. . . . He shall bring forth judgement to the Gentiles . . . the isles shall wait for his law. . . . I will also give thee for a light to the Gentiles, that thou mayest be my salvation unto the end of the earth.'[2]

Not infrequently this sense of an expanding purpose is associated with the figure of one ruler, the divinely appointed King. Thus in the 72nd Psalm we read: 'He shall have dominion also from sea to sea, and from the River unto the ends of the earth. . . . Yea, all kings shall fall down before him: all nations shall serve him.' The date of this psalm, as of the prophecy of Zechariah ix, in which some of these words are repeated, is quite uncertain. But here is depicted a Kingdom which, in contrast to the violent and cruel kingdoms of the world, is to be based upon the law of peace and righteousness; in which the poor and helpless find help and deliverance. This is to be a universal Kingdom, in which all nations are to be blessed. Here is a foreshadowing of a

1. Amos iii: 2; ix: 7.   2. Isaiah xlv: 22; xlii: 1, 4; xlix: 6.

world-wide community, peaceful and blessed under the rule of God's direct representative.

The transition from the third to the fourth pillar of Old Testament belief has in this quotation already been made. The Kingdom of God's chosen ruler is a Kingdom of righteousness. This must be so, since God Himself is righteous.

The identification of God with righteousness, with moral goodness, is to us so self-evident that it is difficult to imagine a time or a situation in which it was otherwise. But unless we can exercise our imagination, and put ourselves back to a stage of thought in which the religious and the moral have not yet become identified, we shall fail to realize the immense significance of the contribution of the Old Testament to the spiritual progress of mankind.

In a famous book, *The Idea of the Holy*, Prof. Rudolf Otto of Marburg developed the view that, if we would understand the origins of the idea of holiness, we must learn to interpret it in the categories of the remote, the uncanny, the awe-inspiring. For this Dr Otto coined the word the *numinous*. Man feels awe in the presence of a *mysterium tremendum*, of that which he cannot understand. This is the feeling that comes upon men sometimes in the presence of the mysterious powers of nature, that falls upon them suddenly in forests or deserts or wild places. If this experience leads men to worship, it is the worship of fear rather than of understanding love and confidence.

The first definition of the holy, then, is that it is that which is separate, mysterious, not to be touched or approached by ordinary men. Certain places, or persons, or objects are possessed by a special power; for this, the anthropologists commonly use the convenient Melanesian word *mana*. That which has *mana* is dangerous to ordinary people, who have not the right of approach or contact, or do not know the formula which gives safety in relation to it. In fact, to use another convenient word, such places and objects are *taboo*.

There is plenty of evidence in the Old Testament for the

prevalence of such ideas among the Israelites in early times. The underlying idea of holiness is, at that period, *separation*. When it is said of the altar in the Book of Exodus, that 'seven days shalt thou make atonement for the altar, and sanctify it; and it shall be an altar most holy: whatsoever toucheth the altar shall be most holy',[1] the meaning is that the altar is to be most rigorously set apart from all contact with unauthorized persons and things, and is to be possessed of such *mana* that anything which touches it will acquire the same *mana* and will become equally dangerous to the profane. The ark of the covenant was held to be the dwelling-place of such a strong *mana* that when Uzzah, with good intent, stretched out his hand and touched it, his rashness was immediately followed by his death.[2]

In the life of man mystery, the numinous, attaches particularly to two things – to blood, and to the whole process of fertility. Blood, which is the very life of man, has always been held to have special powers, sometimes even giving man power over the gods. The processes of reproduction, which man shares with the animals and the whole of nature, seem to make him mysteriously akin to the hidden powers which rule the world, and on a proper relationship to which his continued existence in the world depends.

The excessive preoccupation of men's minds with these two areas of mystery helps to explain that which is most disconcerting in primitive, or ethnic, worship – its constant association with cruelty and with licentiousness. The defenders of idolatry will maintain that to worship an idol is no more than to make visible those mental pictures of the divine, which even Christians form inwardly when they are at their prayers. If this were all, idolatry would indeed be harmless. But here is this strange fact, which I would not undertake to explain, but which seems to me both from my reading and from personal experience to be unmistakable, that when, in the phrase of St Paul, men change 'the glory of the incorruptible god into an image made like to corruptible man, and to birds, and fourfooted beasts, and creeping things',[3]

1. Exodus xxix: 37.   2. 2 Samuel vi: 6–8.   3. Romans i: 23.

these two consequences, cruelty and lasciviousness, invariably follow.

On the one hand, there is the abominable practice of human sacrifice. There are a number of allusions to this in the Old Testament. The blood of animal victims was a powerful charm – but much more powerful the blood of a human victim, in circumstances where there was special need to secure the favour or co-operation of some divine power. For instance, in a moment of special peril the King of Moab 'took his eldest son that should have reigned in his stead, and offered him for a burnt offering upon the wall'.[1] But, in order to bring the matter out of what some may feel the rather remote and 'religious' atmosphere of the Old Testament into the plain light of history, in historic times and in the unimpassioned words of a secular historian, I would refer you to the narrative of Diodorus Siculus, recounting what took place in Carthage in 310 B.C., when the Carthaginians were hard pressed in their war against Dionysius the younger of Syracuse:

They thought also that Cronos was hostile to them because in times past they had sacrificed to him the strongest of their sons, but later secretly buying children and bringing them up they sent them to the sacrifice. Remembering these things, and seeing the enemy encamped against their very walls, they were seized with superstitious panic, because of their failure to pay the god his wonted honour. In their eagerness therefore to set right their past negligence, they selected two hundred boys of the most renowned families, and sacrificed them publicly; and others who were under accusation gave themselves up voluntarily to the number of not less than three hundred. They had a bronze statue of Cronos, of which the hands were stretched out palms upward, but inclined towards the ground, so that a child placed on them rolled downwards and fell into a pit full of fire.[2]

Did not the blood of these innocents cry to heaven for vengeance?

1. 2 Kings iii: 27.
2. Diodorus Siculus xx: 14. Flaubert in *Salammbô* has given with characteristic clarity and precision a terrifying description of such a holocaust.

For the other aspect of idolatry, its connexion with sexual licence as a part of religious worship, you have only to refer to a classic such as Sir James Frazer's *Adonis, Attis, Osiris*, to find the main facts impartially and artistically set forth. St Paul knew well what he was facing at Ephesus, where the great temple of Artemis of the Ephesians was one of the most famous centres in the ancient world of the fertility cult and its evil associations. That temple in course of time so completely vanished that it was only after long search that its site was rediscovered in the middle of the nineteenth century – the cult that was associated with it has long been only a memory in Europe. But what is only a memory in Europe is still a living reality in Asia. In India the great temples which are the centres of pilgrimage are surrounded by the houses of dedicated harlots; a visit to the one is as much a part of the religious ceremonial as a visit to the other. Thoughtful Hindus admit that a young man who goes on pilgrimage is likely to return home morally the worse for his journey; and Hindu reformers are as eagerly concerned as Christians that this ancient abomination should be ended.

Where the identification between religion and morality has not yet been made, morality remains for the most part either a matter of social custom, or of religious techniques and taboos, codified in a complicated series of ritual rules and intended to secure the safety of the worshipper in his approach to the divine.

This was the situation which was faced by the Old Testament prophets – on the one hand splendour of ritual worship and a scrupulous regard for the prescriptions of the ritual code; on the other, the dying out of compassion and the regard for man as man, and failure to see that such things as plain ordinary goodness belong to the realm of religious concern. The great writing prophets, from Amos onwards, were not completely original: they had had their precursors; but their ceaseless insistence on the connexion between morality and religion, and the gradual acceptance of their point of view, constituted a major revolution in the thought of mankind.

Scholars are not agreed as to whether the prophets looked forward to the complete disappearance of the traditional cult and its accompaniment of sacrifice. Certainly they had no hesitation in denouncing the temple and all its doings as hypocrisy displeasing to God. 'I hate, I despise your feasts, and I will take no delight in your solemn assemblies. Yea, though ye offer me your burnt offerings, I will not accept them: neither will I regard the peace offerings of your fat beasts.'[1] So writes Amos. He is echoed by Isaiah: 'When ye come before me, who hath required this at your hands, to trample my courts? Bring no more vain oblations; incense is an abomination unto me; new moon and sabbath, the calling of assemblies – I cannot away with iniquity and the solemn meeting.'[2] But if God is not specially interested in these externals of religion, what is He interested in? It is the positive answer of the prophets to this question that constitutes their abiding importance. 'Let judgement roll down as waters, and righteousness as a mighty stream.'[3] The ideal of judgement and righteousness may be limited, but it is quite specific. It means things like not having false weights and measures, not letting the case of the poor man go by default in the law courts, not making money the primary consideration, not to 'pant after the dust of the earth on the head of the poor'. 'Wherewith shall I come before the Lord, and bow myself before the high God?' asks Micah; and the answer comes back with memorable plainness: 'He hath shewed thee, O man, what is good; and what doth the Lord require of thee, but to do justly, and to love mercy, and to walk humbly with thy God?'[4]

In the book of Deuteronomy the prophetic insights are expanded into a code, which has been well called the Law of Compassion. There, again and again emphasis is laid on fair and kind treatment of the widow, the fatherless, and the stranger; even the bird sitting on her eggs in the nest is not

1. Amos v: 21, 22.
2. Isaiah i: 12–14.
3. Amos v: 24.
4. Micah vi: 6–8.

forgotten.[1] It is for breaches of this simple law of everyday righteousness that the gravest displeasure of God will fall upon His people.

Religions may be classified according to their understanding of the term *spiritual*. In general, the religions of enlightenment, and under this heading may be included Hinduism, Greek philosophical thought, and Gnostic forms of Christianity, tend to identify the spiritual with the incorporeal, the immaterial. The body is the prison, which hinders the free activity of the soul, and from which the soul must be delivered in order that it may realize its own true nature. Judaism and Christianity firmly identify the spiritual with the ethical, the moral, and accept the body as the instrument through which any known truth concerning God is to be expressed in practical conduct. Adherents of all religions would probably accept the sublime remark of Plato in the *Theaetetus* that the highest destiny for man is to be made as much like God as possible; religion acquires a special character, if to be made like God is understood in terms of common honesty, kindness, gentleness, mercy, and good faith. No Christian imagines that morality is the whole of religion; but any religion which does not result in the acceptance of moral principle and express itself in moral action he will unhesitatingly condemn as bad and false.

Let us tentatively accept the prophetic identification of the spiritual with the moral. It is true that righteous action is impossible, except in a world which permits of such moral freedom as makes the individual responsible for his actions. How such freedom can be maintained in a stable universe is a question which may occupy us elsewhere. In the prophetic analysis with which we are here concerned it is assumed that men are not unreasonable when they pass moral judgements on their own actions and on those of other men, and that the prophet has a right to condemn social unrighteousness as an offence against God.

The last of our five pillars is the conviction that God is merciful.

1. Deuteronomy xxii: 6–7.

A sense of ritual uncleanness is not the same as a sense of sin. The term *sin* can have an ethical content only when the idea of God as righteous is wholeheartedly accepted. Purification from ritual uncleanness is a comparatively simple matter; it may be costly, but every ritual system contains provision for purification from every conceivable form of ritual defilement. But if God is righteous, and if offence against Him involves moral guilt and consequent alienation from Him, is there any means by which the guilt can be put away, and a right relationship with God restored? The later books of the Old Testament give evidence of the darkening of this problem in the minds of the people of Israel.

It seemed plain to these thinkers that the consequence of sin must be death. This was stated in plain terms by the prophet Ezekiel: 'The soul that sinneth, it shall die.'[1] So when amid the miseries of the exile in Babylon the exiles reflected on their state, the natural expression of their feeling was: 'Our transgressions and our sins are upon us, and we pine away in them; how then should we live?'[2] But observation showed that the sinner did not always die. In the history of Israel, the outstanding example was that of David. He had sinned against every canon of righteousness human or divine. He had taken the wife of his servant Uriah the Hittite and committed adultery with her; he had treacherously arranged for Uriah to be killed, as though by accident in battle; he had then taken Uriah's wife to be his wife. And yet, when at last David, rebuked by Nathan the prophet, admits his guilt and says, 'I have sinned against the Lord', Nathan is able to reply, in the name of the Lord, 'The Lord also hath put away thy sin; thou shalt not die'.[3]

At once a moral problem arises. The open and flagrant sinner has certainly deserved to die; yet God Himself has declared his deliverance from death. How can this be?

A partial answer was given by the ceremonies provided in the Jewish law for atonement of sin, and in particular by the solemn ceremonial of the Day of Atonement. On that day the scapegoat was to be sent away into the wilderness: the

1. Ezekiel xviii: 4.   2. Ezekiel xxxiii: 10.   3. 2 Sam. xii: 13.

high priest was to 'lay both his hands upon the head of the live goat, and confess over him all the iniquities of the children of Israel, and all their transgressions, even all their sins; and he shall put them upon the head of the goat, and shall send him away by the hand of a man that is in readiness into the wilderness: and the goat shall bear upon him all their iniquities unto a solitary land: and he shall let go the goat in the wilderness'. And on the same day, the high priest, taking the blood of a sacrificed goat, was to go into the holiest place of all, and to 'make atonement for the holy place, because of the uncleannesses of the children of Israel, and because of their transgressions, even all their sins'.[1] Thus year by year a formal and external reconciliation of the nation with God was made.

But it was expressly stated in the law that atonement could be made only for sins of inadvertence, and not for deliberate and wilful transgression: the man who sinned with a high hand was to be cut off from among his people.[2] And here was the very heart of the problem. As the Jews looked back over their history as interpreted by the prophetic historians, they could see that the nation had sinned deliberately, wilfully, persistently, defiantly – and yet it had not been destroyed. How could this be? There could be but one answer: the law, with its insistence on judgement and vengeance, did not contain the sole or the last word of God. Beyond the truth that He is just is the truth that He is merciful, and that, contrary to hope and expectation, a place for forgiveness and for restoration can be found.

It was rather from the experience of the nation than from that of the individual that the Israelite inferred the nature of the divine dealings with man. The span of one man's life is too short, and the event often too perverse or too paradoxical, to serve as a basis for general understanding. It is on the larger canvas of the rise and fall of nations that tendencies appear and moral judgements seem to be confirmed by experience. There is, indeed, in some of the highest expres-

1. Leviticus xvi: 1–24.
2. Numbers xv: 30–31.

sions of Old Testament faith, a curious blending of the individual and the national, and such rapid transitions from singular to collective that it is sometimes hard to tell whether the prophet or psalmist is generalizing from his own experience, or whether he is speaking as the personification of the nation. The psalm which begins so personally 'Out of the depths have I called unto thee, O Lord, Lord, hear my voice', ends with the words: 'O Israel, hope in the Lord; for with the Lord there is mercy and with him is plenteous redemption. And he shall redeem Israel from all his iniquities.'[1] But of one of the most moving passages of all, there can be no doubt that it is spoken of the nation and its fortunes: 'Who is a God like unto thee that pardoneth iniquity, and passeth by the transgression of the remnant of his heritage? He retaineth not his anger for ever, because he delighteth in mercy. He will turn again and have compassion upon us.'[2]

There is a tendency for critics of religion to represent the God of the Old Testament as a gloomy and savage tyrant, and for those who have not read the book itself to suppose that this picture is well-founded in fact. The picture, indeed, is not wholly baseless; there is an element of sternness in the Old Testament, as in the New; there is a certain strain of violence, and occasionally even of vindictiveness, which belong to its historical character, and to the stage of imperfect revelation to which the Old Testament belongs. But to read the Old Testament at large is to receive quite the opposite impression; the emphasis is found to be on mercy, lovingkindness, and reconciliation. The word *ḥesed*, which the translators of the Authorized Version with magnificent disregard for consistency rendered variously as mercy, kindness, lovingkindness, merciful kindness, and pity, occurs more than 200 times; in some contexts, the reference is to such kindness as should exist between men and men, but in the vast majority of cases it is the loving kindness of God of which the writers speak. The characteristic note of the Old Testament insight is: 'For I have no pleasure in the death

1. Psalm cxxx: 1, 7–8.   2. Micah vii: 18–19.

of him that dieth, saith the Lord God: wherefore turn your-selves, and live!'[1]

The writers of the Old Testament were not unaware that, in holding firmly to the idea of God as both just and merci-ful, they were setting forth a paradox; but, like wise men, they were prepared to recognize that honesty in thought not infrequently involves holding to both sides of an antinomy, even though no reconciliation be immediately apparent, and that the abandonment of either involves an improper simpli-fication of the problem. Is not our own experience the same? Natural process is quite remorseless and unforgiving; and we recognize that that unforgivingness of natural law sup-plies the necessary element of stability in our lives. But life in society would be intolerable, if it were impossible for judgement to be tempered with mercy, and if vengeance could never be checked by the exercise of forgiveness. What may present itself as a perplexity in thought is often found to be simple and intelligible, when it is lived out as experience.

For the moment, we must be prepared to leave this prob-lem in suspense. The paradox of justice and mercy will meet us later in our argument, and a possible resolution of it will depend on certain considerations which have not yet come before us. For the moment, we will attempt no more than to summarize our argument hypothetically. If, as the Old Testament affirms, there is invisibly present in the universe a God who is one, active, faithful, righteous, and forgiving, that would account for much which man has discerned in the constitution of the universe, and for much in the moral experience of man in himself and in society. In that case, such a faith should not be discounted as incompatible with the use of reason, or impossible of acceptance by reasonable men. Before asking whether it is in fact acceptable, the next step in our argument must be to consider the figure of Jesus Christ as set forth in the Gospels, and to ask what further light, if any, is shed by His character, His teaching, and His death, upon the problems that have so far come before us as the subjects of our study.

1. Ezekiel xviii: 32.

4

JESUS

SOMEWHERE about the middle of the first century A.D., the Roman authorities became uncomfortably aware of the existence of a new secret society in their midst. They had had experience of secret societies before and did not like them. In 186 B.C., in the famous episode of the Bacchanalia, Roman society had been convulsed by the discovery that it was honeycombed by a society, of a partly political, partly religious character, and that members of the best families in Rome were implicated in the affair. The rapid and violent suppression of the menace was one of the most dramatic episodes in the whole of Roman history. So when the breath of talk began to be directed towards this new society which seemed to have come into existence, *impulsore Chresto*, as a Roman historian wrote, at the instigation of somebody called Chrestus, authority became inquisitive as to its nature and purpose. Festus, the Procurator of Judaea, summed it up with characteristic Roman brevity and accuracy: it all had to do with 'certain questions of their own religion, and of one Jesus, who was dead, whom Paul affirmed to be alive'.[1]

Festus hit the nail on the head. That Jesus, who was dead, was now alive was the very heart of the apostolic message: 'whom God raised up, having loosed the pangs of death, because it was not possible that he should be holden of it'.[2] To this point the Christian witnesses recur, with almost monotonous iteration.

It is important to note what these words meant, and what they did not mean, to the first Christians.

They certainly did not mean simply that Jesus of Nazareth, or His soul, still continued to exist somewhere in God's universe. The Jews, like the Greeks, believed that the souls

1. Acts xxv: 19.   2. Acts ii: 24.

of men, after death, went to the joyless realm of Sheol, in which there was neither life nor light nor knowledge of God, but only a dreadful twilight in which all distinctions were lost in a dreary sameness: 'for there is no work, nor device, nor knowledge, nor wisdom, in the grave, whither thou goest'.[1] But the Christian affirmation was precisely that Jesus had not remained in Sheol. Basing themselves on the sublime aspiration of the Old Testament saint, 'thou wilt not leave my soul in Hades (Sheol), neither wilt thou give thy holy one to see corruption', the Christians affirmed that this hope had been fulfilled in Jesus; David 'foreseeing this, spoke of the resurrection of the Christ, that neither was he left in Hades, nor did his flesh see corruption'.[2]

For this belief, it was not adequate that Jesus should be regarded as a *revenant*, mysteriously able at times to leave the world of the dead and to revisit the scenes of His earthly pilgrimage. The idea of such brief and transitory returns was by no means unfamiliar to the Jews. There is that eerie story in the first book of Samuel about the witch of Endor; at the behest of Saul she called up the ghost of Samuel, and was terrified when he appeared: 'I see a god coming up out of the earth. . . . An old man cometh up; and he is covered with a robe'.[3] But the Christian tradition denied in the most precise terms that the appearances of Jesus after His death were of this character. When the disciples saw Jesus, 'they were terrified and affrighted, and supposed that they beheld a spirit'; but He said, 'See my hands and my feet, that it is I myself: handle me and see; for a spirit hath not flesh and bones, as ye behold me having'.[4]

Christian faith in the continued activity of Jesus did not depend on continued physical or quasi-physical manifestations. It is true that the initial faith in the resurrection grew out of a number of events which those who took part in them described as personal meetings with a living Jesus. Scepti-

1. Ecclesiastes ix: 10.
2. Acts ii: 25–31.
3. 1 Samuel xxviii: 11–14.
4. Luke xxiv: 36–43.

cism may, if it wishes, dismiss these experiences as mere hallucinations, though the record of them is remarkably different from other records of the psychological state called hallucination. But by doing so it does not achieve much in its own cause, since to the early Christians contact with Jesus, who was dead and whom Paul affirmed to be alive, presented itself as a continuous experience, unaffected by time and place and circumstance, and independent of the nutriment which might be supposed to be supplied by visual phenomena.

What the Christians said was that Jesus Christ, though now invisible, was still alive and active, just as you and I are, in this world of space and time. And, as Dr Edwyn Bevan has somewhere pertinently remarked, the basic question that we have to ask about Jesus of Nazareth is, what He has been doing all this time, since those events that concerned Him took place long ago in the procuratorship of Pontius Pilate. The Christian answer has always been that He has been alive and influential in the affairs of men.

Again, it is necessary to be clear as to the precise meaning of the words used, since words can be used to mean different things, and sometimes people appear to be affirming the same things, when in fact their convictions are widely different.

In a sense all great men live on after their death. All wise teachers make considerable use of the Socratic method in teaching: whenever they do so, they are paying tribute to the influence of a man who died considerably more than 2,000 years ago. I suppose that the plays of Shakespeare will be read as long as there are human beings on this planet; in fact, as English comes to be the common language of an increasing part of the population of the world, and as the plays come to be translated into new languages, the influence of Shakespeare continues to grow, and is far greater to-day than it was at the time of his death. But it is to be noted that this posthumous influence is due to the continuing effects of certain things that Shakespeare did and certain words that he wrote while he was alive. If you throw a stone into a pond, the ripple you produce will continue to spread and to expand until it touches the banks on every hand; the growing influence of Shakespeare is like that expanding ripple. But Shakespeare has written no new plays since his death. He has cast no fresh pebbles into the pool of human life. We on the other hand who are alive are always casting in fresh pebbles, though they may be infinitesimal in size, and though the ripples they cause may be microscopically insignificant. The Christian contention is that Jesus of Nazareth has continued, through all the centuries since the days of His human life, to trouble the pool of human life, and that He is as active to-day in moulding human life as He was in His home at Nazareth in fashioning benches and tables.

This general affirmation can be analysed into four subsidiary affirmations, in the truth of each of which the general statement is involved.

1. The relationship between Christians and Jesus of Nazareth is a continuation of that friendship which existed between Jesus and His followers before His death. He is now invisible, and that has changed the character of the friendship; but the most important change is that that friendship is now accessible to all who desire to share it, without limitation of time or country. Human friendships tend to grow cold through long separation; or to die away by change of interest on the part of the friends; or to be broken by misunderstanding. If, as Christians hold, Jesus is ever present and unchangeable, His friendship, not being liable to any of these changes and chances, is perfect and indefectible.

2. The relationship between Jesus and His friends involves two-way traffic, a genuine exchange of love and life. It is said that a Breton peasant, who was accustomed to spend long periods in devotion before the reserved Sacrament, when asked what took place during those times, replied simply, 'I look at Him; He looks at me'. It is this mutuality, this genuine exchange, that is the trade mark of all relationships that are genuinely personal.

Most of the relationships in which we become involved are far below the level of the genuinely personal.

At their lowest, they do not rise above mere awareness. When we are hurrying through a London street to catch a train on the Underground, we are dimly aware of moving bodies about us, and our consciousness records the fact that they are human; but for all the reality they have for us, they might just as well be cows, except that cows on the whole are more dependable in their movements than human beings.

Awareness rises to a higher level when it is required to concentrate itself on an individual. Yet in practice there is very little difference for us between the clerk who issues us with our ticket on the Underground, and the automatic machine from which we can extract the same ticket, if we happen to have the right amount of money in our hand – except again that the automatic machine is a little more reliable than the human.

The relationship between a teacher and his class belongs to a different and higher level. Contact is real, though it may be limited strictly to the intellectual sphere, and in general the teacher is aware of his pupils as distinct and individual human persons. But, as you may remember, it is recorded of that great scholar A. E. Housman that when he was professor of Latin at University College, London, he was wont to apologize to his lady pupils for his inability to remember which was Miss Jones and which Miss Robinson, saying that, if he did remember that, he might easily forget more important things! To him the pupils were only minds which happened to inhabit bodies; and a mind which happens to inhabit a body is something very much less than a person.

Personal acquaintance begins only when each of the two who meet has clearly focused the other as a personal being, existing in his own right, and having his own intrinsic value, and on that basis is prepared to enter with a relationship which involves a willingness both to speak and to listen, both to give and to receive.

Christians may be deluded: but when they speak of their relationship to Jesus of Nazareth they mean emphatically that it is of this personal type. He is not a hero to be admired or an ideal to be followed; He is a friend, who in the relationship of friendship both speaks and acts. He speaks, we hear; we speak, He hears. There is genuine fellowship and exchange.

3. It is affirmed that the Christian through his friendship with Jesus receives guidance as to how he should act, both in the general direction of his life and in particular situations. Guidance for all is provided in the Bible, and in the rules and discipline of the Church. But in addition to this, there is an individual and particular guidance, which is available for all, if they are sensitive and attentive enough to receive it. The prophet of old had written: 'Thine ears shall hear a word behind thee, saying, This is the way, walk ye in it; when ye turn to the right hand, and when ye turn to the left.'[1] What in older days had been a pious hope had, in the Christian dispensation, become a matter of common experience.

4. The Christian affirms that the presence and the friendship of Christ enable him to achieve what would be impossible for him in his own unaided strength.

This power, that helps men to express their highest thoughts and ideals in action, is called in the technical language of theology *grace*. The use of an abstract term tends to be misleading; and the theologians have been much to blame, since they have so often spoken and written of grace as though it were a kind of substance existing independently; whereas it is, in fact, a quality of relationships between persons. There is nothing in the world more purely personal than grace.

It is possible, by analogy with other human relationships, to give some indication of what Christian theology means by the word.

Everyone who has served in the Army knows the difference that can be made almost immediately by the arrival of a new general to take command. If he is the kind of man to spread confidence, that confidence will penetrate to the

1. Isaiah xxx: 21.

very limits of his command, even among those who have hardly seen him, and certainly have never exchanged a word with him. Men know that something which is not themselves has become a part of them, and that to-day they are capable of things that yesterday they would have been unable to achieve.

A painter cannot but give something of himself to his pupils. If he is a bad teacher, he will impose his ways upon them, and so will limit and confine the expression of their natural gifts. If he knows his trade, he will be able to inspire, to correct, and so to enhance the peculiar talent of each. He has entered in and made himself a part of them. In their paintings his influence will be seen, but it will be seen as a liberating and not as a constricting force.

All that and a great deal more is meant by the Christian term *grace*. No analogy can fully express, though it may illustrate, the experience. To the Christian, the experience of grace goes far beyond all human analogies, and that for three reasons. It is unmistakably something other than himself; and yet it is felt not so much as an alien force that works upon him from without, as an indwelling power that re-creates him from within. It is perpetually available, and its operation is hindered only by his own unwillingness to respond. It is illimitable in its power to refashion broken human nature after the likeness of the One who is believed to be its source. For the Christian, grace is always the grace of our Lord Jesus Christ, through whom the love of God becomes a reality to man, and by whom, in the fellowship of the Holy Spirit, the new community of the redeemed comes into being.

To a great many people in the modern world all these assertions about Jesus of Nazareth appear wholly incredible. Words like hallucination, delusion, wishful thinking, and so on are freely used of the affirmations of religious faith. But in the course of our exposition we have not yet reached the point at which judgements are to be made. At the moment we are engaged only in trying to set out the contents of Christian faith. As Mr C. S. Lewis has somewhat petulantly remarked in one of his books, 'I am telling you what the Christian faith is: I didn't invent it'. Whether we like it or not, Christian faith through the centuries has meant sharing in certain experiences, and tracing back these experiences to a certain relationship to that very same Jesus who was dead, and whom Paul affirmed to be alive.

How did these things come about? How did so extraordinary a collection of beliefs become attached to a man, of whose limited human existence at a certain intersection of time and space we have reasonably certain historical evidence?

Let us begin in a very temperate key. At this point we shall say no more than that one of whom such things could be said must, on any showing, have been a most remarkable person.

Lord Rosebery has told us, in his fine study of *Napoleon: the Last Phase*, that Napoleon has permanently enlarged our idea of what it is possible for a human being to achieve. In him a lucid and restless intellect was perfectly matched with a disciplined and undivided will, steadily set on one single purpose, the fulfilment of his own ambition. A lucid intellect, an undivided will, a single purpose: was it the combination of these same qualities which made of Jesus of Nazareth a figure of more than Napoleonic power?

The greatest service which the critical study of the Gospels has rendered in the last 100 years has been the recovery of the picture of Jesus of Nazareth as a man. When we read the Bible or any other book, the impressions we receive are always to some extent determined by the preconceptions which we bring. The halo of sanctity with which tradition had invested the figure of the Founder of the Christian faith made it difficult for men to notice or to give due weight to certain things in the Gospel story, which become obvious as soon as they are pointed out. The minds of most of us are still so much influenced by Sunday-school lessons, sentimental pictures, and the kind of hymns we were taught to sing as children, that it may not be out of place to emphasize this point a little further. New Testament scholars of the

liberal period may have missed certain deeper elements in
the Gospels, of which later scholarship has reminded us;
but they have helped us to remember that the Gospels,
whatever else they are, are the story of *a man*. When I was
a student we were all much influenced by Prof. F. C. Burkitt's
Earliest Sources for the Life of Jesus Christ, and in particular by
his memorable phrase, 'the stormy and mysterious personality', depicted in the pages of the Gospel according to
St Mark. Is the phrase just and well chosen?

Before we look directly at Jesus Christ, it may be useful to
see Him as reflected in the minds of those whom He encountered.

The word that recurs again and again in the Gospel
records is *amazement*. Power and authority in supreme degree
radiated from Jesus, and even the most insensitive could not
remain unaware of it. They were astonished because He
spoke with authority, and not as the scribes. They were
amazed at all the mighty works that were done by Him. At
times this astonishment deepened into the kind of almost
superstitious terror, which men experience when they know
themselves to be face to face with a spiritual power that far
surpasses their understanding. At a critical moment Simon
Peter cried out to Him, 'Depart from me; for I am a sinful
man, O Lord',[1] for terror had come upon him and upon all
that were with him.

This sense of amazement and terror would not allow men
to be neutral in their relation to Jesus. The first overwhelming impression seemed inevitably to translate itself either
into passionate devotion or into unrelenting hatred. On the
one hand, the disciples were inspired to a loyalty that would
follow Him anywhere. When, in a time of stress, He showed
that He was determined to return to the place of greatest
peril, Thomas said, 'Let us also go, that we may die with
him'.[2] Those, on the other hand, who felt themselves rebuked by Him and were not willing to accept the validity
of the rebuke, felt that nothing could meet the case except
to destroy that which they had come to hate: 'And the

1. Luke v: 8.   2. John xi: 16.

Pharisees went out, and straightway with the Herodians took counsel against him, how they might destroy him.'[1]

Jesus Himself was well aware of this consequence of His mission. In face of the challenge which He brings, men cannot for ever remain neutral; as they decide, so they will be judged; as they decide, so they will find themselves divided from one another by their decisions. 'I came to cast fire upon the earth; and what will I, if it is already kindled? . . . Think ye that I am come to give peace in the earth? I tell you, Nay; but rather division: for there shall be from henceforth five in one house divided, three against two, and two against three. They shall be divided, father against son, and son against father; mother against daughter, and daughter against her mother; mother in law against her daughter in law, and daughter in law against her mother in law.'[2] What was true then has remained true throughout the centuries. To this day, the Brahman in India who decides to follow Christ knows that he must do so at the price of being for ever cast out from his own family, and that the funeral rites will be performed for him as for one already dead.

From a study of the life of this very remarkable person, certain facts emerge clearly, apart from any inferences which may seem legitimate to the student, and apart from those dogmatic assertions which the Christian Church was led in the course of centuries to make concerning Him.

Whatever else men may affirm or deny, it must remain for ever certain that Jesus of Nazareth was a genius of the highest order, and that this genius was complex, expressing itself not in one way only but in many.

1. He is unsurpassed in the field of religious poetry.

It is difficult for the English reader to realize this, partly because in our ordinary Bibles the sayings of Jesus are printed as prose, partly because excessive familiarity in childhood has dulled for most of us the splendour of His utterance. To read His words in a language other than our own is a help; yet even this will not carry us far, unless we are prepared also to spread the wings of a lively imagination.

1. Mark iii: 6.   2. Luke xii: 49, 51-3.

> Consider the lilies of the field, how they grow;
>   they toil not, neither do they spin:
> Yet I say unto you,
>   that even Solomon in all his glory
>   was not arrayed like one of these.

By what standards do we judge such words as these? No one has ever yet succeeded in defining the nature of poetry; yet it would perhaps be widely agreed that great poetry is found only where there is a combination of acute observation, deep feeling, and appropriate and memorable expression. Does this one specimen of the poetry of Jesus come short, under any one of the terms of this definition?

2. He is unsurpassed in the brilliance of His dialectic.

It is one thing to be supreme in measured utterance carefully prepared at leisure; it is quite another to be always ready with the telling answer in the heat of dispute. Much of the time of Jesus was spent in controversy with His adversaries; and often, as the record bears witness, their purpose was not to seek the resolution of differences, but to 'ensnare him in his talk'.[1] Again, familiarity tends to rob us of an understanding of the brilliance of His answers. If we can make the considerable effort of imagination required to set ourselves the question and to forget the answer that has been already given, we may better realize both the perilous nature of the snare and the perfect success of Jesus in disentangling Himself from it.

'By what authority doest thou these things? and who gave thee this authority?'[2] This was an exceedingly difficult question to answer. One who follows an established path, the accredited representative of a nation or of a religious system, can always point to his credentials. The innovator, the pioneer, the prophet, has no such ready answer; he stands or falls by the truth of his vision, the intrinsic self-evidencing power of his message. As so often, Jesus answers a question by another question: 'I also will ask you one question, which if ye tell me I likewise will tell you by what authority I do these things. The baptism of John, whence

---

1. Matthew xxii: 15.   2. Matthew xxi: 23.

L.I.F.E. College Library
1100 Glendale Blvd.
Los Angeles, Calif. 90026

was it? from heaven or from men?' This is not a skilful dialectical evasion of the difficulty. It is a legitimate appeal to reason. 'You know the answer, if only you will make use of the knowledge that you already have. You have had before your eyes, in John the Baptist, an example of supreme spiritual authority. Answer my question. By the integrity of your answer, your capacity for insight into spiritual things will be judged. And, if you answer my question rightly, it will be quite unnecessary that I should answer yours, since the answer to your question will already have been given out of your own mouths.'

Is it possible to imagine a more perfect handling of the situation?

3. He is unsurpassed in his capacity to express profound truth in simple language.

As I grow older, I become more sure that there is nothing really important which cannot be expressed perfectly simply, if only people will take the trouble to discover exactly what they mean, and to find the simplest words to match their thought.

Townsend Warner, to whom a great many Harrovians of an earlier date owed whatever capacity they had for expressing themselves in good English, once produced an admirable little book on the writing of English essays. The last chapter consists of a number of accounts of a street accident, in a variety of different styles, none of them highly commendable; the last account is just the parable of the Good Samaritan.

An astonishing proportion of the words of Jesus, in the Authorized Version, will be found to consist of the simplest monosyllables in the English language. 'A wise man, which built his house upon a rock: and the rain descended, and the floods came, and the winds blew, and beat upon that house; and it fell not: for it was founded upon a rock.'[1] The parable of the Pharisee and the publican consists of ninety words only, sixty-nine of them monosyllables;[2] but have all the eloquent discourses on humility ever delivered

1. Matthew vii: 24–5.   2. Luke xviii: 10–13.

really contained anything which was not already implicit in this brief utterance of Jesus?

4. He is supreme in the expression of an ultimate moral standard.

The moral judgements of Jesus fall upon the ear of the sensitive listener like successive strokes of doom. I suppose there is no clergyman of the Church of England who does not feel uncomfortable when the fourth Sunday after Trinity comes round and he stands up to read in the Gospel for the day the familiar words: 'Thou hypocrite, cast out first the beam out of thine own eye; and then shalt thou see clearly to cast out the mote out of thy brother's eye.'[1]

In a day when so many people are convinced of the relativity of all things, and in particular of all ethical judgements and standards, it requires some hardihood to use the word *ultimate* in such a connexion. We are told, not infrequently, that the teaching of Jesus was conditioned by the historical situation in which He lived, that Christian morality was suited to a certain stage in the development of human institutions, and that we may, indeed should, look for a further evolution of thought and standards beyond the point which they had reached in His day. Is this really true or sensible?

Consider, for instance, such a saying as 'love your enemies'. The words must be taken in their full sense, without any attempt to evacuate them of any part of their meaning. Your enemy is the man who is after you with a hatchet to take away your life; or with cruel calumnies to take away what is more precious than your life, your good name. Love, here as almost everywhere else in Scripture, indicates not an emotion, but a total attitude of one human being to another, involving where appropriate redemptive activity. We are to meet our enemy, then, with perfect willingness to endure anything that he may do to us, and perfect willingness to do anything for him that may tend to his lasting good. No doubt there is sometimes difficulty in the application of the principle; but does not the only real

1. Matthew vii: 5.

difficulty reside in the problem of discerning what is genuinely for the enemy's lasting good? Do the other difficulties which people conjure up really express anything more than their unwillingness to accept the words of Jesus in their plain and literal sense?

But, if we are willing to take the words as spoken – enmity the extreme of vindictiveness, love the extreme of serviceableness – is it possible to imagine any ethic which could set a higher standard than this, or make greater demands on those who are willing to accept it? Are we not here face to face with an ultimate? We may, indeed, on Nietzschean or Marxist grounds, reject entirely the Christian view that love and service tend to promote the well-being of men, that they are the only possible foundation for a rational system of ethics. But, if we are prepared, as most people in Britain still are prepared, to agree that in general love is better than hate, does it not appear that Jesus has carried the working out of this principle to the utmost possible limits of human thought?

5. Jesus is remarkable for the supreme mastery over life which is manifest in the records of His career.

As we have already said, it is not the general but the particular which has the power to move the human heart; not the expression of general principles, but the exemplification of those principles in a human life, and the application of them in the myriad complexities of the human situation.

In every human life there are the two elements of the warp and the woof. The warp is that which is fixed and unchangeable by any human effort or desire – the facts of our birth, of particular parents in a particular time and country; our stature, the colour of our eyes, certain natural endowments, such as a musical or an unmusical ear; the situation in which we are placed through the actions of others independently of any volition of our own. The woof is made up of our own reactions and choices within a situation not of our own choosing. We cannot change the past; it may be that our capacity for choice is more limited by heredity than has sometimes been supposed; our power to affect the future may be far less than we desire or hope. But within that field of choice lies the working out of a human destiny; as a man chooses, so is he; once he has chosen, he has set in motion a train of consequences by which he must abide, to a point far beyond the limits of his vision at the time when the choice was made, the action taken. The tension between man with his limited freedom of decision, and the forces beyond his control which have brought him into a certain situation not of his own choosing, is the very stuff of tragedy. Tragedy arises when a man through some inner weakness or failure of nerve abandons that mastery which is his birthright in the situation in which he finds himself, and allows himself to be carried away by the circumstances which it was his duty to control.

No writer has ever brooded more deeply than Aeschylus on the problems of fate and destiny and the responsibility of human choice. He sees men caught up in what appears to be a web of blind fate, working itself out from generation to generation in disaster. Is it no more than blind fate? Has man no freedom? His answer is that man is indeed caught up in the stream of destiny, but he cannot be carried away by it except through his own action and consent. Agamemnon, setting out with his great expedition for Troyland, is delayed by contrary winds; the seers tell him that the only way to secure the favouring breeze he needs is the sacrifice of his daughter Iphigeneia. Then follows the memorable phrase $\dot{\alpha}\nu\dot{\alpha}\gamma\kappa\alpha\varsigma$ $\ddot{\epsilon}\delta\upsilon$ $\lambda\dot{\epsilon}\pi\alpha\delta\nu\sigma\nu$ – he put upon himself the yoke of necessity. He ought not to have done it. He ought to have said 'No', at whatever cost to himself, and by so saying to have broken the nightmare spell, which rested upon the House of Atreus. Instead, by his own choice he made himself subject to the spell, and set in motion those consequences, to himself and to others, that are the subject of the Oresteia.

The Christian faith comes to us as the record of a human life. In the life of Jesus, as in any other, there are the two elements of warp and woof – the raw material which was given to Him, and the pattern that He wove out of it by a succession of choices exactly similar to those which we ourselves are called to make. His triumph is that of the perfect acceptance of a situation which He cannot change, and the perfect response of a human will to the demand of every situation. The life of Jesus is of universal significance, not because it was in any way exempt from the hampering circumstances of particularity, in which we ourselves are involved, but just because of its perfect adaptation to circumstances, its perfect use of these circumstances as the medium through which its own inner mastery was to be expressed.

The warp in the life of Jesus was the unchangeable situation within which He was called to work. He was born a Jew. He accepted fully the limitations imposed upon Him by membership of a despised and oppressed race. His ministry was carried out on a restricted stage. Though conscious that the significance of His work was to extend far beyond the confines of Israel, He always resisted the temptation to seek for Himself a larger sphere: 'I was not sent but unto the lost sheep of the house of Israel.'[1] He must have shared the distress of His people as they groaned under the heavy yoke of Rome; but He never expressed indignation against the Romans, though He saw them also, no less than His own people, as subject to the righteous judgement of God. The pitiless opposition of the scribes and Pharisees was an unpleasant element in the given situation; this too He accepted calmly and without resentment, though He knew well to what in the end it was bound to lead.

All creative work depends on the acceptance of limitation. Milton could not begin to write *Paradise Lost* until he had decided whether he was going to compose a religious drama or an epic. No artist can begin to paint a picture until he has made up his mind whether his genius can express itself better in tempera or in oils. The choice once made, he can set himself to achieve perfection within the limitations he has accepted. Jesus did not attempt to alter the circumstances in which His ministry was to be carried out; within

1. Matthew xv: 24.

those cheerfully accepted limits, He set Himself to the working out of a perfect human life.

He did not manufacture or manipulate situations; He allowed them to develop as they would, through the free action of others. But no situation as it arose ever found Him unprepared; at every point He shows His capacity to make each situation yield all that it can of significance for the manifestation of the will of God and of the purpose of His mission. This power was displayed specially in situations that in themselves were unpleasant and disconcerting.

Simon the Pharisee desired Him that He would eat with him, and then omitted the usual courtesies with which any guest would be received – a serious matter in the formal and elaborately courteous East. That Jesus felt the insult keenly is clear from the mournful and weighty cadence of His rebuke:

> I entered into thine house,
>> Thou gavest me no water for my feet;
> Thou gavest me no kiss:
>> Mine head with oil thou didst not anoint.[1]

But from this unpropitious beginning Jesus turns by contrast to the sinful woman, whose sins which were many could be forgiven because she had loved much; and from the unpleasantness of social discourtesy plucks the jewel of one of His most memorable utterances.

This mastery is perhaps the best point from which to start consideration of the Christian affirmation concerning the sinlessness of Jesus. How do we know that Jesus never sinned?

It is impossible to prove a negative. Even if we had a complete record, such as is in any case unobtainable, of all the words and works of Jesus, we should still lack evidence concerning the world of thought, in which are the roots of all evils, and in which many of the gravest defects of character reside. It is true that in the fourth Gospel Jesus is recorded to have said, 'Which of you convinceth me of sin?'[2] It is true also that nowhere in the Gospels do we find any sign that Jesus, who so emphatically called others to

1. Luke vii: 44–46.   2. John viii: 46.

repentance – 'Except ye repent, ye shall all likewise perish'[1] – Himself felt any need for repentance. This point is important and we shall recur to it again. It is not the great sinner but the great saint who is most sensitive to imperfection in himself; as men make progress towards the ideal, they become more acutely aware of their inability to attain it. If Jesus, who on any showing manifested in superlative degree the most admirable of human characteristics, never displayed any sense of guilt or imperfection in Himself, it is at least possible that this was because He was in fact free from such guilt and imperfection.

But this line of argument is inconclusive, since it starts from the confused idea that goodness is simply the absence of badness, and that to abstain from what is wrong is in itself virtue – whereas in fact it may be no more than cowardice. Goodness, in any sense in which a valid ethic will admit the term, is not negative; it is a positive, dynamic, creative power. It is the capacity to take hold of a situation, any situation, and to extract from it the maximum of good which it can possibly be made to yield. The great leader is the man who can snatch victory from the very jaws of defeat. The human spirit is at its height, not when all is pleasant and favourable, but when it shows its capacity to rise superior to thwarting circumstance, and to win from it the fruits of heroism and gentle strength.

It has already been suggested that the greatness of Jesus is to be seen in His capacity to accept situations as they came, without resentment and without dismay, and to make each serve His purpose. If we find that even in the abandonment and desolation of the cross He was in fact still master of the situation, and that never was His capacity to bring good out of evil so conspicuously seen as in His death, we may be led to grasp the positive character of sinlessness, and may be prepared to consider whether, on the evidence available in the Gospels, the Christian claim that Jesus was unique as being sinless is reasonable and worthy of the consideration of thoughtful men.

1. Luke xiii: 5.

The friends of Jesus believed that His unique power to deal with human situations derived from a unique intimacy with God.

When He began to preach, the first thing that His hearers, friends and enemies, noticed was that He spoke with authority and not as the scribes. There is an immense difference between speaking with authority and speaking from authorities. The scribe was the man who could cite for every statement that he made the chain of authorities reaching back from teacher to teacher to the original authority by whom the statement was first made. It was widely recognized in Israel that this scribal method was necessary during the period when the prophetic gift was in abeyance. The prophet is the man who speaks boldly, saying 'Thus saith the Lord'. He can offer no credentials other than the intrinsic power of His utterance. He can appeal to no authority other than the invisible authority of God. Not unnaturally, when Jesus began to preach the people took Him for a prophet – 'the prophet which is of Nazareth in Galilee'. When He began to say, 'Ye have heard that it was said unto them of old time . . . but I say unto you', the claim that He could set aside the ancient law was indeed a tremendous claim, but did not necessarily expose Him to a charge of personal arrogance, since one prophet could advance on the revelation given to another; had not Jeremiah proclaimed a new covenant of God with His people, which should in time replace the old? But it could not but seem reasonable to the Pharisees that they should ask for a sign, in authentication of such tremendous claims.

Such a sign Jesus firmly refused to give. His authority rests only on an inner intimacy with God; and such authority can authenticate itself only to those who have spiritual perception at least in some measure akin to that of the one who speaks with authority.

It is central in the teaching of Jesus that every single individual is the object of the direct, detailed, continuous, and personal attention and care of God: 'Are not two sparrows sold for a farthing? and not one of them shall fall on the ground without your Father: but the very hairs of your head are all numbered. Fear not therefore; ye are of more value than many sparrows.'[1] The Old Testament had asserted that the plea of the widow, the orphan, and the fatherless ascended up to God, and that His ears were open unto their cry. Jesus takes up this insight of the Old Testament, and makes it at the same time more far-reaching and more intimate.

What He proclaimed to others was evidently the principle by which His own life was guided. His actions and movements do not depend on His own unaided will and judgement; in everything He is guided by the will of His Father. Nothing that He does is done in His own strength; all power is received directly from God, and received in just such measure as is needed. In the fourth Gospel the inner life of Jesus and the intimacy of His relationship with the Father are set forth in a multitude of different ways. 'Mine hour is not yet come.' 'His hour was not yet come.'[2] For everything there is an appointed time fixed by the Father's will. Jesus will not run ahead of this, since to choose His own time would be to transgress the Father's will. 'The Son can do nothing of himself, but what he seeth the Father doing: for what things soever he doeth, these the Son also doeth in like manner.'[3] 'For I spake not from myself, but the Father which sent me, he hath given me a commandment, what I should say, and what I should speak.'[4] 'I have meat to eat that ye know not. . . . My meat is to do the will of him that sent me, and to accomplish his work.'[5]

Is such intimacy between God and men a possibility? Or

1. Matthew x: 29–31.
2. John ii: 4; vii: 30.
3. John v: 19; see also viii: 28.
4. John xii: 49.
5. John iv: 32–4. It is well known that the fourth Gospel is later than the other three, and contains a larger measure of interpretation. But even if the sayings quoted are not so much a transcript of the original words of Jesus as an interpretation, the interpretation is congruous with the total presentation of Jesus in the four Gospels; and for the purposes of our present argument, that is sufficient.

were the friends of Jesus, who observed Him and have left us the record of His life, deluded in thinking that He enjoyed it? Is what He taught on the basis of that intimacy really true? These are among those questions which are much easier to ask than to answer; but perhaps an analogy from human relationship may help to make clear what is involved in the question.[1]

Personal relationships are, as we have already indicated, *sui generis*, and demand at least a measure of mutual attention, interest, and exchange. But, even when genuinely personal relationships have been established, no human being can see another human being exactly as he is. There are always two factors in the situation – B as he really is; and the preconceptions, misconceptions, and fancies which A brings into the relationship. This is what is called by psychologists the element of projection. We all project on to every human relationship something which is in ourselves, and not in the actual situation. This is not to say that there is no real meeting of person with person. But there is also the possibility of much misunderstanding and disillusionment. The classic case is that of the young man who wakes up from the dream of love, to find that he has really been in love with love, and has never seen in the clear light of day the girl on to whom his inner dreams have been projected.

To put the matter diagrammatically, what A sees is not B, but a point X, somewhere on the semicircle which unites A and B. The point at which X is seen is determined by the strength of the element of projection which is mixed by A with the reality of B. And, of course, X may and should be a moving point; as understanding and observation develop, X should move from A towards B; though, with the imperfection of even the most perfect human relationships, X will never precisely coincide with B. In certain cases, such as a happy marriage of many years' duration, X may come very near to B. At the other extreme, where the element of

1. Deeper questions concerning the relationship of Jesus to God the Father have been deliberately postponed to the last chapter of this book, where a discussion of them will be found.

projection or preconception is very strong, X may be very close indeed to A, or indeed may be within the mind of A. I once worked for a year with a group of people who, before I joined them, knew something of my previous history and my academic record, and had formed such a clear idea of what I must be like that when I arrived they were not able to see the real me at all. The point X never moved out of their minds on to the semicircle between them and me.

If this is true of our relationship with our brother whom we have seen, much more is it likely to be true of our relationship, if any such is possible, with God whom we have not seen. Even those who admit the validity of religious experience are bound to admit that in all such experience the element of projection enters in. This accounts for the contradictions and uncertainties in the evidence even of those who profess to worship the same God. The sceptic readily makes use of such imperfections to discredit the whole idea of religious experience. But, as we have seen more than once, to say that a thing is imperfect is not the same as to say that it is non-existent or wholly invalid. We do know one another, though in this life we can never know one another perfectly. We cannot know God perfectly; this is not in the least the same as to say that we cannot know Him at all. In human relationships there are as many degrees of perception as there are people; but some men and women do stand out as endued with such gifts of understanding and penetration that it seems evident that in them the element of projection, of distortion, is very small indeed. We must allow for the possibility that the same may be true in relation to the divine. Most of us, even if we believe in God, have such woolly ideas about Him that the admixture of our own fancies and illusions is all too plain. But is it not possible that there are some men so sensitive to the divine that in them the element of projection is very small? And is it not also possible that, if there were a sinless person, the factor of distortion would be reduced to its very minimum, or in fact might not exist at all?

Is it possible that Jesus spoke as He did of God, because

He had Himself seen and known God, as no other man before or since has ever seen and known Him? It is clear from the records that He had a unique capacity to penetrate the secrets of men's hearts, and to know them as they really were; in the simple words of the fourth Gospel, 'He knew what was in man'. What He has to say about God is marked by an extraordinary simplicity, lucidity, and conviction. Is it possible that this was because, exempt from the muddled confusions of our spiritual vision, He was seeing God as He is, and recording in the simplest and plainest way what He had seen? If we see reason to think that He was in fact sinless, the clarity and sureness of His vision of God, which makes Him unique as a spiritual teacher, may be connected with that other inward quality that distinguishes Him from other men.[1]

Jesus seems to bring into the world a new attitude towards suffering.

Those who have not themselves greatly suffered indulge in a great deal of foolish talk about suffering. It is supposed to have a naturally purifying and elevating effect on the human spirit. Those who have suffered know well that, though good can sometimes miraculously come out of evil, the real effects of suffering are as different as possible from those which imagination has painted.

The first effect of severe suffering is a kind of paralysis. It produces such a concentration of the mind upon itself that the sufferer becomes almost unaware of anything outside himself. The mere effort demanded by endurance of the suffering is so exacting that no energy is left over for anything else. The mental faculties become dulled and lucid thought becomes difficult. The long continuance of suffering results in a terrible burden of weariness which always seems to have reached the limit of what can be endured, and yet always opens out afresh into deeper depths of weariness. It is not surprising that suffering quickly reveals the real

1. Here again it must be noted that the uniqueness of Jesus, as He is presented to us in the Gospels, raises many questions, of which consideration is postponed to Chapter 9.

character of the sufferer, and brings to light all the weaknesses that in days of health may have been concealed.

There seem to be in fact four possible attitudes towards suffering.

There is, first, the yielding of despair. Fortunately this is not very common. Even those who say that they despair generally have somewhere within them at least a spark of hope; they are not wholly beyond the reach of human kindness. Genuine despair is a very terrible thing. It means the death of the spirit, of everything that enables a man to react to his environment and in a measure to control it.

Much commoner and more familiar is the attitude of angry resentment. 'Why should I have been made to suffer like this? What kind of a world is it in which such suffering is possible?' For my generation, that attitude was fixed and expressed for ever in the poetry of A. E. Housman. Housman shook his fist at the universe, and cursed whatever brute or blackguard made the world. The highest that the spirit of man can reach is a kind of wry and rueful resignation:

> The troubles of our proud and angry dust
> Are from eternity, and shall not fail;
> Bear them we can, and if we can we must;
> Shoulder the sky, my lad, and drink your ale.

Thirdly, there is the Stoic attitude. The ideal of the Stoic wise man was ἀπάθεια, freedom from inner perturbation. His aim was to live in an ivory tower of his own detachment and fortitude, to look out impassively on the vicissitudes of life; and, if suffering or misfortune should come upon him, to regard it as an external event that in no way inwardly concerned him, and could not in any case disturb his peace of mind.

The great Stoics of the Roman Empire, contemporaries of Jesus and of Paul, were men of conspicuous nobility. Many of them were in continuous opposition to the empire, and looked back nostalgically to the simpler and more austere days of the republic; in consequence, their lives were never safe, and they never knew when they might be called to meet the executioner; or if such favour were given, to anticipate his arrival by a voluntary death.

As an illustration of the spirit and the temper of these men, I have transcribed the last page of the mutilated *Annals* of Tacitus. It is the story of Paetus Thrasea, who in the reign of Nero was accorded the privilege of the free choice of his own mode of death. On the day appointed for his death he gathered a company of friends together in his house:

His chief attention was given to Demetrius, a master of the Cynic creed, with whom he was debating the nature of the soul, and the divorce of spirit and body. Then, taking the decree of the Senate, he led Helvidius and Demetrius into his bedroom, and offered the arteries of both arms to the knife. When the blood had begun to flow, he sprinkled it on the ground, and calling the quaestor nearer, he said, 'We are making a libation to Jove the liberator. Look, young man (may heaven indeed avert the omen!): but you have been born into times when it is expedient to steel the mind with instances of firmness'. Later, as the end was long in coming, and he began to suffer grievously, he turned his eyes upon Demetrius. ...[1]

At this point the manuscript breaks off, and the rest is hidden.

It would be hard to find in history more admirable examples of adherence to principle and courage. Yet the Stoic creed is not always attractive. It is a creed for strong men, and has no place for the weak. But most of us are conscious that in ourselves we are weak, and that, if we are to stand against all the ills that life may bring, we have need of a courage not our own. For such as we are the Stoic has no message. The bad side of Stoicism is its hardness and its arrogance, which, while heroically enduring suffering, is not free from austere contempt for those who cannot attain to the same high standard, and for those who have inflicted the unmerited suffering.

In the story of the death of Jesus no place is found for either hardness or contempt.

Others have sometimes seemed to overcome suffering by expelling it, by guarding within themselves some iron-bound

1. Tacitus: *Annals* xvi: 35. The phrase to which I particularly wish to draw attention is this: *Ceterum in ea tempora natus es quibus firmare animum expediat constantibus exemplis.*

sanctuary, to which the suffering cannot penetrate. It is not so with Jesus. He does not wilfully run on suffering; until His hour is come, He regards His life as a gift to be carefully preserved. But when the time of suffering comes, He opens His arms to receive it, allows it, so to speak, to hurt Him as much as it can, lets it find its way to the inmost recesses of His being. 'My soul is exceeding sorrowful, even unto death.'

In the midst of agony He never loses His perfect serenity and self-control. As we have said earlier, suffering tends so to concentrate the attention of the sufferer on his own struggle, that for the time being others outside himself almost cease to exist. It is not so with Jesus. He has leisure of spirit, even in that crisis, to be aware of others and their needs – to speak a word of hope to the robber who has been crucified with Him, to remember the needs of His mother, to speak to the daughters of Jerusalem, who stood weeping for Him as He went along the sorrowful way.

His judgement on those who have done the wrong is clear and uncompromising. Yet in this judgement there is no trace of personal vindictiveness, of contempt or hatred. Those who have crucified Him are sinful men, standing under the divine judgement, and so in desperate need of the divine mercy; therefore His first word from the cross is a word of forgiveness: 'Father, forgive them, for they know not what they do.'

He is convinced that there is no irrational purposeless suffering in the world. When such things as the Crucifixion happen, the sun's light fails and there is darkness at noon; it seems that all the courses of the world are out of joint, and that blind chaos has taken charge. To Jesus, it is not so. There are dark and terrible forces of evil at work in the world; but even these are not outside the control of the Father in heaven, who can use even the evil for the working out of His majestic purposes. This death has been contrived by the malice and cruelty of Pharisees and Herodians and chief priests. Jesus sees it in another light: 'The cup that my Father giveth me, shall I not drink it?'

He is convinced that innocent suffering, meekly and

courageously borne, has redemptive value. Through it something is achieved that could not be achieved in any other way. 'For verily the Son of man came not to be ministered unto, but to minister, and to give his life a ransom for many.'[1]

If a ransom is to be paid, then there are captives who need to be delivered. If a redemption is to be achieved, it follows that there are men who need to be redeemed.

From what do men need to be redeemed? How is redemption possible? The New Testament has an answer. Is that answer true, and relevant to the human situation?

The consideration of this problem must be the next stage in our argument. For the moment we shall do no more than note the paradox that, in the experience of men through nineteen centuries, the cross of Jesus has proved itself to be light and strength and hope. To those immersed in tragedy and near to the point of despair, it has brought firmness to endure in a strength not their own; serenity of spirit through renewed faith in a loving Father; and hope that their suffering is not mere meaningless agony, but somehow has its place in a redemptive purpose.

It is remarkable that one of the most impressive testimonies in the English language to this fact comes from a poet who was not himself a believer in the One whom he proclaimed – Percy Bysshe Shelley:

> A power from the unknown God,
>   A Promethean conqueror came;
> Like a triumphal path he trod
>   The thorns of death and shame.
>   A mortal shape to Him
>   Was like the vapour dim
> Which the orient planet animates with light;
>   Hell, Sin and Slavery came,
>   Like bloodhounds mild and tame,
> Nor preyed until their Lord had taken flight.
>   The moon of Mahomet
>   Arose, and it shall set:
> While blazon'd as on heaven's eternal noon
>   The cross leads generations on.

1. Mark x: 45.

5

MAN THE PROBLEM

MAN's chief problem has always been man himself.

What is man? The answers given to this question in different epochs and by different thinkers have swung between the extremes of arrogance and of self-depreciation.

Medieval man lived in a tidy geocentric universe. The earth remained fixed, as God had in the beginning created it. Round it revolved the nine heavens of the sun, the moon, the planets, and the fixed stars, emitting as they moved the heavenly music of the spheres. Man was the crown of creation, the last created, made in the likeness of God, the one for whom this world was made, and who had been originally ordained by God to rule in it.

But man is fallen from his high estate. Through the malice of the devil corruption has entered into the world, and has so extended its empire that in all the race of men there is nothing clean. Mankind is a *massa perditionis*, the object of God's wrath and judgement, and doomed to everlasting destruction.

This doctrine was accepted in its severest and most literal form, and found the crudest expression on the lips of medieval moralists and revival preachers. Such was the strength of its hold on the minds of men that it long survived the abandonment of the Ptolemaic in favour of the Copernican astronomy. Some of the most characteristic expressions of it are to be found in the writings of Jonathan Edwards, the pillar of the New England theology in the eighteenth century:

The God who holds you over the pit of hell, much as one holds a spider or some loathsome insect over the fire, abhors you and is dreadfully provoked . . . you are ten thousand times so abominable in his eyes, as the most hateful and venomous serpent is in ours.

Children, he tells us, are

young vipers, and are infinitely more hateful than vipers.

On this last passage Leslie Stephen commented, with a not wholly unsympathetic tartness: 'That Edwards should have been a gentle, meditative creature, around whose knees had clung eleven young vipers of his own begetting, is certainly an astonishing reflection.'

The life of medieval man was not wholly darkened by this gloomy theology. He managed to get a good deal of fun out of existence, as can be learned from Miss Helen Waddell's two charming books, *The Wandering Scholars* and *Mediaeval Latin Lyrics*; or indeed, to go no further afield, from the merrier parts of Chaucer's *Canterbury Tales*. But apart from a few sceptics like the Emperor Frederick II, *Stupor Mundi*, medieval man in the Christian West would, if questioned, almost certainly have expressed his acquiescence in this traditional interpretation of the Christian doctrine of original sin and its consequences for man; and the medieval ecclesiastic if asked, as Christ was once asked, 'Are there few that be saved?' not feeling himself bound by the reticence of his Master, would probably have replied, 'Very few indeed'.[1]

The Renaissance was marked by a violent reaction against this traditional estimate of man.

Three strands may perhaps be discerned in what may be called in general the Renaissance tradition.

There is, first, the renewed faculty of accurate observation. Nothing in human history is stranger than the gradual dying out in Europe, with the disruption of the ancient Graeco-Roman culture during the fourth and fifth centuries, of the impulse to observe and understand. That ancient culture never wholly disappeared; there was a kind of apostolic succession, which went forward through men like the Venerable Bede, Alcuin of York, and the philosopher Johannes Scotus Erigena. Thought was more active than is sometimes supposed; but it was almost entirely about things that were

1. Many references in G. G. Coulton: *Five Centuries of Religion*, Vol. I (Cambridge 1923–50).

already known; there were few additions to the raw material of thought through fresh observation, and little of the stimulus that comes through discovery. When Aristotle began to make his way back to the consciousness of the West, mainly through Latin translations from the Arabic, his methods and habits of thought came upon men's minds with the shock of a creative revolution.

With the growth of the Renaissance spirit, all this was changed. Men looked out upon the world with new eyes. This material universe was no longer regarded as a vale of tears, to be escaped from as soon as possible, but as a kingdom of discoverable riches and infinite delight, to be surveyed, explored, and subjected, and used to the glory of man. Though the birth pangs were long, out of this renewed faculty of observation and wonder modern physical science was born.

Secondly, Renaissance man claimed the right to direct his critical intelligence on anything and everything in the world. His view might be summed up in the formula that there is no alleged truth so sacred that it cannot be doubted, no canon of thought so widely accepted that it cannot be questioned, and no institution so venerable that it cannot be criticized. This new spirit of criticism had its unpleasant and unattractive sides, as in the coarse and shallow scepticism of those Roman ecclesiastics, who made a mockery of the most solemn rites of the Church which they had been ordained to serve. At the same time, however, this critical spirit was forging, in its better and more valid forms, an instrument of the utmost value for the recovery of vanished truth. The medieval world had without question accepted as genuine the document called the Donation of Constantine, in which it was related that the first Christian Emperor Constantine, having been healed of leprosy by Pope Sylvester, deliberately transferred the seat of the Empire from Rome to Constantinople, in order that he might leave the successor of St Peter in unchallenged and unrivalled dominion in the West. In the fifteenth century Laurentius Valla proved that this precious document was a forgery.

From that time on, whatever other arguments might be advanced in favour of the papal supremacy, it was impossible ever again to claim that it had been legally instituted by the action of the Roman Emperor.

In the third place, the Renaissance tradition had unbounded faith in man and in his natural perfectivity. At a time when almost every year was being marked by some transcendent achievement of human genius, particularly in the visual arts, this new confidence in man, and this new understanding of the world as his kingdom, is not surprising. It was a much later poet who sang 'Glory to man in the highest, for man is the highest of things'; but the words are an echo of the true Renaissance spirit.

As has often been remarked, this new attitude to man, and to man's body as the home of his restless, questing spirit, can be traced clearly in the development of Italian painting. The exquisite effects of the school of Fra Angelico are attained almost entirely by the skilful arrangement of surfaces. To look at those still, expressive figures, is hardly to guess that blood and muscles are at work beneath their skins. Even in the great pictures of Botticelli, with a far more developed and naturalistic technique, there is little attempt to look beyond human pose to the principles of human activity. A new range of observation begins with painters like Luca da Signorelli and perhaps Carlo Crivelli. The process is complete in Michelangelo. The colossal statue of David, which once stood (and now stands in replica) outside the Palazzo della Signoria in Florence, is perhaps the most perfect expression of the Renaissance concept of man, in the full vigour of muscular and harmoniously developed youth, going out to conquer and to subdue the world. There must have been many who, as they looked at the great fresco of the Last Judgement on the east wall of the Sistine Chapel in the Vatican, have felt that the figure of Christ as Judge is uncomfortably like the figure of David. Is it really the natural man, with all his capacities, his ambitions, his insatiable desire of self-expression, who has the last word in judgement on all things in heaven and earth? Is he, as a matter of fact, exempt from any judgement other than his own?

Renaissance thought, and its development in humanism, obviously challenges to the heart the traditional Christian understanding of man and his world. Christian theology has in the main depicted man as weak, and desperately in need of the grace of God; humanism looks upon him as strong, if only he will rise up and exercise the strength that is latent in him. Christian theology finds that man's blessedness increases in direct ratio to his dependence upon God; humanism demands for him complete independence – every man should be the master of his fate and the captain of his soul. Above all, Christianity has thought of man as essentially sinful, and unable, without divine intervention, either to perceive and know what things he ought to do, or to have power to fulfil the same. Humanism regards man as naturally good except in so far as he has been perverted by ignorance or priestcraft, and able, if set free to live according to the law of his nature, to arrive in this life at a state of almost unalloyed happiness. Christian faith taught that true happiness for man lies only in the eternal world. Humanism, with its new delight in the material and visible world, relegated the unseen world to a very great distance, and bade man exchange a heavenly for an earthly paradise.

It is curious that the political thought of the Renaissance and post-Renaissance period, starting from the new idea of the autonomy and self-direction of man, moved in two sharply contrasted directions. The vitality of the thought of that time will be apparent if we consider how closely the two great opposing political forces in the world to-day correspond to these two types of thought about man and his nature.

If each man is free to exercise his infinite capacity and desire for self-expression, untrammelled by all those rules of Christian charity and divine sanctions, of which medieval man was always conscious even when he was most flagrantly disregarding them in action, it seems fairly certain that the world will become the scene of an internecine conflict between opposing wills. So thought Thomas Hobbes. His solution of the problem is the authority of the State. His thought, in fact, served as the theoretical justification for that new type of state which was coming into being with the collapse of the medieval world – a strong, centralized, autocratic monarchy, able to control the aberrant wills and purposes of its subjects. Hobbes may be called, without too flagrant an anachronism, the father of all totalitarians.

The other, and optimistic, stream finds expression in the political thought of Locke, with its profound belief in the reasonableness of man, and of the power of reason to assert itself in human affairs; but still more clearly in the romanticism of Rousseau. 'Man is born free, but is everywhere in chains.' So begins *The Social Contract*. Man is essentially and naturally good; if he can but be set free to follow the dictates of his unperverted nature, evil and cruelty will disappear, and mankind will be happy as bounteous Nature always intended him to be. This optimistic philosophy clearly prepared the way for the French Revolution, and underlies the American Declaration of Independence and the first Constitution of the United States of America. This optimism concerning man's nature and capacity, and of the beneficent effects of 'liberty' – a concept rather assumed than critically analysed – has been characteristic of American thought up till the present day.

The two great branches of Western Christendom have reacted differently to the continuing challenge of the Renaissance and of humanistic thought. Protestantism has on the whole compromised with it, and has tended to substitute the humanistic kingdom of man for that Kingdom of God, which orthodox Christian thought had proclaimed as the end and the judge of all human enterprise. Thereby it has become deeply secularized, and has at times been in danger of losing altogether its spiritual vitality. Roman Catholicism has on the whole repudiated the Renaissance. Its thought is largely determined by the canons of a pre-critical, pre-scientific age. This, on the one hand, tends to imprison Roman Christendom within the narrow limits of obscurantism, and to produce by reaction that fierce anti-clericalism which is endemic in some countries of Europe, epidemic in many other parts of the world; on the other hand, it has given to that Church a stability and an enduring spiritual vitality which cannot but be the envy of Protestants.

The nineteenth century, for all its mechanical progress, and the general optimism of the Victorian era, found man once again perplexed as to his place and function in the universe.

That universe had turned out to be much vaster and more complex than anyone had imagined. As astronomy began to calculate the distances of the fixed stars, and man learned to think in light years, the frontiers of space seemed to recede to illimitable distances, and the earth to be reduced to the dimensions of an insignificant speck of dust.

Geology had carried back the origins of the world, and even of life on it, by hundreds of thousands if not millions of years. Even in my boyhood a great many of the Bibles sold in England carried on each page a chronological indication, based on the calculations of Archbishop Ussher in the seventeenth century; and the creation of the world was neatly dated in 4004 B.C. If you read the sermons of John Donne, and note the repeated references to 6,000 years as the measure so far of man's tenure of life on this planet, you will realize that in the seventeenth century this was the time-scale that was taken for granted even by learned men. It is sometimes hard to remember that this continued to be true until late in the nineteenth century. It was not without an effort that men adjusted their minds to the new demands of geology and palaeontology.

One of the severest shocks to orthodox and traditional thinking was administered by the publication of Charles Darwin's *Origin of Species* (1859) and *Descent of Man* (1871). Those who picture the Victorian age as a calm and complacent time would be astonished, if they were to turn up the files of old periodicals, and to discover the vehemence and the virulence of the storms which raged over the new hypothesis of evolution. If man was no more than a highly developed animal, what became of his uniqueness in the universe? And the uniqueness of man, as the object of God's special favour and of a divine act of redemption, was the very basis and foundation of orthodox religion. But it was not only Christians who were dismayed; others, too, felt themselves shrunk and diminished before this appalling and ruthless majesty of the physical universe, and wondered whether it was still possible to hold the traditional views of the significance of the life of man.

All this is very familiar to-day. I have set it forth at some length only in order that we may try imaginatively to put ourselves back into the position of those to whom all these discoveries were new, and recapture the disarray of spirit into which many of them found themselves cast. That uncertainty, as it affected the student world, was well expressed by Bishop (at that time Professor) J. B. Lightfoot in a sermon preached in the chapel of Trinity College, Cambridge, in 1876:

What is man, nay, what is all humanity, but an atom in this limitless universe, a drop in this ocean of infinite space?

What is man, even on this earth of his own, but a fleeting apparition, a thing of yesterday, a term in an endless series, one ripple in the stream of the ages, one moment in infinite time?

What is man? Half akin, nay, more than half akin to the brute. And the son of man? A superior mammal, a developed mollusc, a creature among creatures, a finer sample of a vulgar type.

The universe appeared as vast, cold, bleak, and unsympathetic, a scene of ceaseless conflict, and reckless sacrifice not only of the individual but of the type.

In face of this new situation, thoughtful men tried in various ways to make terms with what they believed to be truth, and to find some way to live honestly and uprightly in a world the moral foundations of which seemed to have been cast down.

Some, like T. H. Huxley, adopted without compromise the attitude of rebellion against an intolerable world. In 1894 that distinguished scientist wrote:

Let us understand, once for all, that the ethical progress of society depends, not on imitating the cosmic process, still less in running away from it, but in combating it.

But is there any sense in combating a universe which is so much stronger and more enduring than we? When Thomas Carlyle was informed that Margaret Fuller of Boston had announced her decision to accept the universe, his abrupt comment was, 'Gad, she'd better'.

Others, realizing that Huxley's gesture of defiance is all in vain, yet conclude that it has to be made. Our ship must go down, but at least let it go down with all its colours flying. Bertrand Russell, in eloquent and glowing terms, told an earlier generation of students that there was no other course open to us but to build our lives upon the foundation of un-yielding despair. A century earlier a much greater man, Giacomo Leopardi, face to face with the new world, in which, as he judged, knowledge was destroying imagination and science banishing inspiration, wrote in his *Dialogo di Tristano ed un amico*:

Whether my feelings are the product of sickness, I do not know; I only know, that, sick or well, I spurn the cowardice of men, I repudiate every consolation and every childish deception; I have the courage to endure the loss of every hope, to look without dis-may upon the desert of the world, not to hide from myself any part of the unhappiness of men, and to accept all the consequences of a philosophy which though sorrowful is true. That philosophy, if it has no other usefulness, at least wins for brave men victory over the hidden and mysterious cruelty of human destiny.

Others accepted the law of the survival of the fittest through conflict, but developed for it applications in the realm of social and political life to which Mr Darwin would hardly have lent his name. The consequences of this view were worked out to their furthest limit, with the fire and passion of genius, by Friedrich Nietzsche, whose philosophy is summed up in the title of one of his works, *The Will to Power*. Only through the elimination of the slave morality of service and weakness can the strong be emancipated, and set free to do 'what is, according to the true principle of life, according to the doctrine of the will-to-power, the right thing to do: to use their power and to dominate the weak'.[1] Only through frank acceptance of the law of universal conflict can true manhood emerge – the manhood of the superman.

Yet others found a way to optimism by giving a different twist to the Darwinian hypothesis. Darwin, as a biologist, was concerned with the principle of *changes* in the natural world, and never committed himself to any moral judgements, such as would have involved the use of the terms 'better' and 'worse'. But let change be identified with progress, and immediately the hypothesis takes on a wholly different aspect. Then it is possible to interpret the whole process optimistically. Nature is indeed growing and travailing in pain; but the whole process is upwards, and when the goal is attained it will be evident that all the suffering was justified by the result which without it could not have been attained. Probably man is not the last word in the process of evolution; it is enough for him that he plays his part in the gigantic scheme of progress, of which, inevitably, all but a tiny fragment is for ever hidden from his eyes.

This type of philosophy suffered from evident defects. It lived on the idea of progress, but could give no clear answer to the question 'Progress towards what?' It drew its origin from the Darwinian doctrine of the survival of the fittest. But again, to the common-sense question 'fittest for what?' it seemed impossible that it should return any answer other than 'fittest for survival' – a tautological answer which is not calculated exactly to encourage or inspire. Thirdly, this optimistic interpretation of the universe did not take seriously enough the phenomena of retrogression and decay, which are as clearly evident in nature and in history as the more encouraging phenomena of development and progress.

If such questions were asked in the years of optimism, they

1. Emil Brunner: *Christianity and Civilisation* (London 1948), p. 135. Dr Brunner adds in a note (p. 165): 'There was nothing accidental about Hitler's choice of Nietzsche's works as a present for his friend Mussolini, even though he himself is hardly likely to have read much of them.'

were sometimes judged to indicate merely a timid lack of faith in the future of the universe and of mankind. Since then tremendous force has been lent to them by the sinister and tragic history of the Western world in the second quarter of the twentieth century.

We have watched the increasing momentum of the advance in man's capacity to destroy his fellows and in the end himself.

The most tragic thing of all about this history is that the disease of destructiveness attacked mankind not at his lowest level but at one of the highest points of civilization. The Germans are a great people. Their contributions to civilization, particularly in the realms of philosophy and music, are unsurpassed by those of any other modern people. Their enterprise, industry, and self-discipline, virtues to some extent offset by a certain lack of imagination and sensitiveness, have deservedly won the respect even of their rivals in various fields. But for twelve years, from 1933 to 1945, this great people had placed itself in subjection to a power, ruthless and unscrupulous, which came to supremacy through destruction, and at its end seemed prepared to see its own fall accompanied by the annihilation of the German people. The liquidation of 6,000,000 Jews was, as it were, the outward and visible expression of a spirit which seemed bent on the massacre of all those spiritual principles, all those strivings after justice, which in earlier centuries had made Europe great.

Most Germans now maintain that they knew little of what was going on in their own country. Other nations looked on in timid uncertainty. But it is precisely the blindness and timidity of the virtuous that provides the opportunity for destructive violence. Violence breeds violence; destruction opens the way for further destruction. The Americans had for years held it to be their privilege to lay down moral principles and to give good advice to less free and democratic peoples; but in the end their contribution was the launching of the first atomic bombs on Hiroshima and Nagasaki.

That was the beginning of the nightmare. After the atomic bomb the hydrogen bomb; after the hydrogen bomb the cobalt bomb; and with this last development man seems at last to have in his hands the power to make all life impossible in the world that God has given him.

Fear does not help clear thinking, and there seems to have been a good deal of confusion as to the real issues involved in the problem so starkly posed by the development of nuclear fission. It is not just that in Hiroshima the best part of 100,000 human creatures died in a few moments. Sooner or later they would have died anyhow. The influenza epidemic after the first World War, the Bengal famine of 1943, claimed an immensely larger number of victims in a few weeks or months. It is not the bomb that is the problem; as always, it is man himself who is the problem. What is man? The answer seems to be that he is a nasty and destructive animal – and always has been; strangely balanced between an unquenchable impulse to build and an implacable impulse to destroy.

Man has been given a rich, fertile, and productive world. Why then does he set himself to turn it into a desert? It seems that many of the deserts now in the world are man-made. Man cuts down the primeval forests, and undoes in a few years the work of centuries. The result is the terrible scars of erosion, through which rich lands can in a generation be irretrievably ruined. Man racks the earth to secure quick harvests, forgetful of the rule that he can continue as a tenant upon the kindly earth only on condition that he treats her kindly and puts back into the soil as much as he has taken from it. The result is a gigantic dustbowl.

But why is it so? Why is it that man, endued with every gift needed to master the universe, is so wholly incapable of ruling himself? Why is it that man, made to love and to be loved, should expend so much of his energy in useless hate? Why, when his tenure of life upon the earth is in any case, as we have seen, so precarious, should he seem to take delight in rendering life not merely precarious but impossible? What is this strange disease at the heart of things?

And given the disease, is there any possibility of healing?

In the days of optimism a great scientist, Sir Oliver Lodge, told us that Western man was not worrying about his sins. As far as the individual is concerned, I believe that this is still true. And yet it seems plain that to-day a very large number of people are worrying a very great deal about other people's sins.

What is sin? The very idea has dropped out of contemporary consciousness to such an extent that the word has an almost archaic flavour.

One of the most distinguished of living philosophers has written that he does not know what is meant by a sense of sin, but that he supposes that, when his friends use the expression, they are describing an experience rather like the feelings of a man who has just committed a social *faux pas*. Oddly enough, that is a remarkably acute piece of observation. The same feelings can be produced by different causes; and the nature of an experience must be determined in relation to that which has caused it and to that to which it is directed. A lapse from the standards demanded by a social code and an offence against a moral code do produce much the same sense of confusion and disarray. But beyond that there is a sharp distinction. The requirements of the social code can be summed up in the phrase 'one does' and 'one does not'; the demands of the moral code always find expression in the words 'I ought' and 'I ought not'.

What intelligible content can be given to these words 'I ought'?

Most men are aware of having within them three selves. There is the first self that I show to the world – always a compound of truth and falsehood, of sincerity and acting, of reality and conformity to the extraneous and largely irrelevant demands of society. Secondly, there is the self that I know that I could be, if I were always true to my own best insights and convictions as to the truth. Finally, there is the self that I know I really am, or, as the Christian would say, myself as I am in the sight of God. And that real self is so often the traitor self; the self that through laziness or cowardice betrays the ideals that it has itself professed; and awakes from the illusion of self-complacency to a disturbing realization of what it is and what it does.

Almost all of us know what it is to be ashamed of ourselves. Shame is the peculiarly human quality. It is not found in the animals which live by natural instinct, except in so far as dogs and other domestic animals through long association with human beings acquire by training certain almost human characteristics. When the prophet wishes to express the extreme degradation of his people, he says twice over: 'were they ashamed when they had committed abomination? nay, they were not at all ashamed neither could they blush'.[1]

To be ashamed is to be able to stand outside ourselves, and to judge ourselves by an objective standard, to which we ought to have attained and of which we have fallen short. This inner shame and self-condemnation is something entirely different from being put to shame before men by the discovery of something which we have done and of which they will disapprove. Even if what I have done should never be known to another soul, I am still aware of my own failure; I know that what I have done, whatever the excuses I may find it reasonable to make for myself, would be wrong at all times for all people in any circumstances, and that the whole universe is permanently a poorer place because of what I have done. Anyone who has ever lost his temper and spoken harshly to a child knows exactly what I mean.

All this is true, even though no one but myself should ever know what the traitor self has done. But the point can be reinforced by my knowledge of the kind of judgement that others will pass on me, if what I have done should come to their knowledge. If I have made a social gaffe, they may write me off as a fool or as a boor; but for certain other actions they will think of me as a cad, and my own inner self will affirm their judgement to be just. There is all the difference in the world between saying 'It was a pity that he did that', and saying 'He ought not to have done that'.

1. Jeremiah vi: 15; viii: 12.

So far we have been considering what we may call the raw material of a sense of sin. The pain and discomfort of a sense of shame only becomes a sense of sin if two further steps are consciously or unconsciously taken.

The first is a recognition that God is concerned in our moral struggles and failures. Shame is strong in relation to those things which are felt to be of universal obligation. 'I can't let the other fellow down.' Why not? Because trust between man and man is the only thing that makes life in society possible. That is, so to speak, part of the grain of the universe; to go against the grain produces jolts and dislocations, which are reflected in the inner discomfort of the one who has done the wrong. But, as long as this order of the world is thought of as impersonal, there can be no sense of sin. The word 'sin' has meaning only in relation to a belief that the order of the world is as it is only because God has so appointed it, and that breaches of that order are something with which He is directly and personally concerned.

The sense of sin becomes acute, only if the wrong is understood in terms of injury to the love of God. Offences against the law of a strong and righteous God may well provoke His anger and vengeance; and, if He exists at all, to be under His displeasure is obviously a dangerous state for man. But, if God is rightly called Father, and if to break His law causes Him such pain as most disorderly sons have at one time or another seen in the eyes of earthly fathers or mothers – the situation is entirely changed. The failure is seen now, not in relation to the one who has done the wrong, not in relation to an abstract and impersonal law, but in relation to One who has been injured and wounded by the wrong, just because He cares for the wrongdoers.

The most remarkable thing about wrongdoing is that it is universal. We are not always as conscious of it in ourselves as we should be, but we are very conscious of it in other people. If anyone should be so incautious as to assert that he had never done anything wrong, it is unlikely that the judgement of those who had lived with him would bear out his claim; indeed, paradoxically, since arrogance is at the root of so many forms of imperfection in action and character, it is probable that such a claim is at once disposed of by the very fact of having been made.

For the strange fact of the universality of wrongdoing the theologians have invented the term 'original sin'. The detailed discussion of this term, and of the various views of its meaning that have been held, belongs to technical theology. For our purpose it is a useful label, indicating both that Christian faith takes seriously this consciousness of failure in us all, and also that it recognizes it as one of the most perplexing factors in the human situation.

The positive aspect of the idea of original sin is its recognition of a real unity of the human race. From the biological point of view such a unity seems to be probable. The experts will not commit themselves to a judgement as to whether the human species as we now know it took its origin in one place or not. But, even were its origin proved to have been multiple and not single, in the course of the ages there has been so much mingling of stocks and crossing of genes that each of us is, in a real sense, an heir of the whole history of the human race; if there is any flaw in the general substance of humanity, it is certain that each one of us will have inherited it. In religious parlance this participation is a common humanity and a common history is expressed in the phrase, 'As in Adam all die, even so in Christ shall all be made alive'.

The reference to Adam directs our minds back to the early chapters of Genesis. Now that it is generally accepted that those chapters are not historical in the usual sense of the term, there is perhaps a tendency to dismiss them as 'mere mythology'. One of the many services that Prof. Reinhold Niebuhr has rendered to the thought of this generation is his affirmation that certain aspects of religious truth can hardly be conveyed in any other form than that of myth, and that, the more the Genesis stories are studied, the profounder appear their insights into the nature of reality, and of man as a part of that reality.

The story of Adam and Eve, and the eating of the forbidden fruit in the garden of Eden does not explain, and does not set out to explain, the origin of evil in the universe. It does offer a quite extraordinarily penetrating analysis of the whole process of wrongdoing and of its consequences. Much of what follows can be verified by everyone from his own experience; those who have children can observe the same process at work, as moral choice and responsibility come to be realities in their experience. (A colleague of mine once remarked that only a bachelor could ever have doubted the doctrine of original sin!) We are on the track of what Kierkegaard meant by his dark saying that the individual is both himself and the race.

The first and crucial point in the story is that a moral crisis cannot arise until there is a definite command to be obeyed or disobeyed. The second is the strange, inexplicable, but unmistakable fact that simultaneously with the giving of a command arises the impulse to disobey it. In the world of secular mythology, the forbidden door in the story of Bluebeard's wife is the symbol of this dilemma; Bluebeard's wife knows that to open the door and to look beyond it will be disastrous, yet she feels herself drawn, as though by an irresistible power outside herself, towards it.

The impulse to disobey is followed by plausible debate, in which the arguments in favour of disobedience are set forth almost under the guise of virtues. The tempter says that there are great advantages in a variety of experience: 'God doth know that in the day ye eat thereof, then your eyes shall be opened, and ye shall be as God, knowing good and evil.'[1] And so Eve looked on the forbidden tree, and saw that it 'was good for food, and that it was a delight to the eyes, and that the tree was to be desired to make one wise'. On this debate follows the decision to sin. But what is not usually remarked is that the fortress has really been surrendered long before the decision is made. There is a red light a long way before the precipice is reached; that red

1. The Serpent in *Paradise Lost* states this part of his case with truly memorable eloquence.

light is passed with the beginning of the plausible debate, and once it is passed return is hardly possible.

The next point is the most penetrating of all. When man has done wrong, almost his first thought is to provide himself with a companion in wrongdoing. 'She gave also to her husband with her, and he did eat.' How else is it that evil spreads so rapidly through a whole community? How else is it that it is so successfully propagated from generation to generation?

Immediately upon wrongdoing, recognized as such, follows that shame of which we have already spoken: I ought not to have done it; I need not have done it, but I did. 'They knew that they were naked; and they sewed fig leaves together, and made themselves aprons.' Then fear: 'the man and his wife hid themselves from the presence of the Lord God amongst the trees of the garden.' When challenged and confronted with the offence, the immediate impulse is to make excuse and to blame someone else. Alas! poor humanity. Was there ever a cup broken in the scullery which did not 'just come to pieces in my hand'? 'And the man said, The woman whom thou gavest to be with me, she gave me of the tree and I did eat. And the Lord God said unto the woman, What is this that thou hast done? And the woman said, The serpent beguiled me, and I did eat.'

So the final stage is reached of discord and alienation. Adam and his wife are banished from the near presence of the Lord God, from the garden of all delights, and sent forth into a world which henceforth will bring forth thorns and thistles, and in which they are to live a hard life, maintaining themselves by the sweat of their face.

In Adam all die. This is, fortunately, not the whole truth about humanity; but he would be a bold man who would deny that this is the kind of thing that is actually happening every day among men. Every man is to some extent his own Adam and his own Eve. Most of us, with John Donne, have to deplore 'that sin by which I have won others to sin, and made my sin their door'.

To recognize the fact of evil is the first stage in progress.

The second is to ask, if this is the disease, what is the remedy that ought to be applied? Our view as to the remedy will obviously depend on our understanding of the nature of the disease.

When the evolutionary philosophy was in its heyday, there was a strong tendency to regard evil as merely *atavism* – a reversion or a yielding to the animal elements in man's nature. Biological science has shown that man is akin to the other animals; by the long, slow process of evolution he has risen so far above them; but the animal nature is not wholly bred out of man, and will assert itself, unless it is kept under by the higher factors of reason and spiritual instinct. There is in us something of the tiger, and that may easily express itself in acts of violence and ferocity. We recognize in ourselves the nature of the snake, with its cunning and malice. The nature of the pig still drives us to gross seeking after the merely material pleasures of life.

There may or may not be a measure of truth in this analysis. But, in any case, it is clear that it misses what is essential in the problem of man. Evil is not simply the misdirection of certain instincts; it is a deliberate choice made by that most central part of man, his will. The heart of it all is man's inordinate pride, his desire to make himself independent of all other selves, including God, to make himself the centre and unquestioned lord of his own universe. 'I want to do it, because I want to do it; I will do it, and nothing shall stop me.' We do not perhaps usually express ourselves in quite such crude terms; yet, when we are quite honest, is this not really what we have often said to ourselves?

In favour of this understanding of evil, we may quote some of those who have had the most profound understanding of the human heart and of its motives.

Augustine writes that sin is 'a perverse desire of height, in forsaking Him to whom the soul ought solely to cleave. . . . What is pride but undue exaltation? And this is undue exaltation, when the soul abandons Him to whom it ought to cleave as its end, *and becomes a kind of end in itself*'.

Pascal says: 'This I is hateful. It is essentially unjust, in that it makes self the centre of everything; and it is troublesome to others in that it seeks to make them subservient; for each I is the enemy, and would be the tyrant, of all others.'

Each of these men of genius finds the heart of evil in self-will and self-assertion, against God and against other selves – not in one specialized instinct or another, but in the very core of the self as such.

If the evolutionary hypothesis as set forth in the earlier years of this century were true, in the course of time the undesirable and animal elements should be bred out of man, leaving him purely and simply man. But we have a right to ask when this is going to take place, and whether there is any sign of its taking place. We have rather full records of the doings of the human race for 5,000 years; is any marked change in human nature observable? 'We boast that we are much better than our fathers,' says Diomedes simply in the Iliad; are we, 3,000 years later, quite so sure as he?

Another view of evil is that sin is really stupidity and ignorance, and that the remedy for it is knowledge.

This view is as old as the Greeks. The philosophers, sometimes even Plato among them, held that virtue is something that can be 'taught', and that the remedy for the ills of human life is to be found in the spread of education. The same idea recurs in the positivist philosophies of the middle of the nineteenth century, and is perhaps still popular among their heirs to-day. The liberation of man through the spread of scientific knowledge is one of the cardinal elements in the Communist's hope for the future.

No one who has lived in a country where 80 per cent of the population is illiterate, and where oppression flourishes in the soil of ignorance, will question for a moment the value of education, or will doubt that its widest possible extension is desirable. But, obviously, education of every kind will not serve our purpose. The accumulation and dissemination of knowledge has in itself no moral significance. As recent history has shown, mere knowledge can be turned to the basest and most destructive uses; and a clever devil is far more dangerous than a stupid one. Part of the problem of the modern world is that it has lost certainty as to what education is for, and as to how its purpose can be attained.

Xenophon tells us that among the Persians boys of noble family were taught to shoot straight and to tell the truth. Plato held that among the essential parts of education were music and gymnastics. Each is pointing out that education aims at the formation of a complete man. We may find it useful to analyse a little further this concept of completeness. Any education worthy the name must include the training of the mind in the weighing of evidence. The mark of an educated man is that he has some idea of what kind of statements can be proved by what kind of evidence, and that he can distinguish between what, though not proved, is probable, and what is so improbable (e.g. that the world is flat), as to make it not worth the while of a serious-minded man to waste his time on it. Secondly, education must lay the foundations of at least elementary aesthetic appreciation. If our civilization is not to founder altogether in a universal welter of ugliness, it is necessary that the young should be exposed, as far as may be, to great literature, great pictures, and great music, and given at least some clues to the understanding of why some things are called great. Finally, education must include the training of the moral sense. Some historians are now so cautious that they interpret their task only in terms of understanding, never of approval or condemnation. This will not do; even recognizing the fallibility of our judgements, we must have the courage to distinguish between good and bad, and to stand to our judgements. '1066 and all that' is sometimes wiser than the professionals. When, on a great occasion, Mr Churchill referred to Adolf Hitler just as 'that bad man', the conscience of the world applauded his utterance.

What I have set down as the three essentials in all true education clearly correspond very closely to the three traditional ultimates, the true, the beautiful, and the good. If all modern education did include these essentials, if the young of today could honestly say with Cleopatra

> and then, what's brave, what's noble,
> Lets do it after the high Roman fashion,
> And make death proud to take us.[1]

we should have gone far to escape from the pettiness, the vulgarity, and the limited horizons of contemporary civilization.

Education could do much to meet our need. But are not those who pin their whole faith to it still victims of the Victorian illusion that 'we needs must love the highest when we see it', and that no man will ever consciously do what he sees to be wrong? This is an illusion. If it were true, the world would be a great deal simpler a place than it is. It is unfortunately the fact that men very often do things which they see perfectly clearly to be wrong and harmful to themselves and to others. I once had a friend whose more pious friends thought that it would be very good for him to give up smoking a pipe. He told me that his answer was: 'I know it's expensive; I know it's bad for you; I know it's dirty. But I like it, and I shall go on doing it.' We are not always so admirably honest as my friend. There is more than a little painful truth in the accidental transposition of the child's prayer:

> May my friends be all forgiven,
> Bless the sins I love so well.

Though human vanity finds it hard to admit it, the real reason that we sin is that we like our sins; if this is not true, at least on some occasions and in some degree, why do we go on sinning?

Others find the cause of human evil in a bad organization of society, and look to social change to effect also the moral redemption of mankind.

Here again we must recognize the element of truth in this contention. Environment plays an immense part in the formation of human character. Poverty, disease, and overwork grievously limit the possibilities of human development. But, even when we recognize the legitimacy of social change, may we not also recognize that the advocates of such change

---

1. *Antony and Cleopatra*: Act IV, Sc. XIII.

often claim more for it than it can possibly achieve? If tyranny has existed in the past, why has it existed? What is it in human nature that produces and maintains injustice? Even if old tyranny is destroyed, is it not possible, does not history show that it is likely, that it will reconstitute itself in new forms?

Marxist Communism makes for itself the highest possible claims as the deliverance of humanity from the evils of the past. Has it fulfilled, or does it show signs of fulfilling, these claims? Marxism has developed a kind of mythology of the sinless proletariat. Through all the centuries the proletariat has been the innocent victim of oppression and exploitation. Itself sinless, it has paid the price for the sins of others. Let but the proletariat assert its claims and take control of its own destinies, let it but take the leap from necessity into freedom and all the ills of human life will take wings and fly away. The facts, as far as they are now before the world, hardly seem to justify this optimistic expectation. The great Communist experiment has involved the enslavement of one country after another that has loathed and feared the idea of coming under the Communist yoke. Suspicion finds its expression in the erection of an iron curtain, in purges and trials for treason, in rigid control of the press, and in ceaseless distortion of the truth. Liberty has been abolished in the name of liberty.

It may be that all these things are merely unpleasant phenomena of the transitional period before the dominance of the proletariat is fully established. But it is also possible that the myth of the sinless proletariat is a myth, and that the proletariat is just as sinful, though perhaps in different ways, as any other part of the community; and that any new order of society will have in it its own particular form of sinfulness, its own contradictions, its own inner principle of decay.

When we have boxed the compass in our search for explanations for the disease and disarray of the life of man, when we have given all possible weight to external things, we come back to man himself. Man's chief problem is man himself. 'Not in our stars, dear Brutus, but in ourselves', is our disease and the issue of our destiny. Evil resides not in heredity or in environment, not in conditions nor in traditions, but in the heart of man himself.

As evidence for this, I would cite not necessarily the Bible but almost any one of the great poets, whose insight into the depths of human nature has made them classics.

As one reads the four greatest tragedies of Shakespeare – *Hamlet, Lear, Othello,* and *Macbeth,* or even more that concentrated expression of bitterness, *Timon of Athens* – it is hard to doubt that at some time in Shakespeare's life a crack had opened in the solid ground beneath his feet, and that through bitter experience of his own he had been led to perceive the full extent and power of evil in human life. Is Hamlet merely out of his wits that he says: 'It goes so heavily with my disposition that this goodly frame, the earth, seems to me a sterile promontory, this most excellent canopy, the air, look you, this brave o'erhanging firmament, this majestical roof fretted with golden fire, why it appears no other thing to me than a foul and pestilent congregation of vapours'?

The continuing power of these great plays to draw and move the hearts of men is evidence that what we are dealing with in Shakespeare is imaginative insight, and not mere imagination. With infallible precision he has drawn out the nature and consequence of evil. First, it blinds the man who yields to it. Macbeth has listened to the first promptings of ambition. Why can he not see whither inevitably it will lead him? Secondly, sin weakens the will. We all suppose that, having embarked on a certain course, we can go just so far, and that we shall be able to draw back when we feel that we have gone far enough; only to find that the tyranny of habit is far less easily broken than we had supposed, and to admit ruefully with Macbeth that 'to go back is tedious as to go o'er'. Finally, sin corrupts. It can become so much the atmosphere a man breathes that he is no longer aware of it as evil; at first resisted, it becomes at length a custom that is acquiesced in and taken for granted. And the end of it all is the piteous cry of Lady Macbeth in the sleep-walking scene, 'All the perfumes of Arabia will not sweeten this little hand'.

And after all it is true; Duncan is dead – 'Who would have thought the old man to have so much blood in him' – and neither prayers nor tears will ever bring him back to life.

This is the analysis not of a theologian but of a dramatist. The theologian can only be grateful that his work has been so well done for him by a supreme artist, whose understanding of the human situation is free from any suspicion of theological *parti pris*.

But, if we are willing to follow Shakespeare and to admit that this is the human situation, what then do we do about it?

One way of facing the situation is simply to assert that human nature does not change; that is the kind of people that we are, and we must make as good a use as we can of the material with which we are supplied. This adaptation of means to ends is perfectly legitimate for the politician. The King's government must be carried on; it must be carried on through men who are all to some extent selfish or dishonest, and by securing the necessary measure of consent from people very few of whom are wholly disinterested in their aims. The politician is aware that what he can achieve may be very far short of his ideal. His concern is with the possible – to get expressed in legislation and administration as much of his ideal as at that moment is practicable. If he tries to go beyond, he may well fall short of it, just because of the unworkableness of unpractical idealism in practical affairs.

Another solution is to cut our coat according to our cloth, and not to set up moral standards higher than are attainable by the ordinary decent man.

Part of the appeal of Islam undoubtedly lies in the fact that, whereas it represents an ethical advance on the standards of primitive peoples and is seriously exacting in certain matters of external practice, such as the fast of Ramadan, it is gentle towards many human weaknesses, and does not make demands greater than the majority of men can meet. The apologists of Islam defend it on precisely this ground, affirming that, while the ethical teaching of Jesus is so exalted as to have lost touch with the world of everyday life, Islam is the practical code of ethics for men who have to live in a very imperfect world.

Much the same may be said of the code of morals with which most of us are most familiar – that of the English gentleman, or of the old school tie. That there are many admirable features in this code no sensible person would deny. But its limitations are also obvious. It has never been distinguished by generosity towards the internal and external proletariats – those lesser breeds without the law, whose existence has been tolerated rather than approved; and on the whole it has been content with a very mediocre level of attainment in sexual morality.

But we have to reckon with the ineradicable tendency in the human mind to press towards the absolute. The ethical halfway house, though pragmatically convenient, does not prove itself ultimately satisfactory.

If the standard demanded is low, the attainment of it easily produces self-complacency and arrogance – in itself an unpleasant disposition; and, as previously noted, arrogance is the root of many other sins.

If the standard is high and approaches the ideal, then the man who takes it seriously is faced with the constant problem of defeat and failure to attain to the standard which he has set before himself.

The third possibility is that which is implicit in Christian faith – to accept open-eyed both the ethical standard set forth in the teachings of Jesus Christ, and the despair that follows upon human failure to attain it. 'O wretched man that I am, who shall deliver me from the body of this death?'

I think that it is this uncompromising acceptance of the reality of evil that more than anything else makes it possible for me to remain a Christian. I do not find a similar realism elsewhere.

Some systems treat sin as a mere illusion; as imperfect or undeveloped good, or good misplaced; or something that, in relation to the totality of things, can be seen to make its due contribution to the whole.

Others regard 'sin' as a neurotic symptom, as an imaginary burden of guilt, which it is the business of the psychiatrist to remove. There is much truth in this. And yet, after all, Duncan is dead, and neither prayers nor tears will ever bring him back to life. The question 'who killed him?' raises issues of very much more than imaginary guilt.

Yet others find ready excuse for sin. We are all in the same boat; it cannot be helped; and perhaps we shall find reason to think that it is not so bad after all.

Christian faith admits of no blinkers, and no palliation. It takes human nature seriously, both in its nobility and in its radical and desperate badness. It regards sin as in essence deliberate rebellion against the known will of God, and therefore as treachery to the whole order of the world. It regards it as cruelty, since it nearly always involves a lack of respect for the personality of others as persons, and so causes a diminution of their value. It regards it as a betrayal of the self by the self – what a startling phrase in the Epistle to the Hebrews calls the contradiction of sinners against themselves.[1] And yet, taking this exceedingly dark view of the situation, Christian faith still bids men both despair – and hope.

Paradoxically, in this faith, hope is not something to be held on to in spite of despair; the despair itself is the ground of hope.

Why do you despair? Only because, even though you may have sinned, you have never wholly and with the whole of your being yielded to the sin. No writer has ever set forth this inner conflict more dramatically and penetratingly than St Paul: 'To will is present with me, but to do that which is good is not. For the good which I would I do not: but the evil which I would not, that I practise. But if what I would not that I do, it is no more I that do it, but sin which dwelleth in me.'[2] Even in the act of sinning, there is something that stands outside, a self which though

1. Hebrews xii: 3. This is quoted from the Revised Version; note the change from the wording of the Authorized Version.
2. Romans vii: 18–20.

involved in evil, is yet able to judge and to condemn. I myself am prisoner at the bar, witness for the prosecution, judge, and jury – and, it may be, 'mine own executioner'. It is just this inner conflict, of which almost all of us are in some measure aware, that is the evidence that we have not sunk beyond the possibility of being saved.

Consider some other possibilities. If we were in truth no more than intellectually developed animals, presumably we should share the complacency of instinct and the perfect adaptation of the animal world to environment. If we had become wholly identified with the evil in ourselves, as is theoretically possible, there would be no more place for conflict. It seems to me that in Iago Shakespeare has purposed to delineate such a character. Perhaps that is why most of those who read or see *Othello* feel that Iago is too inhuman ever really to come to life. Perhaps that is why the commentators find themselves in difficulties. Though we can theoretically admit the possibility of the complete identification of an individual with the evil in him, we have no experience of such a situation, and have difficulty in forming a mental picture of a man in whom evil has become so much a part of him as to be beyond all possibility of healing. However, if such identification had taken place, there would be no more conflict; there would instead be perfect peace, the peace of death. As long as there is conflict there is hope. As long as there is despair – not now the cosmic and in part irrational despair of Leopardi, but the cool, rational despair of an unfavourable moral judgement on the self – the self is not beyond the possibility of redemption.

Christian faith unflinchingly accepts the proposition that in Adam all die. It is only because it so firmly holds to this first part of the Pauline affirmation that it is able also to affirm the second part, and to hold with equal assurance that all in Christ may be made alive. How this may be so must be the subject of the next stage in the development of our argument.

6

CHRIST THE RECONCILER

In the last chapter we tried to set out the real needs of man as attested by inner experience, by the penetrating analysis of great poets and seers, and by the evidence of the Bible. We found that these needs are threefold. Man needs pardon, because he stands guilty before a tribunal the verdict of which he accepts as just and valid. He needs cleansing, because imagination is defiled, and from this is produced the vicious circle of new sin continually stimulated by the memory of old. He needs renewal, because his will has been weakened by self-indulgence, and can no longer be relied on to make such decisions as will implement the findings of the intellect.

All these – pardon and cleansing and renewal – are included in the message of the Gospel under the term forgiveness or its equivalents. That this forgiveness is freely available to all was the essentially new element in the earliest preaching of the followers of Jesus; it recurs with almost monotonous iteration in the records of what they said. 'Him did God exalt with his right hand to be a Prince and a Saviour, for to give repentance to Israel and forgiveness of sins.' 'Be it known unto you therefore, brethren, that through this man is preached unto you the forgiveness of sins.' 'To open their eyes, that they may turn from darkness to light, and from the power of Satan unto God, that they may receive remission of sins and an inheritance among them that are sanctified.'[1]

In closer correspondence with our analysis of man's three-fold need, we may cite from the Epistles such passages as these: 'God was in Christ reconciling the world unto himself, not reckoning unto them their trespasses, and having committed unto us the word of reconciliation.'[2] 'How much

1. Acts v: 31; xiii: 38; xxvi: 18.　　2. 2 Corinthians v: 19.

more shall the blood of Christ, who through the eternal spirit offered himself without blemish unto God, cleanse your conscience from dead works to serve the living God.'[1] 'Ye have put off the old man with his doings, and have put on the new man, which is being renewed unto knowledge after the image of him that created him.'[2]

It must be recognized at once that the Christian proclamation of forgiveness through the life and death and resurrection of Jesus Christ is met by fierce criticism from a number of different quarters.

A contemporary philosopher of great distinction has told us that he could not respect a God who could forgive. This chimes with the unchanging attitude of classical Hinduism. The Hindu holds that, in a world governed by the iron law of retribution, forgiveness is impossible. If it were possible, it would be immoral, since if God were to tamper with the law of *Karma*, just retribution for deeds done, He would break down the foundation on which the whole moral order of the world rests. A Hindu lawyer once said to me: 'To us, sin is exactly like a tennis ball which you throw against a wall; precisely in proportion to the force with which you throw it, it will rebound and come back to you.' It is written that each man shall eat the fruit of his own deeds. Can this law be changed? If a window has been broken, can it be put together again? Only in the cinema, where a film can be played through in either direction: if the action is reversed, the broken fragments will come together and leap up, and miraculously fit themselves again into an unbroken pane of glass. But can such things happen in the real world? Is not forgiveness a fiction produced by wishful imagination out of fear?

From another direction comes a precisely opposite objection. For the Moslem, everything depends on the inscrutable will of God. If it is His will to forgive, He can easily forgive. Why then all this fuss and controversy? We are reminded of the saying of the French cynic: 'Le bon Dieu me pardonnera: c'est son métier.'

1. Hebrews ix: 14.   2. Colossians iii: 9–10.

Such objections can be answered only by developing at some length the whole Christian doctrine of redemption and renewal.

In the first place, it must be emphasized that no one can be more concerned than the Christian with the moral stability of the world. Accepting, as he must do wholeheartedly, the saying of the great Bishop Butler that 'things are what they are, and their consequences will be what they will be; why then should we wish to be deceived', he is bound to reject from the start any doctrine of forgiveness which involves juggling with the natural consequences of human action, or with the moral law of the universe.

But also, since he is pledged to give due weight to every single fact that comes under his observation, he is bound to take note of the fact that forgiveness is something which does exist in the world. Dr H. R. Mackintosh, in his admirable book *The Christian Experience of Forgiveness*, asks, in a footnote, 'Do we not forgive one another every day?' On this lesser man might be inclined to comment, 'Well, perhaps not every day; but at least sometimes'. Yet in one of the best short studies of the meaning of Christian marriage that I have ever read, the writer states that happiness in marriage is possible only on the basis of the continual and *daily* exercise of mutual forgiveness. In any decently organized family the attitude of parents to their children is one of endless patience; in some cases, perhaps, this patience is no more than an amused tolerance; but ordinarily it includes something which cannot be described by any word other than forgiveness. And when forgiveness is thus manifest, the general conscience of mankind finds it admirable – far more admirable than the taking of vengeance, that strict justice which demands the exaction of an eye for an eye and a tooth for a tooth, or the contempt which cannot bother any further about the wrongdoer.

It may be said that we are not entitled to argue from the human to the divine, from human relationships to the problem of man's relationship to God. But that is not what at the moment we are concerned to do. We are merely pointing out that, even in a universe in which consequence follows hard upon action, forgiveness does actually exist. We have no right, therefore, *a priori* to exclude it from consideration, or, taking as established the moral consistency of the universe, to regard it as an impossibility.

To those who think that forgiveness is easy we shall be inclined to reply simply in the famous words of St Anselm, *Nondum considerasti quanti sit ponderis peccatum* – you have not yet considered the seriousness of sin.

What is the actual consequence of wrong-doing as between men? It tears the fabric of personal relationships. All personal relationships depend upon mutual confidence, and this is a very delicate and easily injured thing. Some injuries, such as those which arise from a hasty or ill-considered word, are easily put right. But what is to be done with a child who has told a deliberate and wilful lie? Confidence has been destroyed. There is no easy and immediate solution. This is not to say that restoration is impossible; but the way back cannot but be hard and difficult. If anyone denies this, we can only conclude either that he has never been in this situation; or that, having been in it, he has failed to treat it as seriously as it deserved.

To anyone who is willing to consider the seriousness of sin, it must be evident that forgiveness is a difficult business.

It is certainly felt to be so from the side of the one who feels upon him the obligation to forgive. I happen to remember the occasion on which this was first vividly brought home to me. In some story written for children, the much beloved dog belonging to the boy who was the hero of the story had been stolen by a tramp; when it came to bed-time, the boy found that he could not say the Lord's Prayer, because he could not forgive the man who had stolen his dog. I knew at once that, in similar circumstances, I should not have been able to say the Lord's Prayer either.

It is worth noting that, in speaking of forgiveness, Christ more than once uses the similitude of *debt*. This has the advantage that it makes visible and measurable something that in most human relationships is invisible and incommensurable with anything else. There is the very simple parable of the two debtors, who owed respectively 50 and 500 pence. And when they had nothing to pay the creditor frankly forgave them both.[1] The question at once arises as to who pays the price of forgiveness. The answer evidently is that the debtors pay nothing, and that the whole price is borne by the one who forgives. Is this just? Clearly in such a transaction justice as we ordinarily understand it is made to stand on its head. Justice demands that the debtor should pay his debt in full and with interest, that the wrong should be thrown back on the wrongdoer in such a way that he bears the whole weight of it. But, where forgiveness enters in, the one who forgives pays the whole price of the wrong – and gets nothing from it other than the satisfaction of having forgiven.

Is this possible? We can only answer that this is something which does actually happen; and therefore we must conclude that, for some reason, this universe is the kind of universe in which such things can occur.

Sometimes we find better theology in the moralists and the poets than in the theologians. I do not know any finer expression of this paradox than is to be found in Francis Thompson's poem *The Veteran of Heaven*:

O Captain of the wars, whence won Ye so great scars?
In what fight did Ye smite, and what manner was the foe?
Was it on a day of rout they compassed Thee about,
Or gat Ye these adornings when Ye wrought their overthrow?

''Twas on a day of rout they girded Me about,
They wounded all My brow, and they smote Me through the side:
My hand held no sword when I met their armèd horde,
And the conqueror fell down, and the Conquered bruised his pride.'

What is this, unheard before, that the Unarmed makes war,
And the Slain hath the gain, and the Victor hath the rout?
What wars, then, are these, and what the enemies,
Strange Chief, with the scars of Thy conquest trenched about?

1. Luke vii: 41–3.

'The Prince I drave forth held the Mount of the North,
Girt with the guards of flame that roll round the pole.
I drave him with My wars from all his fortress-stars,
And the sea of death divided that My march might strike its
    goal. . . .'

What is *Thy* Name? Oh, show! – 'My Name ye may not know;
'Tis a going forth with banners, and a baring of much swords:
But My titles that are high, are they not upon My thigh?
"King of Kings!" are the words, "Lord of Lords!";
It is written "King of Kings, Lord of Lords".'

The New Testament frankly accepts this paradox. Mercy glories against judgement. There is a principle of justice in the world; but this is not God's last word. The principle of forgiveness belongs to a higher order; it follows its own laws, which are different from those of distributive justice, and cannot be understood or interpreted in the light of any spheres of operation other than their own.

The error in most theories of the Atonement is that they endeavour to square justice and forgiveness, to introduce forgiveness into the sphere of law, and to show that it is somehow compatible with the principles of law. What lies behind these attempts is the laudable feeling that the moral stability of the universe must at all costs be preserved. It is true that in our universe law and forgiveness can both exist, and that each has its own sphere of activity and its proper function to perform. But to attempt to interpret one in the categories of the other is necessarily hopeless. Forgiveness breaks through the categories of law and escapes into a freer air. St Paul saw this clearly, and expressed it quite uncompromisingly. There is a world of law, the principle of which is retribution; there is a world of grace, the principle of which is release. It is impossible to live simultaneously in both worlds.

This distinction is so generally overlooked or misunderstood that it may be well to pursue it a little further, and to elucidate the nature of the contradiction between the two worlds.

Justice is an assertion of the will to live.

Forgiveness is an expression of willingness to die.

Justice is an activity of the instinct of self-preservation. This is undoubtedly one of the strongest instincts in human, as in animal, nature. Some psychologists would class it, with the instinct of reproduction, as one of the two basic and indispensable impulses in man. When anything threatens, or is felt to threaten, life or security, the whole strength of the organism is immediately drawn together in the effort to repel the menace and to preserve the self. We may remember the apophthegm of Bacon that revenge is a kind of wild justice. In extreme cases the impulse of self-preservation may be carried to the point of the annihilation of the aggressor; and in civilized though not usually in primitive codes of law, killing in self-defence is not accounted murder.

Crime is anything which a society judges to be a menace to its existence or its way of life. The process of legal justice is the expression of that society's will to live, of its instinct of self-preservation. The aggressor must be repelled; the wrong that he has attempted to do to the society must be thrown back upon him. In extreme cases the reaction of the society against threatened or accomplished wrong may involve the annihilation of the offender.

Forgiveness involves the abandonment of self-assertion and self-defence. It submits to the wrong without resistance, and is itself prepared to pay the price of it. In a sense, therefore, forgiveness is contrary to nature; or perhaps we should rather say springs from a secondary and higher instinct; and this works in precisely the opposite direction from that of the primary and immediate instinct, which we share with the animals. Just because of the strength of the impulse of self-preservation, its inhibition by its contrary, and the direction of the self towards the patient enduring of wrong, may be felt as sharp conflict and even as agony.

The wrongs that most of us are called to forgive are so trivial that the real nature and cost of forgiveness may not be immediately apparent. But, if we are in a position to ask anyone who has actually forgiven an intolerable wrong what, in those circumstances, it feels like to forgive, the answer will almost certainly be, 'It feels like death'. It feels like death because it really is a kind of death. Here again a piece of accurate observation by a not always very sensitive novelist may help us to appreciate Christian insights in this matter. In almost the last scene of Galsworthy's *Forsyte Saga*, when Jon Forsyte, who has been unfaithful to his wife and has fallen into sin, returns to his home, the wronged wife is immediately and instinctively aware of what has happened. Her set purpose is to take her husband back, and not to let the wrong stand between them; but she must pass through a moment of the agony of death, in which she cries out, 'Don't touch me', before she can win through to the world of reconciliation and new life. This illustration is all the more valuable that, in all his many volumes, Galsworthy shows no trace of any understanding of the meaning of the Christian faith. He was a good enough observer to know that forgiveness is something that actually does occur in the lives of men and women.

If it is difficult to forgive, it is almost equally difficult to be forgiven. The one who has done the wrong, no less than the one whom he has wronged, has to learn to abandon self-assertion and self-defence; and no one in the world finds this an easy lesson to learn.

Our first impulse, when we are faced with the fact of our own wrong-doing, is to make excuse. After all, in such a case there are generally wrongs on both sides. He must not press his case too far. Would it not be much more sensible to arrive at a peace by negotiation and exercise the blessed virtue of compromise?

Undoubtedly there are cases in which this is the right procedure. Where quarrels have arisen over rather trivial affairs, impartial friends of the disputants can often devise a solution by compromise. But what is to be done when there have not been wrongs on both sides, when the offence has been unprovoked, gratuitous, and indefensible? It is only the extreme case that makes clear the real nature of the problem.

L.I.F.E. College Library
1100 Glendale Blvd.
Los Angeles, Calif. 90026

The next and perhaps the favourite evasion is to say, 'Of course I have done wrong, but I will put it right'.

This is not a contemptible attitude; at least it indicates a willingness to accept responsibility. The weakness of it is that there are so few cases in which it is applicable. In matters of property, where injury is measurable and direct reparation is possible, an apology and prompt payment may meet the case. But generally our words and actions are like arrows which we have shot into the air, and which, cry as we will, will never come back to us. Take the common case of malicious gossip. If you have repeated something to a person's discredit, and afterwards find it to be untrue, what can you do? You may seek out the one to whom you had spoken and withdraw your words. But can you find all those to whom he has passed on the false report, and all those to whom they have repeated it? You may have set in motion a process which, try as you will, you cannot check or reverse. Of what use then to say 'I will put it right'?

'Well, I cannot put it right, but at least I am man enough to bear the consequences of my own act.' If only we could, how simple life would be. If you have been helping yourself to money which is not your own, probably, and very properly, you will go to prison. But it will not really be you who will suffer; it will be your innocent wife and children and all your friends. This is inevitable, because God has bound us all together in one bundle of life, and, in the words of Scripture, 'None of us liveth to himself, and none dieth to himself'.[1] Who, then, can limit to himself the consequences of his own wrong-doing?

The recognition of our own complete helplessness, in relation to the wrong that we have done, is the pre-condition of repentance and restoration.

As long as man is concerned with himself he is capable of remorse, and, as is well known, remorse never leads to any real deliverance. It expresses itself in such terms as 'I have let myself down, I have injured my own self-respect'. This is a kind of sorrow, which may be painful, even agonizing.

1. Romans xiv: 7.

But it is, in the very striking phrase of St Paul, the sorrow of the world which worketh death.[1] In point of fact, the close connexion between remorse and suicide emphasizes the aptness of the apostle's word.

Repentance can begin only when a man has ceased to be concerned about himself, and is wholly absorbed in the interests of others and in the consequences to them of what he has done. It involves a complete acceptance of the helplessness which is the consequence of wrong-doing. It does not stand upon any imagined rights; it makes no claim for itself. It does not attempt to strike a bargain. But the acceptance of such a position of self-renunciation and humiliation is also for proud, arrogant, human nature a kind of death.

When a man has reached this point of genuine repentance, it is possible for him to be forgiven. But if he is to be lifted out of his humiliation, forgiveness must be of the right kind; it must restore to him his sense of worth, or humiliation and despair may become permanent, and then there is no deliverance.

For a beautiful delineation of the wrong kind of forgiveness, let us turn again to a novelist, this time to *Mr Skeffington*, by the authoress of *Elizabeth and her German Garden*. Here there is a painful scene, in which the wealthy heroine, returning home suddenly, finds her servants engaged in having a pleasant party at the expense of her larder and her cellar. Naturally, she dismisses them on the spot; and then, reflecting that so complete an upheaval will be a great nuisance, decides to cancel the dismissal and to keep them all; but, after she has done so, and sees the servants slinking about the house like guilty spectres, feels a certain sympathy with God, who must find it so troublesome to be forgiving people all the time.

People often speak of forgiveness in such a connexion, when what they mean is 'condonation'. But such misuse of terms can lead on to grave confusion of thought. True forgiveness is always healing and uplifting. Condonation masquerading as forgiveness may well be based on contempt; if

1. 2 Corinthians vii: 10.

people are not taken seriously as responsible and valuable persons, then what they have done need not be taken seriously either, and, if other considerations make it desirable, may just be passed over. That this is a dishonouring kind of forgiveness is too evident to need fuller explanation. Perhaps this throws light on a dark saying. At a time when there was some difference of opinion between those two eminent scholars, A. E. Housman and W. P. Ker, Prof. Ker wrote, not perhaps altogether seriously, 'Forgiveness is the last refuge of malignity: I will not forgive Professor Housman'. If forgiveness has in it that element of contempt, and involves a patronizing attitude towards a fellow creature, I do not think that malignity is too strong a word for it. Such forgiveness, so far from restoring the one who has done the wrong, can only further imprison him in his alienation and despair.

True forgiveness can never spring from anything other than love. Love recognizes an infinite value in all other human beings, even the least deserving, because, whatever human nature may be now, no limit can be set to what it may become. Love is indignant at wrong-doing, not from any feeling of personal injury or vindictiveness, but because of the harm it has done to the wrongdoer; it has marred the dignity of his manhood. In order that that lost dignity may be restored, love is prepared to take upon it the form of a servant, to go down to the offender where he is, to share the shame, the indignity, and the consequences of the wrong, and by sharing them, to break the prison bars and set the captive free.

If I am still loved, in spite of my wrong-doing, I am valued; if I am wanted back, if I am really wanted back, I can endure to be forgiven.

This is splendidly brought out in Marjorie Kinnan Rawlings's book *The Yearling*, another example of admirable, though unconscious, theology in a novelist. You may remember that the lad Jody has had to kill his beloved yearling fawn Flag, because his pet was doing too much damage on the farm. It hurt him so much to do it, that, having done it, he told his father straight out that he hated him; and then, concluding that no one would want him after that, ran away from home. Some days later he has to creep back, tired, sick at heart, hungry, because there was nowhere else to go. He finds to his amazement that his disappearance has caused utter desolation in the home, and has nearly killed his father. 'It was unbelievable, said Jody to himself; *he was wanted.*'

It is unbelievable; but it may also be true. To the sinner, to be valued, to be really wanted, is life out of death.

Human analogies can do no more than prepare the mind for the staggering possibility that forgiveness may be the determining factor also in the relationship between God and man.

If men sometimes forgive one another, and if forgiveness is seen to be an admirable thing, we might hesitatingly infer that in the relation of God to man also forgiveness might be a possibility. If the Christian faith is true, then the cross of Christ proclaims in unmistakable terms that forgiveness is a fact, and gives us certainty concerning what otherwise we might have hoped for, but could never have surely known. 'God was in Christ reconciling the world unto himself.'[1]

If this is true, the first aspect under which the cross presents itself to us is as a revelation of the nature of God. It shows us 'what it feels like to God when we sin'. This is not the first thought that comes to us, when we are conscious of having done wrong; we need to be shown it in a way that we cannot mistake.

An Indian evangelist, whose name is unknown to me, expounding the parable of the Prodigal Son to an audience of non-Christians, explained to his hearers that the moment at which the prodigal son really repented was when he reached home and saw that in his absence his father's hair had gone white. This is not to be found in the parable as originally told by Jesus; but surely it was inspired comment. On a cursory reading, the parable draws attention to the sufferings of the young man, whose folly and selfishness

1. 2 Corinthians v: 19.

eventually bring him down to the level of the swine that he is sent out to feed. More careful consideration shows that the real hero of the parable is the father. It is he who has really suffered, he who has carried the heavy end of the log. Once in India, preaching in the open air to a large crowd of educated non-Christians, I made the same point: 'In that story who suffered most? Many people say that it was the son who ran away from home. But not one of you who is a father would ever say that.' At that point my speech was interrupted by a wholly unexpected round of applause.

If God is no more than a convenient term for an impersonal power behind the universe, then the parallel has no meaning. But if it is true that the very hairs of our head are all numbered, that every single human individual is the object of the unremitting, tender, personal care and affection of God, then it is obvious that, every time we do wrong, that wrong goes directly to the throne of God, and wounds that tender love by which we are encompassed.

The cross of Christ, understood as revelation, shows us once for all the real nature of sin. It is a deliberate and wilful assault on uncomplaining and unresisting love. Once done, it goes out beyond our control, and is infinitely destructive in its effects. Sin is magnified by the love against which it is an offence; where there is little love, it is not seriously felt; where love is great, the dimension of sin is enlarged. Since the love of God is infinite, sin becomes infinitely harmful and infinitely hateful. But in the end love proves stronger than hate:

> And victory remains with love,
> Since Love himself was crucified.

The Cross is the manifestation of forgiveness.

During the centuries Christian theology has elaborated many theories of the Atonement. Almost all of these contain some element of value, drawing attention to one aspect or another of what, in actual fact, the death of Christ has meant in the experience of men. But in the process of elaboration formal theology has often withdrawn into such realms of technicality and abstraction that it is almost impossible for the ordinary man to understand what it is all about, or to feel that it has very much to do with him. Yet when all is said and done, all these complicated theories in the end rest on one very simple fact – that on the day of the Crucifixion Jesus did actually forgive those who had done Him the utmost wrong. In the whole story there is no word of reproach or hatred. There is clear condemnation of the wrong; He says to Pilate, 'therefore he that delivered me unto thee hath greater sin'.[1] But the key-word is the first word from the cross, 'Father, forgive them; for they know not what they do'.[2]

To orthodox Christian theology Jesus is the very word of God; His death is a redemptive act from the side of God, in which are made manifest both God's attitude towards sin, and His willingness to forgive even the worst sin of man. Even if we find ourselves at the end unable to accept the orthodox doctrine, and see in Jesus nothing more than the greatest and the best of men, we may feel that, more than anything else that has ever happened, the cross sheds light upon the nature of the universe. Shall man be greater than God? Jesus forgave from His heart the utmost and bitterest wrong. Will God do less than this? Such inference from man to God can never be more than precarious. Yet, though this lower interpretation of what Jesus was could not suffice to give us certainty, even that might well lead us to hope that what we shall find at the heart of the universe will be patient endurance of wrong and generous willingness to forgive.

But, if God is willing to forgive, why should the expression of His forgiveness have to take this particular form? God is by definition eternal and omnipotent. What is the significance in relation to Him of an event in time and space?

If the cross of Jesus is in some sense an act of God, it must be in its nature sacramental – that is, it is an outward showing, as far as it can be outwardly shown, of something beyond itself; an indication of a mystery which must for ever remain hidden from human eyes.

1. John xix: 11.   2. Luke xxiii: 34.

Redemption, to be moral, cannot be arbitrary. As we saw earlier, forgiveness involves for the one who forgives a kind of death, through the voluntary surrender of his right to self-defence and self-assertion. The cross suggests that, even for God Himself, there is no other way. He can forgive, only as He Himself is prepared to bear the wrong and pay the price. The cross is the manifestation of the mystery of God's willingness to die.

As soon as man sinned God chose to die. But the cross must never be represented, as in history it sometimes has been, as a kind of dodge, through which it became possible for man to escape the consequences of his sin. It is moral and genuinely redemptive only if it corresponds to an inner necessity in the being of God Himself. That necessity seems to be connected with the fact that God is Creator. He is not in time and space, but we are; if this visible universe and the creatures that dwell in it are to be redeemed, that can only be done from within; and that involves a manifestation of God's redeeming love and power, under the conditions of time and space, at a particular point of history. And since forgiveness always involves something that is of the nature of death, in no other way could the redemption of the world so appropriately be accomplished as through an actual death in time and space, under the actual conditions of humanity, and at a particular point of human history.

As long as men were content to think of the divine in terms of gods many and lords many, there was no special difficulty in the idea of a dying God. In fact almost everywhere in the temperate zone, so clearly marked by the annual death of nature in winter and the annual resurrection in spring, the story of the god who dies and rises again is a regular part of the structure of mythology. Classical scholars meet him in the lament of Bion for Adonis: 'I cry woe for Adonis – the beauteous Adonis is dead'; and the last lines of the poem remind us that this is not the commemoration of one single event which happened once but the mythological presentation of something that happens once a year: 'Give over thy wailing for to-day, Cytherea, and beat not now thy breast any more; thou needs wilt wail again and weep again, come another year.' Among the abominations denounced by the prophet Ezekiel was something very similar: 'Then he brought me to the door of the gate of the Lord's house, which was towards the north: and behold, there sat the woman weeping for Tammuz';[1] we meet them again in *Paradise Lost* – the Syrian damsels lamenting Tammuz

With amorous ditties all a summer's day.

These and similar tales were widespread and familiar in the Levant in the days of Jesus; it has not been difficult for those who would over-emphasize the similarities and overlook the differences to suggest that the Christian interpretation of the death of Jesus takes its origin in this world of ideas, and to reduce Jesus to the level of a Levantine Saviour God.

Polytheism can readily make room for a dying God; but an austere monotheism, belief in a single Creator God, can hardly be so accommodating. God is, by definition, the principle, source, and origin of all life; how can He have anything to do with death? Muhammad felt the difficulty to be so great that Islam has rejected the idea completely; God the eternal cannot die; it is impossible that a prophet should be so forsaken by God as to be left to die a shameful and agonizing death; since, then, Jesus was a prophet, though not the equal of Muhammad, He cannot have been crucified; the Jews were deluded in supposing that they had crucified Him. Thus the very basis of the Christian doctrine of redemption is rejected as a falsehood, a corruption by Christians of their own original Scriptures.

But if the Crucifixion of Jesus is a historical fact, and if it is in some way, as Christians have believed, the dying of God Himself, then this is the point at which we can really understand what God is like. Death is an ultimate, a final and irrevocable step; 'greater love hath no man than this, that a man lay down his life for his friends'.[2]

1. Ezekiel viii: 14.   2. John xv: 13.

If this is true, one great difficulty is immediately taken out of the way. We have already said that no true forgiveness can be given *de haut en bas*, in the patronizing spirit of self-conscious innocence. If we may speak in human terms, the problem for God was to find some method by which He could grant forgiveness without permanently humiliating His creatures and so depriving them of their self-respect. But if He is so concerned about our sins as to carry His identification of Himself with us to the point of dying for them, then everything is changed. A God who came to us in the guise of power might overawe and overwhelm us; a God who approaches us in utter weakness and helplessness makes a very different appeal. He comes not as one who confers a favour out of His superfluity; He comes asking a favour of us. He stands as a beggar at our door; He makes no effort to break in upon our independence; He merely pleads that we will be so good as not to refuse the gift which He has travelled so far to bring. This may sound paradoxical language; but it is no more than a careful expansion of what St Paul has said in a classic passage on the death of Christ: 'We are ambassadors therefore on behalf of Christ, as though God were intreating by us: we beseech you on behalf of Christ, be ye reconciled to God.'[1]

And, of course, it is always possible for each one of us to say No.

But we must return from these deep speculations to the historic fact of the Crucifixion of Jesus, and ask what it was that was there actually achieved. How can one man's death avail for many? Even if that One were the Son of God, how can His single death be a principle of redemption for all mankind?

The Christian answer is that Jesus on the cross fulfilled the destiny of the human race, and that therefore His death is the turning point in the history of the world.

We find it difficult to understand this, because we have grown too accustomed to thinking in an individualistic, even atomistic, fashion of man in relation to the race. We forget

1. 2 Corinthians v: 20.

or ignore that real unity in which all things are bound together. It is literally true that, when I cross a room, my movement alters the balance of the earth and therefore shakes the stars; that the commotion I have made is infinitesimally small does not alter the fact that I have made it. In the same way, I cannot live to myself alone; whatever I do or fail to do affects the whole life of man everywhere, though there are very few among us so placed that the effects of their character and actions are visible or measurable beyond a tiny circle.

Sometimes, however, we can see that one man has acted representatively on behalf of the whole human race. When once one man has discovered something new, no other man need make the same discovery again. Pythagoras proved that the square on the hypotenuse of a right-angled triangle is equal to the sum of the squares on the other two sides. This was a permanent addition to human knowledge, a solid rock of truth on which other men could build. If one climber has found the way to the top of a virgin peak, the back of the difficulty is broken, and no other man need ever wrestle with it in the same way; thousands may share for themselves in the thrill of discovery, but what the original pioneer achieved remains unique; he achieved it both for himself and for all those who might come after him. If, in a shipwreck, one man has descended into the boiling surf and carried a rope to shore, there is no need that any of his companions should endanger his life in the same way.

In all these spheres there is a 'once-for-allness' about certain achievements which makes them unique, though a thousand other men should follow in the footsteps of the pioneer. That such uniqueness exists also in the moral and spiritual spheres is not susceptible of certain proof or disproof; but, human nature and human life being what they are, the balance must be held to incline in favour rather than against. What was there about the death of Jesus which made two New Testament writers ascribe to it in explicit terms precisely this quality of 'once-for-allness'? 'For the death that he died, he died unto sin once for all: but the life that he liveth, he liveth unto God.'[1] 'By which will we have been sanctified through the offering of the body of Jesus Christ once for all.'[2]

This question can be answered only in relation to the most far-reaching question of all – what was the purpose for which the worlds were made? Let us start from the answer, for the moment put forward only as a hypothesis, that God made this world in order that He might see His own love perfectly reflected in a free and answering love. If that is a true answer, from the beginning onwards God had never seen what He desired. Natural things, inanimate and animate, up to the level of the animals, each perfect in its own order, all perfectly fulfil the will of God; yet none can supply that which is desired, since none has those God-like qualities of self-consciousness and freedom which mark man out from all other existent things. And men, because of that instability of the will and that darkening of the understanding that had come in through sin, were never able to make more than a hesitant, confused, and uncertain response to God. Thus the universe failed in that very thing for which it was made. It was frustrated at the cardinal point of its being. Frustration is precisely the word chosen by St Paul to express this condition: 'The creation was subjected to *vanity*, not of its own will, but by reason of him who subjected it, in hope that the creation itself also shall be delivered from the bondage of corruption into the liberty of the glory of the children of God.'[3] The picture is that of a plant which goes on growing, but never can gather its strength together sufficiently to flower.

Then Jesus came, and the universe flowered. What God had so long looked for at last He saw – in a human mind that was able to grasp His purpose, in a human heart that manifested perfectly the divine quality of love, in a human will perfectly surrendered to His will even unto death. And what Jesus achieved, He achieved not for Himself only, but,

1. Romans vi: 10.
2. Hebrews x: 10; and see also vii: 27 and ix: 12.
3. Romans viii: 20–1.

because of that real unity of the human race in which we are all bound together, for us all.

The first flowering is a tremendous experience in the life of a plant; it involves chemical and biological changes which make it radically different from what it was before. If the universe flowered in Christ, then it is no longer exactly the same universe as it was before He died and rose again.

The age of frustration is over, and the age of achievement has begun. It was in terms such as these that the first Christians interpreted the new experience that had come to them through Jesus Christ. 'If any man is in Christ, he is a new creature: the old things are passed away; behold, they are become new. But all things are of God, who reconciled us to himself through Christ.'[1] The old epoch, which was the epoch of disappointment and death, culminated in the death of Jesus; the new epoch, which is characterized by life and victory, began with the resurrection of Jesus from the dead. And what Jesus achieved, He achieved not for Himself only, but for us all: 'Because I live, ye shall live also.'[2]

The word of the Cross is to Jews a scandal, and to Greeks foolishness. The Moslem dismisses so impossible an event by denying that it ever happened. When we have done our best with explanations and theories, we are still left with the element of paradox. Why did He do it? Why did it seem to Him worth while to do and to endure all this to redeem a world? We can only answer that the logic of love is different from the logic of calculation, and reaches different conclusions.

Redemption through the death of Jesus Christ makes sense only on the presupposition that God attaches an infinite value to the souls of human creatures:

> Whose souls, condemned and dying,
> Were precious in Thy sight.

There has been a good deal of discussion, some of it highly technical, in recent years on the nature of love. A distinction has been drawn between love which derives from the recog-

1. 2 Corinthians v: 17–18.   2. John xiv: 19.

nition of value in that which is loved, and that which confers value on the object of love by the act of loving; or, to put the same thing in simple language, between love which loves the already lovable, and that which loves the unlovely, because it can be made lovable only by being loved. In practice, I think we should find it difficult to affirm that any of our own feelings could be assigned precisely and exclusively to either type; most human feelings are far too mixed to fit into any academic categories. But I believe that, in principle, the distinction is true and helpful, and, just at the point which our argument has reached, can lead us into certain necessary insights.

The message of the Gospel is that God loves sinners. And it is precisely this that men find it extraordinarily hard to believe and to accept. The Pharisees did not regard sinners, at least if they were Israelites, as wholly beyond the limits of God's concern; if only they would repent and improve themselves a little and turn back to God, God would be willing to receive them. And that is exactly what is preached today from a great many supposedly Christian pulpits. Comb your hair, cut your nails, put your clothes a little to rights, and perhaps, even though your wedding garment is not very adequate, you may secure admission to the festival of the great King.

Repent, and you will be all right. 'And vacant chaff well meant for grain.' Of course, if I could repent I should be all right; but to be a sinner is just to have lost the capacity to repent. If you ever had occasion to try and help one who has become an alcoholic or a drug-addict, you will know exactly what that means. If only the drunkard would pull himself together, he would no longer be a drunkard; but to be a drunkard is to have lost the power to pull yourself together. These pious injunctions, ceaselessly reiterated, as they are from most Christian pulpits in Advent and Lent, are not a message of hope to those who know that they are baffled by the imagination and imprisoned within the weakness of their own wills.

As is now well known, parallels to almost all the sayings of

Jesus can be found somewhere or other in the teachings of the Rabbis. The great and magnificently honest Jewish scholar, C. G. Montefiore, asking himself at what point, if any, the teaching of Jesus is completely new and original, finds the point of originality here. The Rabbis had said that if the sinner returns to God, God will receive him: they had not said that the love of God goes out to seek the sinner where he is. But in the Gospels it is so. Of course, if the lost sheep finds its way back to the fold, it will be let in. But this is not what is said in the parable of the lost sheep; there it is the shepherd who goes out to seek the lost sheep in the wilderness; and it is declared, to the scandal of all virtuous souls who have never gone astray, that there 'shall be joy in heaven over one sinner that repenteth, more than over ninety and nine just persons, which need no repentance'.[1]

You will find one of the finest expressions of this truth where you might not expect to find it, in Moody and Sankey's *Sacred Songs and Solos*, in the hymn by Elizabeth Clephane, first sung in this country by the American evangelist Ira D. Sankey, to a rather vulgar tune of his own composition:

'Lord, Thou hast here Thy ninety and nine;
  Are they not enough for Thee?'
But the Shepherd made answer: 'This of mine
  Has wandered away from Me;
And although the road be rough and steep,
  I go to the desert to find My sheep.'
But none of the ransomed ever knew
  How deep were the waters crossed;
Nor how dark was the night that the Lord passed through
  Ere He found His sheep that was lost.

The Gospel affirms that God loves sinners, not when they clean themselves up and make themselves respectable, but just as they are, in all their dirt and alienation; or, what is much more difficult, in all the armour of their respectability and self-righteousness. Now it is quite evident that if God really loves people such as you and I know ourselves to be, He must be a very odd God. That He does so love us

1. Luke xv: 7.

– that and nothing else – is the very heart of the Gospel.

The Jews need not have found this doctrine as strange as they did, since it is indicated more than once in the Old Testament in connexion with the election of Israel. It is emphasized more than once that God's choice of Israel depended not on any special merit that He had discerned in that people more than in any other, but solely on His own unbought and unconditioned love. 'The Lord did not set his love upon you, nor choose you, because ye were more in number than any people; for ye were the fewest of all peoples: but because the Lord loveth you, and because he would keep the oath which he swore unto your fathers, hath the Lord brought you out with a mighty hand, and redeemed you out of the house of bondage, from the hand of Pharaoh King of Egypt.'[1] In even more picturesque terms the prophet Ezekiel pictures the contrast between what Israel was by nature, and what she had become by grace: 'As for thy nativity, in the day thou wast born . . . none eye pitied thee . . . to have compassion upon thee; but thou wast cast out in the open field, for that thy person was abhorred, in the day that thou wast born. And when I passed by thee, and saw thee weltering in thy blood, I said unto thee, Though thou art in thy blood, live; yea, I said unto thee, Though thou art in thy blood, live. . . . Now when I passed by thee, and looked upon thee, behold thy time was the time of love; and I spread my skirt over thee, and covered thy nakedness: yea, I sware unto thee, and entered into a covenant with thee, saith the Lord God, and thou becamest mine . . . thus wast thou decked with gold and silver; and thy raiment was of fine linen, and silk, and broidered work; thou didst eat fine flour, and honey, and oil: and thou wast exceeding beautiful, and thou didst prosper unto royal estate. And thy renown went forth among the nations for thy beauty; for it was perfect, through my majesty which I had put upon thee, saith the Lord God.'[2]

But, in fact, this part of Old Testament teaching had been forgotten; and when Jesus came putting into practice what

1. Deuteronomy vii: 7–8.   2. Ezekiel xvi: 4–14.

these older Scriptures had described as the attitude and action of God Himself, respectable ecclesiastical authorities were affronted. Conventional morality always expects a virtuous teacher to find pleasure in association with the virtuous; the seeking of lost sheep is never a popular profession. Thus it came about that the Church's Founder came to be described as the friend of sinners; the words 'this man receiveth sinners and eateth with them' were originally spoken not as a compliment but as a criticism.

It is evident from the Gospels that the love of Jesus for His friends was in the main not of that type which recognizes existing value, but of that which confers value which did not exist.

In His relationship with His disciples we can see a great deal of normal, natural human friendship; He was glad to have them with Him, and counted on their support in His time of trouble. But it is evident that He looked beyond what they were to what He could make of them. His faith in them is even more remarkable than their faith in Him. Who but Jesus, looking upon the impulsive and unstable Peter, would have compared Him to a rock? Who but Jesus, of whom it was asked, 'How knoweth this man letters, never having learned?'[1] would have believed that a group of 'unlearned and ignorant men', by the sole fact that 'they had been with Jesus',[2] would acquire the capacity to turn the world upside down?

The disciples at least belonged to the more respectable class of society. But Jesus carried His mission far beyond the limits of respectability. He was found surrounded by publicans and sinners. He went into the house of Zacchaeus, the oppressive and unjust tax-gatherer – and of course was immediately followed by criticism: 'And when they saw it, they all murmured, saying, He is gone in to lodge with a man that is a sinner.'[3] This association of Jesus with the outcasts of society was entirely free from that sanctimonious air of doing good to others, which has so often made the charitable efforts of Christians loathsome in the eyes of those

1. John vii: 15.   2. Acts iv: 13.   3. Luke xix: 7.

whom they have tried to help. It is evident that Jesus liked being with people like that, and that they liked Him. He gave them freely and spontaneously the best gift of all, His own personality and His own love, and they responded. He gave back to them that which society had taken from them, the sense of infinite value in the sight of God.

Why did Jesus act in this way? We must turn again to the inspired interpretation of the life of Jesus given in the fourth Gospel: ' The Son can do nothing of himself, but what he seeth the Father doing: for what things soever he doeth, these the Son also doeth in like manner. For the Father loveth the Son, and sheweth him all things that himself doeth: and greater works than these will he shew him, that ye may marvel.'[1] Jesus of Nazareth, who, to put it at the lowest, had an unrivalled insight into the spiritual issues of human life, affirmed that God loves sinners, even while they continue in their sin; it was therefore natural to Him to model His own life on His apprehension of the divine, and to make that life a continuous manifestation of love for sinners, even while they continued in their sin. Conversely, He invited those who saw Him to believe that in seeing Him they saw the Father; to carry their inferences upwards from His visible actions and behaviour in time and space to what is being done all the time by the Father, who though not Himself in time or space has been pleased to concern Himself most intimately with them; to find in Him *the truth*, that inner reality which underlies the universe and holds in one all the principles by which it is maintained.

This attitude, this activity of God, is set forth with wonderful power in the parable of the Prodigal Son. But the reality is greater than the symbol. In that parable the father waits with infinite tenderness, for the son to return; in the reality, the Father says, 'I will go and find my son'. In the parable, the son who by his own folly has lost his right to sonship says to the father, 'Make me as one of thy hired servants'; only to find himself overwhelmed by the exuberance of a welcome which includes the best robe, the

1. John v: 19–20.

ring for his hand and shoes for his feet, and the killing of the fatted calf. Many other prodigals have come back timidly, hoping that they might perhaps be allowed to stand outside and hear something of the music of the feast, and perhaps gather up some of the broken meats that fall from the Master's table; and have been astonished when the heavenly attendant comes and says, 'They want you inside'. ('It was unbelievable,' said Jody to himself, 'he was wanted.') In every experience of reconciliation with God there is always this element of surprise, of the incredible. If the wayward son is genuinely sorry for what he has done, he takes it for granted that he can never be restored to what he was before; he has forgotten that God's ways are so much higher than ours that to us they seem incredible, and that He is a God who delights to perform the impossible.

Perhaps this surprise is something by which all eternity will be permeated. Perhaps we may think that we detect it on the faces of the redeemed in Fra Angelico's Resurrection, as they step so blithely over the flowery fields of Paradise; it seems incredible to them that they should be there. Who has ever expressed this better than one of our own poets:

> Love bade me welcome; yet my soul drew back,
>   Guilty of dust and sin:
> But quick-eyed love, observing me grow slack
>   From my first entrance in,
> Drew nearer to me, sweetly questioning
>   If I lack'd anything.
> 'A guest' I answered, 'worthy to be here.'
>   Love said 'You shall be he'.
> 'I, the unkind, ungrateful? Ah, my dear,
>   I cannot look on thee.'
> Love took my hand, and smiling did reply,
>   'Who made the eyes but I?'
> 'Truth, Lord, but I have marred them: let my shame
>   Go where it doth deserve.'
> 'And know you not', says Love, 'who bore the blame?'
>   'My dear, then I will serve.'
> 'You must sit down', says Love, 'and taste my meat.'
>   So I did sit and eat.

7

THE NEW COMMUNITY

NOTHING in the contemporary scene is more striking than the general regard which is felt for Jesus Christ and the general dislike of the organized Church which bears His name.

There have been, of course, those who like Friedrich Nietzsche detested Jesus as the great deceiver and betrayer. Occasionally attempts are made to rob Him of His place of central importance in human history. Some years ago a curious book called *An Outline for Boys and Girls and their Parents* was published under the editorship of that generally admirable writer Naomi Mitchison; the contributors appear to have made it their aim silently to deny Jesus by excluding Him altogether from their pages; they were not altogether successful, and His name twice slipped in unawares. It is not surprising that the book can now be read rather as a curiosity than as a serious contribution to popular education. Mr H. G. Wells in his *History of the World* included Jesus among the great figures of history. Bertrand Russell, albeit a little patronizingly, has given him a section in his *History of Western Philosophy*. In India countless thoughtful Hindus who have no intention whatsoever of becoming Christians recognize that the teaching of Jesus evokes in them a deeper response than anything that they have elsewhere encountered.

But somehow the Church as an institution fails to attract. 'I love and honour Jesus Christ; but must I join a Church?' This question is very often heard on the lips of young people, who are appalled by the contrast between the adventurous idealism of the teaching of Jesus and the conventional stuffiness of the Church as they see it before their eyes.

There was a time when an individualist or idealist interpretation of the Gospels was widely current in the theological world. The central concern in religion was held to be the relationship between God and the individual soul. As A. N. Whitehead has expressed it, 'religion is what a man does with his solitariness' – a view which, in spite of its popularity, would make nonsense of the Christian Gospel. Jesus, it was maintained, came to proclaim the great truths of the fatherhood of God and the brotherhood of man; He came to introduce a new spirit into human affairs; but the Church, by substituting for this simplicity the complications of the Creeds, and by giving it concrete expression in an institution with laws and regulations, has driven out the spirit of Jesus. Jesus came to bring to man liberty of thought and action; the Church has always desired to imprison both Him and His followers in the traditions of men.

In the last fifty years there has been a sharp reaction against the individualistic view, and many of the best writers on theology have given expression to the conviction that the Church is an essential part of the Gospel, and that the primary concern of Jesus was not with the individual but with a community. This is not new doctrine. Rather surprisingly, it was John Calvin who said that it is not possible for a man to have God for his Father, unless he also has the Church for his mother. But this recovery of the corporate sense of the Gospel enables us to read the New Testament more nearly as it was written and first read by those who lived in the exhilaration of the first days of a new community. To those who ask whether it is not possible to accept Christ and to dispense with His Church, we must answer, in the light of the New Testament, that it is impossible. Jesus Christ is always an offence, a scandal. To the Pharisees it was a scandal that He came as an unlettered carpenter. To the whole ancient world it was a horrible offence to be offered salvation in the person of a crucified Jew. But the offence could not be avoided. To-day it is a trouble to many people that the message of Jesus is offered to them through a Church, all too human and imperfect, which seems often to conceal rather than to manifest the lineaments of the Master. But so it is. This poor Church is

Christ's Church. Christ will not separate Himself from those who are called by His name; we may not attempt so to separate what God has joined together.

It is perfectly true that the word ἐκκλησία, Church, occurs only twice in the Gospels. Both instances are in St Matthew; both occur in parts of the Gospel which most scholars would attribute rather to the later and interpretative element in the Gospel than to the original words of Jesus Himself. But nothing could be more dangerous, in theology as elsewhere, than to base an argument solely on words, and particularly on the absence of certain words from certain documents. It is only recently that I have noticed that the word ἐλπίς, hope, does not occur once in the four Gospels; but are they not full of hope – hope for men today – hope of the establishment of the Kingdom of God with power at the end of the world? The word πίστις, faith, is not found in St John's Gospel. In the same Gospel there is no word for either forgiveness or remission. If we were to base any arguments on these omissions, we should reach some strange theological conclusions.

The fact is that, in the Gospels as we have them, the calling out and preparation of a new community, in which the work of Jesus will be continued and perfected, is central to the whole of His ministry. It could, indeed, hardly be otherwise. Jesus deliberately worked within the framework of the Old Testament tradition, though that framework could not permanently contain what He came to do; He regarded His work as the fulfilment of the law and the prophets, though inevitably the Old Testament bottles were burst by the pouring in of the new wine of the Gospel. Now the whole of the Old Testament is the record of God's dealings with a chosen people, and with individuals only as they were concerned in or served the destinies of that people. If the work of Jesus was to complete that of the Old Testament, it is reasonable to expect that it would follow the same pattern of a universal purpose of God going forward through a people, a community, specially entrusted with the knowledge and the service of His will.

At the start the message of Jesus was directed to the whole people. There was always the possibility that the whole people would repent and turn to God, and so become capable as a whole of fulfilling its destiny as the servant of the Lord. Before long it became clear that this universal repentance would not take place; parallel with the growth of faith in some was the growth of unbelief and increasingly bitter opposition in others. Then the method of Jesus changed. The choice of twelve disciples, to form the inner nucleus of His followers, was a turning point in His ministry. The number twelve is significant; in relation to the new community, these twelve specially chosen disciples were to play the same role as had the twelve sons of Jacob, the twelve patriarchs, in relation to the old. As it became increasingly clear that the career of Jesus would end in death and disaster, more and more time was given to the training of the twelve for leadership in a community which would persist when Jesus was no longer visibly present to lead His people.[1]

These and other arguments can be drawn from the historical conditions under which the work of Jesus was accomplished. A simple and perhaps even more convincing argument can be drawn from the teaching of Jesus at one of its highest points. The two great commandments, 'Thou shalt love the Lord thy God with all thy heart, and with all thy soul, and with all thy might', and 'Thou shalt love thy neighbour as thyself', are already found in the Old Testament, but in separation.[2] Jesus brought them together, and showed the dependence of one upon the other. A man cannot truly love God unless he accepts the responsibility of loving also all those in whose welfare God is concerned; as a later Christian writer expressed it, 'he that loveth not his brother whom he hath seen, cannot love God whom he hath not seen'.[3] Conversely, if love for the neighbour is to rise

---

1. The evidence is clearly and fully set out in Dr Newton Flew's *Jesus and His Church* (London 1949).
2. Deuteronomy vi: 5; Leviticus xiv: 18.
3. 1 John iv: 20.

above a general philanthropy, that neighbour must be seen as a child of God, as one whose value is determined by the fact that he is the object of God's interest and regard.

The writer of what is known as the second Epistle of Peter draws a distinction between φιλαδελφία, love of the brethren, and ἀγάπη, love; 'Supply . . . in your godliness love of the brethren; and in your love of the brethren love'.[1] For this distinction there is good authority elsewhere in the New Testament: 'A new commandment give I unto you, that ye love one another; even as I have loved you, that ye also love one another. By this shall all men know that ye are my disciples, if ye have love one to another.'[2] All men are to be regarded as falling within the sphere of our responsibility; by allegiance to the God revealed in Jesus Christ all human relationships are to be transformed and renewed. But within the fellowship of those who are bound together by personal loyalty to Jesus Christ, the relationship of love reaches an intimacy and intensity unknown elsewhere. Friendship between the friends of Jesus of Nazareth is unlike any other friendship. This ought to be normal experience within the Christian community. That in existing Christian congregations it is so rare is a measure of the failure of the Church as a whole to live up to the purpose of its Founder for it. Where it is experienced, especially across the barriers of race, nationality, and language, it is one of the most convincing evidences of the continuing activity of Jesus among men.

It has seemed necessary to lay emphasis on the corporate and communal nature of religious experience, as understood by the Christian, in view of the widespread revival of interest in mysticism.

It is not easy to define mysticism. An appendix to Dr W. R. Inge's famous lectures on Christian mysticism makes available for us no less than forty-seven different definitions, none of them perhaps wholly satisfactory. Sometimes the word is used almost as a term of abuse; the mystical is opposed to the practical, to the disadvantage of the former.

1. 2 Peter i: 5–7.   2. John xiii: 34–5.

Sometimes the term seems to be used so indefinitely as to cover any religious experience which includes a vivid sense of the existence of an eternal world and of personal communion with God.

Perhaps it is best not to attempt definition but to ask what mysticism is, in its purest and most classical forms, as for instance in the philosophy of Plotinus, the great fountainhead of all Western mysticism, or in the traditions of orthodox Hinduism; and to consider whether what is sought and perhaps found in these traditions is the same as what is offered in the Christian Gospel.

1. The mystic seeks absorption in the eternal, and the cessation of separate existence. Separateness is an illusion or a disaster. The individual soul desires to fall as a drop of water into the limitless ocean of being – ἄπειρον πέλαγος οὐσίας is a phrase of the fourth century Greek Father Gregory of Nazianzus – or, as a divine spark that has somehow fallen into imprisonment in the flesh, to be reunited with the primal fire.

2. The mystic, after he has progressed beyond the most elementary stages in the quest for God, tends to regard the presence of other selves as a hindrance to his progress, and to resent their intrusion upon his solitariness. His progress is, in the magnificent phrase with which the *Enneads* of Plotinus end, 'the flight of the alone to the alone'.

3. The mystic regards external rites and ordinances as a necessary discipline for beginners, but as a hindrance to those who have progressed beyond the level of the sensuous and the seen. In the quasi-mystical discourse on love of Diotima in the *Symposium* of Plato, the aspirant makes his first experience of beauty as manifest in forms and colours and visible beings; but he must pass forward, if he can, to the vision of beauty itself, the idea, unincorporate, selfexistent, and eternal. To be content with beauty expressed in forms is to exchange the substance for the shadow.

4. The mystic regards the return from rapt contemplation to the sordid realities of the visible world as bitter deprivation, as an almost unendurable fall:

Swift as the radiant shapes of sleep
  From one whose dreams are Paradise
Fly, when the fond wretch wakes to weep,
  And Day peers forth with her blank eyes. . . .

If he could, he would be always on the mount of contemplation, and have done for ever with the mist and distractions of this world of evanescent things.

This is what the great mystics have meant by mysticism. We shall not argue here whether there is any sense in which it is legitimate to speak of Christian mysticism, though noting that those who are commonly referred to as Christian mystics have on the whole themselves been most careful to avoid the term. But we must take cognisance of the fact that what the Christian Gospel offers, under the four headings listed above, is wholly different from what is sought and desired by those who follow the classic way of the mystics:

1. The Christian desires a perfect unity of his will with the will of God, such as was manifested in Jesus of Nazareth; but this is not that absorption into the divine being which the mystic seeks. The Gospel is expressed in terms of $\dot{a}\gamma\acute{a}\pi\eta$, love. Such love always involves a mutuality, an 'I – thou' relationship of loving and being loved. The Christian expects and desires that this 'I – thou' relationship will continue to all eternity. Eternal life to him means the ever-increasing vision of God, and the ever-increasing fulfilment of the self, as it is enabled to respond in love to the love of God.

2. The Christian rejoices in the fellowship of other selves. So far from finding in them a hindrance to his own progress, he knows that the discipline of consideration for others and concern about their needs, that growth in the love of the neighbour, is an indispensable condition for growth in the love of God. The Gospel, for all its particular care for the individual, knows nothing of an individual salvation.

3. The Christian is prepared unashamedly to accept the condition of, to use a favourite expression of Baron von Hügel, *creatureliness*. He may look forward to a state in which

he will no longer be concerned with a body occupying space and gnawed perpetually by the tooth of time. He may expect a Kingdom of God, in which there will be no place for sign and sacrament, since the reality which the sign sets forth is perfectly and eternally enjoyed. But he is not there yet. It does not disturb him that Christianity is the most material of the great religions, taking the body as seriously as the spirit; that in professing it he cannot escape at any turn from the hard, historical realities of the flesh and blood of Christ, and that at the very heart of the most spiritual worship of the Church he will find the crude physical realities of bread and wine. Christian faith holds out to him no hope at all that he will ever, in this life, attain to such a level of spiritual achievement, as will enable him to dispense with these physical things as the food of his soul, and as the sacramental means of the most intense and intimate fellowship with God.

4. To the Christian, return from the high realms of adoration to the world of contingency and frustration is felt not as an agonizing deprivation, but as a fulfilment of that which in adoration had been sought. It is not for the servant to be above his Lord; if the Lord found His happiness in opening the eyes of the blind, in cleansing the leper, and in preaching the Gospel to the poor, the servant can find it in no other way. 'In as much as ye did it unto one of these my brethren, even these least, ye did it unto me.' The highest spiritual experience in this life is not rapt contemplation of the divine, but the rendering of disinterested service to the poorest, the lowliest, and the lost. Times of withdrawal and contemplation are necessary, but only in order that the one who has scaled the Mount of Transfiguration may be strengthened to bring the spirit of Jesus into those problems of daily life that are inescapable in the plains.

What has here been stated somewhat schematically is also historically true. The Christian Church in its early days survived because it was a fellowship of peculiar intensity and mutual loyalty.

At the start it appeared as though the Christian group

might continue as an inner fellowship within Judaism. It was not long, however, before the radical differences began to appear. As Stephen first discerned, when the principles of Jesus came to be practically applied they would make temple and law and sacrifice otiose; the new religion involved a temple of God as wide as the whole created universe, a priesthood coextensive with the human race, and a sacred season extending from one end of the year to the other. If Christians came to realize this, so did Jews. By the time that the fourth Gospel came to be written, 'the Jews' are already the enemy *par excellence*; the name is never once used with any other significance than this.

But the Jews were not the only adversaries. The Gospel strikes too near the heart of man in his traditions, his superstitions, and his economic interests to be easily tolerated. Elymas the sorcerer, the priests of Zeus at Lystra, Demetrius and his fellow silversmiths around the great temple of Artemis at Ephesus, all found the new message inconvenient, not to say alarming. Roman authority was not by habit given to persecution; but it was always on the watch against anything that might promote civil disorder, and ruthless to any movement which might even seem to question the supreme authority of the Emperor; it was not difficult for hostile mobs to call in the aid of the Government to their panic or to their ill-will.

Persecution from without does promote fellowship. In times of peace the boundary between the Church and the world becomes ill-defined. In time of persecution, on the contrary, the Church does not need to be told to be separate from the world; the separation is sharp and unmistakable – and on both sides. No half-hearted supporter is likely to commit himself at his own peril to an unpopular cause. The Communist party in Spain does not welcome members who are likely to change their minds and to betray the secrets of the party to its enemies.

Such a close fellowship must have its distinctive marks and badges, by which wholehearted loyalty is expressed and renewed. Those who have lived all their lives in peaceful surroundings do not always recognize this necessity, and regard the Christian sacraments as an appendage to Christian faith rather than as integral parts of it. Things look different on the frontier and in times of persecution. There, even if there were no theological significance in the sacraments at all, their use could be defended on the grounds of their pragmatic value alone. They both express and make effective the character of this new society.

In India the high-caste Hindu attaches such significance to baptism as would satisfy the most high-flying Christian orthodoxy. A Hindu, if he wishes, may accept in his heart all the tenets of the Christian faith; he may be regular in attendance at Christian worship and may contribute largely from his means to the support of the Christian Church. He may even openly profess himself to be a friend and follower of Jesus. If he stops short of baptism, and is careful not to offend against the rules of his caste, his position in the Hindu community is unendangered and unimpaired. But let him once take the fatal step, and all is altered. He is at once cut off from home and family, from all social ties, and from all his ancient roots in the life of his community. To his own people he is as one dead. It is baptism alone that makes the separation irrevocable.

This works also in the contrary direction. Hundreds of young men, deeply attracted by the character and teaching of Jesus, have held back from baptism, in order that they might continue to live and witness among their own people. The convert is cut off from all his past; he no longer has any access to his own people, and has no opportunity to bear any witness to them about his new-found faith. As an unbaptized Christian, he can move about among them freely, and let character and conviction bear their own quiet witness. The argument is painfully plausible. All that can be said is that facts are stronger than logic. Scarcely one of those who have started out, with whatever sincerity of conviction, on this course of inner Christian allegiance without overt Christian confession, has been able to resist the soothing influence of compromise; not one of them has ever succeeded in creating un unmistakably Christian movement among his own people.[1] The saying that no man can serve two masters is hard; but if it is eliminated from the Gospel – then what remains is no longer the Gospel.

The Holy Communion has unhappily become a subject of controversy among Christians, and what ought to be the unchanging centre of union has become the point of bitter separation. But, amid all the conflict of doctrines, on the two points which are relevant at this stage of our argument Christians of all the various Churches would agree.

First, the Holy Communion is the most democratic institution in the world, since, in the simple act of eating and drinking at the table of the Lord, accidental differences of rank or worldly position cease to have any significance. All are one in the fellowship of the Holy Spirit, the fellowship created by the Lord. When in old days the squire danced with the kitchen-maid at the servants' ball, there was usually a certain amount of constraint on both sides. If the squire and the kitchen-maid meet at the Lord's Table, and both are Christians in heart as well as in name, no such constraint is felt in receiving the body and blood of the Lord.

No one perhaps can so well realize this significance of the Holy Communion as one who has lived and worked under the conditions of the Indian Church. In India, where the traditions of Hinduism are still strictly kept, members of different castes do not eat together. Two men may be intimate friends and partners; yet, if they do not belong to the same caste, neither can invite the other to a meal in his own house. Nothing is harder for the high-caste convert than the acceptance of the common chalice at the Holy Communion, from which he will drink with others of lower social status than himself. But in Christ the middle wall of partition is broken down. I have celebrated the Holy Communion in a tumble-down schoolhouse in a remote village; and, on turning round for the administration, have noticed that my little congregation included converts from six different Hindu

1. Several have successfully started reform movements, which have stopped short of a full and unmistakably Christian allegiance to Christ.

castes, all of whom in Hinduism had been separate, all of whom in Christ had been made one.

Secondly, the Holy Communion is a fellowship of those who are prepared to die for Christ, as Christ has died for them. A few years ago the expression of such a sentiment in peaceful England might have sounded melodramatic and unreal. Events of recent years have caused us to think again. Many of us have German friends who spent years in Hitler's concentration camps, just because they were Christians and would not condone such measures as the persecution of the Jews. Some of us have had friends who went into Hitler's concentration camps and never came out again.

Throughout the centuries, the Church of Christ has survived only because there has been within it a sufficient number of men and women who were willing, if need arose, cheerfully to die for Him. This was conspicuously true of the Church in the first three centuries; it was the martyr Church. Persecution was not continuous or always intense; on the whole, the Roman authorities seem to have disliked persecution, and as far as possible tended to let the laws against the Christians sleep. Nevertheless, the law was the law, and what the law said was *Non licet esse vos*, 'It is not permitted that you should exist'. Christians knew that at all times their peace was insecure, and that it might be their calling to glorify God by facing the fire or the wild beasts in the arena. And yet the Christian society both survived and grew. Clearly it had something to offer that men and women in that decaying world felt that they desperately needed.

What was it which this society offered, and which men felt that they could not find elsewhere?

First of all, perhaps, the Church offered hope. In the old legend of Pandora's box, when all the other good things had been lost and all evils had been let loose upon mankind, hope remained. As so often, the legend pictorially expresses profound truth. Man cannot live without hope. If hopelessness descends upon tribes and peoples, they fail to reproduce their kind, die out, and disappear. In the second and third centuries despondency was beginning to settle down upon large masses of people in the Roman Empire; the pressure of government was growing daily heavier; the threats of the barbarians beyond the frontier were becoming daily more ominous. As so often in times of distress, men sought to call in a new world to redress the balance of the old, and asked whether religion could offer, on the far side of the grave, such happiness as earth denied. For the most part religion returned an ambiguous or disheartening answer.

In the greatest days of Greece, life in this world was so full of enterprise and achievement that men had not much attention to spare for what might come after death. Greek religion gave little hope; but the youthful zest of that great age enabled men to face death with such dignified and splendid resignation as found expression in the funeral speech of Pericles as recorded by Thucydides, and in the funerary sculptures of the best period of classic art.

As the pulse of life beat lower and the need for consolation was more ardently felt, crowds of men and women sought assurance of a better life after death through initiation into one or other of the mysteries. Long before, Pindar had written of the blessedness of those who in this life had made due preparation for the endless way: 'For them the sun shineth in his strength, in the world below, while here 'tis night; and, in meadows red with roses, the space before their city is shaded by the incense-tree, and is laden with golden fruits ... beside them bloometh the fair flower of perfect bliss. And o'er that lovely land fragrance is ever shed, while they mingle all manner of incense with the far-shining fire on the altars of the gods. From the other side, sluggish streams of darksome night send forth a boundless gloom.'[1] Those who still read the works of Tennyson may recognize the concluding lines of *Tiresias*:

> and every way the vales
> Wind, clouded with the grateful incense-fume
> Of those who mix all odour to the Gods
> On one far height in one far-shining fire.

1. Pindar: fragment 130, translated by J. E. Sandys.

To some, no doubt, the mysteries made real the consolation that they promised. But they suffered from two grave and, in the end, fatal defects. They provided emotional satisfaction, but they had no theology; they could give no answer to those questions which, sooner or later, must be asked by every intelligent man. Religions can last for a time in the strength of an emotional impetus, but only those survive which have a philosophy, a body of doctrine which can, for a time at least, quiet the restless intellect of man. Secondly, though the mysteries demanded exacting measures of ritual and outward purification, they failed to give an inner power and purity to correspond with the outward requirements. Just from the fact that so many ran from one initiation to another, it is easy to see that what the mysteries provided was an anodyne and not a cure, and that they belonged to that class of institutions which, like the Jewish law, made nothing perfect, and could never be more than a shadow of good things to come.[1]

The beliefs and thoughts of ordinary men are most clearly shown in the sepulchral inscriptions, many of which have been preserved in the Greek Anthology. To read at length in this collection is a desolating experience; there in abundance are despair, regret, bitterness, cynicism, sometimes a wry resignation; but scarcely ever a gleam of hope.

'Child, be not overly distressed; no man is immortal.'
'I was not, I was born, I lived, I am not; that is all – –'

'All we are kept for death, fed like a herd of swine that are butchered, without rhyme or reason.'
'Here lie I, Dionysius of Tarsus, sixty years old, unwed; would that my father had been the same.'

Christianity burst upon this ageing, weary world, with hope of everlasting life through participation in the resurrection of One who had been dead but is alive, and has the keys of death and of Hades.[2] Contrast the tone of the inscriptions quoted above with the jubilant expression of St Paul: 'having the desire to depart and be with Christ; for

1. Hebrews vii: 19; x: i.   2. Revelation i: 18.

it is very far better'.[1] It was the almost universal conviction of the ancient world that this life is the real life, and that what lies beyond the grave cannot be at best more than a shadow of the reality that exists here. Occasionally some bold spirit like Euripides raised the question, 'Who knoweth whether this life be not truly death, death life?' Socrates, under sentence of death, ends his *Apology* with the words, 'And whether they [his accusers] or I are going to a better thing, none knoweth save God only'. The confident proclamation that life here was worth living well, because it is a preparation which has its fulfilment, its consummation, in another and eternal world, was the monopoly of the Christians. One will not find in pagan sources close parallels to this conclusion of Paul's great chapter on the resurrection: 'Wherefore, my beloved brethren, be ye steadfast, unmoveable, always abounding in the work of the Lord, forasmuch as ye know that your labour is not in vain in the Lord.'[2]

What the Christians professed they also practised. Such classics of the days of the persecutions as the letter of the Churches of Lyons and Vienne (A.D. 177), and the Passion of Saint Perpetua (*c.* A.D. 200), the earlier part of which was certainly written by the noble matron Perpetua herself, breathe a spirit of quiet and sanguine hopefulness in the face of death, in which there is no trace either of hysteria or of bitterness. Perhaps the triumph of the Christians over death was more powerful in winning new adherents to their cause than the witness of their words.

But, though Christianity must always be in a sense a world-renouncing religion, since its heart and its hopes are set elsewhere, the thing that impressed observers about the early Christians was that their faith had given them new zest for living precisely in this world of space and time.

Zest was what most men lacked. The Empire had brought peace, but it had brought at the same time the end of political experiment and of the human vitality which that both expresses and inspires. Literature was for the most part an echo of classic forms and tones. Art was content to copy,

1. Philippians i: 23.   2. 1 Corinthians xv: 58.

and not infrequently to debase, the traditions of a better day. It was not an exciting world to live in; the best people lacked even the energy to fight to defend their homes, and were prepared to pay barbarians to do it for them.

The discouragements of daily life were reflected in religious belief. Everything seemed to be under the domination of iron Fate; the destiny of man is written in the stars and he cannot escape it. But since that destiny is based on no intelligible or moral principle, it seems equally reasonable to say that the affairs of men are ruled by chance – fickle, unpredictable, frequently malignant. In the alternations of fatalism and feverish desire, men turned to astrology, in the hope that they might at least learn the fate that was written in the stars, even though no power on earth or in heaven could avail to stop or to avert it.

For the Christian, the bondage of fate and chance had finally been broken by the manifestation of Jesus Christ once for all. History was no longer a phantasmagoria or an endlessly recurring cycle; it was the scene of the one all-embracing purpose of the heavenly Father. So far from history running downwards towards annihilation, it was in fact working up to its consummation. Soon, perhaps very soon, the Son of man would appear from heaven and take the Kingdom to Himself. In the meantime, there was a work to be done and a Kingdom to be proclaimed. As far as the interval of time permitted, the word of the Gospel was to be proclaimed to all nations. And, since Christians had been instructed to do all that they did in the name of the Lord Jesus, even the most trivial occupations and the routine demands of daily life acquired a new glory, as they were seen in the light of a divine purpose. Although this world was passing away, Christians were always to live in it as 'children of God without blemish in the midst of a crooked and perverse generation, among whom ye are seen as lights in the world'.[1]

Thirdly, the good news of God in Christ gave to man a new power of self-rule.

1. Philippians ii: 15.

In matters of morality and personal conduct, it is very difficult to distinguish one age from another. When so many individuals are involved, and so much of individual conduct escapes the scrutiny of others, generalizations are always hazardous. Nevertheless, there would probably be agreement that England was a kinder, more orderly, more moral country in the middle of the nineteenth century than it had been at the end of the eighteenth. Similarly, when Romans under the Empire contrasted their own age unfavourably with the austere and purer times of the Republic, they had grounds for their judgement other than the mere peevishness of the elderly *laudator temporis acti*.

It was a profligate age. Reckless expenditure on the part of the rich was matched by an iron callousness as to the fate of the poor. The spectacles of the circus and the amphitheatre hardened and coarsened the minds and nerves of ordinary men. Licentiousness was almost unchecked. It must always be so in a slave-owning society; the slave took vengeance for the bitterness of his servitude by spreading corruption of every kind among the ruling class and their offspring. For our knowledge of these and other prevalent ills we are not dependent on the denunciations of ill-tempered Christian Fathers; the evidence of the pagan writers is unanimous, and leaves us in no doubt as to the character of the society in which the early Church grew up.

This is not to say that there were no better elements in pagan society. We have already considered some examples of nobility, and to these many others could be added from every century, until the ancient world finally went down in ruin. Nor can it be maintained that the Christians were perfect or blameless; that most candid of books the Bible makes it quite clear that the first Christians were a mixed bag, no less strangely compounded than we of good and bad; the evidence of Councils and Fathers confirms what is clearly written in the New Testament. But when a comparison is made, judgement comes down every time on the side of the Christians. They achieved what others spoke of. In an age when the passions of man seemed like an angry torrent carrying everything before it, they assumed that, if the Spirit of Jesus Christ was in control, the order of a life transformed after the likeness of Christ would take the place of the chaos of inordinate and unbridled passion.

They restored the ideal of a pure and healthy family life, in which husbands and wives loved one another, and remained faithful to one another until death.

They were willing to accept children with thankfulness as a gift of God and to delight in them. Old Roman society was dying out for the single reason that it was not reproducing itself; men and women alike refused the burden of bringing children into the world and caring for them – a sure sign of deep-seated inner decay.

Christian life was marked by simplicity and discipline, but it was as yet free from any bitter asceticism, or from any trace of a Manichean fear of things that are pleasant and beautiful, as though they must of necessity be evil in themselves.

Early Christian preaching, in New Testament days and after, was marked by a strong ethical emphasis. Men were invited into a society in which it was possible for them to be good in the most ordinary sense of the term; they joined the society because they felt that there the inextinguishable human desire for goodness might find satisfaction.

There is always a tendency to idealize the Church of the days of the persecutions, and this must be resisted. The early Christians were men and women such as we are, affected by the same weaknesses and follies, liable to the same betrayals as we. And yet the first three centuries are a time unparalleled in the later history of the Church. Those early Christians lived nearer than we to the events of the New Testament; perhaps their lives were more consciously lightened by the stupendous miracle of the Resurrection. Without help of favour or patronage, 'not many wise . . . . not many mighty, not many noble',[1] faced all the time by powerful enemies, and intermittently threatened by cruel persecution, they held on, and not merely maintained them-

1. 1 Corinthians i: 27.

selves, but spread their infant communities into every province of the Roman Empire and beyond.

If that were the whole history of the Christian Church it would have few critics, and few would hesitate to admit themselves overwhelmingly in its debt. Unfortunately what follows later is far less attractive; and, pledged as we are not to exclude any phenomena from our survey, we must frankly take account of what is unfavourable, as well as of what is favourable, in the Christian story.

In A.D. 313 Constantine made Christianity a permitted religion in his dominions, and gradually accepted it as the official religion of the Empire. This liberation was naturally followed by an immense increase in the number of Christians, and in the strength of the Churches. But there have been many in later Christian centuries who have bewailed what at first appeared as a heaven-sent blessing as the worst disaster that has ever befallen the Church.

Dante twice refers in terms of lamentation to the wealth which Constantine bestowed upon the Church:

> Ahi, Constantin, di quanto mal fu matre,
> non la tua conversion, ma quella dote
> che da te prese il primo ricco patre.[1]
> Ora conosce come il mal dedutto
> del suo ben operar, non gli e nocivo,
> avvegna che si il mondo indi distrutto.[2]

It is the word *ricco*, rich, that makes the quotation from Dante specially relevant. The Church professes to follow the Poor Man of Nazareth, who had nowhere to lay His head; yet throughout so many centuries of its history it has been marked by a passionate enthusiasm in the service of Mammon. It is almost impossible that a Church should exist wholly without property in land or buildings or money; yet, as it acquires these things, it becomes involved in a relation-

1. 'Ah Constantine! to how much ill gave birth, not thy conversion, but that dower which the first rich Father (Pope) took from thee.' *Inferno* xix: 115-7.

2. 'Now knoweth he that the ill deduced from his good deed hurteth not him though the world be destroyed thereby.' *Paradiso* xx: 58-60.

ship to the world which is immediately perilous to its soul.

Part of the trouble is that institutions, unlike individuals or even human families, never die, and therefore the possibilities of accumulation are literally illimitable. All the monastic orders started out with the ideal of godly poverty. Even if they had desired strenuously to maintain it, the admiration and the charity of their friends would have made this almost impossible; ere long gifts of lands and houses began to flow in upon them, and were accepted to the greater glory of God. One section of Dr G. G. Coulton's great history of *Five Centuries of Religion* bears the significant title *Getting and Spending*. Every new reform called men back to the ideal of poverty. Francis made poverty his bride, and established utmost renunciation as the rule of his fellowship. But not many years had passed before the strict observance of his rule was condemned as heresy. At the time of the Mexican revolution earlier in this century, it was computed that the Roman Catholic Church actually owned one-third of the total land surface of the country.

It is not the possession of money but the love of it that is condemned in the Gospels. But it is very hard to own money without coming to regard it as important; it is very hard to be concerned with the affairs of the world without losing that detachment from them which Christian faith demands.

With love of money tends to go love of privilege, and therefore not infrequently the blind support of the *status quo* and of the powers that be. Liberalism in politics and a welcoming attitude towards new truths have not always been characteristics of the Church of Jesus Christ.

Most people in the West now accept without question the principle that there should be no discrimination between individuals, and no inequality of social and civic privilege, on the ground of religious conviction or allegiance. It is easy to forget that this belief in religious equality grew very slowly; much of the feeling between Anglicans and Free Churchmen in Britain is due to the almost fanatical desire of the Established Church to cling to privileges that it would have done much better to allow to sink into obsolescence. It is today almost incredible, yet late Victorian biographies make it unmistakably clear that as late as the third quarter of the nineteenth century Anglican opinion could be worked up almost into a frenzy on the question whether nonconformist ministers should be permitted to conduct services at the burial of members of their flocks in churchyards.

One of the last of nonconformist grievances to be removed was the refusal of admission to the ancient universities except to those who were willing to sign their names to the Thirty-nine Articles of the Church of England. There may have been a time when such restrictions were defensible; by the middle of the nineteenth century it was the opinion of most people that that time had passed away. Yet when at last the bulwark fell and nonconformists were admitted on equal terms with Anglicans, so great a man as Henry Parry Liddon, in the judgement of many the greatest preacher of the age, wrote mournfully that Oxford would never be the same place again. He was quite right; Oxford never was the same place again. But perhaps, in view of the part which the universities play in the life of the nation, it is good that Anglican and nonconformist and Roman Catholic undergraduates, and those of no religious profession at all, rub shoulders in the process of a common education.

The darkest shadow of all on the life of the Church has been its alliance with the State and its belief in coercion and violence as means for the promotion of belief or the cure of unbelief.

The year A.D. 385 stands out marked with peculiar infamy, as that in which for the first time, as far as history bears record, the blood of Christians was shed by Christians, and that in a matter affecting the faith. In that year the bishops of southern Gaul handed over the Spanish heretic Priscillian to the civil power; and the civil power, as so often too complaisant to the wishes of the ecclesiastical, had him and his companions executed. We know little of the opinions and character of Priscillian, and most of what we know comes from the not impartial evidence of his enemies. A high authority tells us that he was as orthodox as Jerome – what-

ever that may mean – I would not myself wish to share all
the opinions of the eminent translator of the Bible into
Latin. But even if Priscillian had professed the most abominable doctrines, those bishops who sought his death still stand
under the shame of introducing into the Christian Church a
plague of which it has never yet been able to free itself. This
is not a twentieth-century judgement; it was that also of one
of the greatest of contemporary Christians, the saintly Mar-
tin, Bishop of Tours, who knew all the facts, and expressed
his opinion by refusing to communicate with the bishops
who were privy to the judicial murder of Priscillian.

It is not difficult to adduce arguments in palliation of
religious persecution. We must judge men, we are told, by
the standards of their age and not of ours. In the Middle Ages,
heresy was certainly believed to be the very worst of crimes,
and it was held that the judgement of heaven would fall on
the country or kingdom that did not cleanse itself of the vile
infection. To persecute the heretic, and if necessary to burn
him alive, was regarded as the kindest thing for him, since
temporal agony might lead him to repentance and so to
eternal gain. Much confusion was caused by failure to distinguish between the Old Testament and the New. Yet,
when we have thought of every excuse that we can, is it not
still necessary to maintain that these things ought not to
have been done, and that they could not have been done, if
man had been willing to let Christ rule in the Church which
is called by His name?

There is hardly a Christian body in the world which is
free from blame.

In 1572 the massacre of St Bartholomew, in which 70,000
French Protestants perished, was hailed in Rome with jubilation, the ringing of bells, and the striking of a commemo-
rative medal. English Protestants remember with thankfulness the martyrs under Mary, who lighted a candle which,
by God's grace, has never yet been put out in England.
They sometimes forget the Roman Catholics who suffered
death in the reign of Queen Elizabeth. It is true that no real
comparison is possible. Under Mary, 300 innocent victims

were burned alive in a few months. In the forty-five years of the reign of Elizabeth, only 180 Roman Catholics were executed, and all of these were fatally compromised politically by the tortuous policy of the Vatican. But even those who are most thankful that the Jesuit campaign for the reconversion of England to Rome ended in fiasco are free to regret that among the victims was the gentle and saintly Edmund Campion, surely one of the purest of all those who have given their lives for what they judged to be the cause of Christ.

Puritans left England for America in the cause of religious liberty; yet they carried with them the dreadful tradition of religious persecution. In the years between 1658 and 1661 four Quakers were hanged in the colony of Massachusetts, one of them a woman.

And so the horrible tale goes on. It continues to our own day, with the breaking up of Protestant chapels in Spain, and the beating up of Protestant missionaries in Colombia. The apostles of toleration and fair-dealing have more often been sceptics and unbelievers than Christians.

All these are grave charges against the Churches. Yet, if I were not already a Christian and a Churchman, I think that what more than anything else would keep me back from accepting the responsibilities of Church membership would be the apparently irredeemable triviality of the Churches. To read the ordinary Church paper is to enter a world which seems as remote as Jupiter from the concerns of men and women who have to live their lives where the real work of the world is carried on. To listen to the conversation in most theological colleges is to receive the impression that the salvation of the world depends upon the shape of ecclesiastical vestments or some peculiar liturgical innovations – or the refusal of them. Far too many allegedly Christian sermons are trivial little discourses on trivial little themes: 'but they are not grieved for the affliction of Joseph'.

If we were simply to make a list of all the things that can truly be said against the organized Churches, we should probably end by crying out with Voltaire 'Ecrasez l'infâme'.

But one of the phenomena of which we have to take note is that a considerable number of thoughtful men and women have managed to remain not merely sincere Christians, but also devoted and earnest Churchmen. In the days of William Temple, it was of considerable advantage to the Church that the most intelligent man in England happened also to be Archbishop of Canterbury. And others who have started as sceptics and unbelievers, like the philosopher Prof. A. E. Taylor[1] or the poet T. S. Eliot, have come to find their home in a very imperfect visible Church; the quality of their work after their conversion suggests that the change was not due to softening of the brain.

How does this come about?

It is right to give due weight to everything that can be said in criticism of the Church. It would not be right to give less weight to those things that can be said on the other side.

The Christian Church through the centuries has manifested certain remarkable characteristics, which must be entered in making up the main account.

First, the Church has shown an astonishing power of renewal from within; and that renewal has generally been associated with the appearance, within the Church, of characters whom the whole world, Christian and non-Christian alike, revere for their saintliness and likeness to Christ.

The eighth century was a hard and brutal time. With the culmination of the barbarian invasions, the grandeur of Rome had collapsed in smoking ash; wars and rumours of wars filled the western world. The barbarization of the Church had gone so far that chastity and sobriety were hardly expected even of its leaders. It is just in that period that we encounter the Venerable Bede, one of those very few characters in history of whom it is possible to say that no

---

1. When Dr Taylor was showing signs of becoming a Christian, his colleague at St Andrews, G. F. Stout the logician, was heard to remark, 'I can't think what has come over Taylor these days; I wouldn't be surprised if it had something to do with that baby of his' – a saying not unworthy of attention.

single evil thing is recorded of them. If violence and brutality ruled the world, learning, gentleness, and humility had found a refuge in remote Northumbrian monasteries. At the same time Ireland, which in the general *débâcle* had become the island of the saints and the last refuge of Christian culture, began to overflow with that flood of generous Christian activity that reached as far as the monastery of Bobbio in northern Italy.

Those who idealize the Middle Ages forget how much of strife and savagery had survived from the dark centuries. The brilliant civilization of the north Italian cities of the early Middle Age was marred by ceaseless violence, treachery, and war. Those cities almost expected periodically to be burnt to the ground. The difference from our own day is that, whereas we know that we cannot replace Coventry Cathedral by anything half as beautiful, the men of the Middle Ages knew that, if anything fair and noble was destroyed, they could rebuild even more splendidly and nobly than their fathers. But out of that turbulent and often squalid background emerged in a single century Francis of Assisi, Thomas of Aquino, and Dante of Florence. It is not surprising that Bishop Creighton, than whom few men have been better qualified to judge, was wont to say that so far the thirteenth was the greatest of all the Christian centuries.

Eighteenth-century England was not the scene in which one would expect to encounter a great spiritual revival. Outwardly it was a time of splendid, rational, polished civilization. And a good deal more real piety had survived than has sometimes been allowed for in the past. But morals were at a low ebb, and the formal, uninspired divinity of the pulpits showed little power to guide or to control the passions of men. It is recorded that the great Bishop Joseph Butler refused the Archbishopric of Canterbury, on the ground that he did not wish to take the responsibility of heading a Church which it was already too late to save. And yet it was in that society, and in the face of those disadvantages, that the Wesleys launched their great campaign of evangelization, and thereby set in motion a process by which in course of time the character of English society was changed. For threequarters of the nineteenth century the Methodists were the proletarian Church, that body which more than any other succeeded in reaching down to the new industrial masses in their poverty, and in bringing light and warmth and colour to their starved and straitened lives.

The Methodists were on the whole rigidly conservative and anti-revolutionary in politics. In an age such as ours, which is so largely influenced, consciously or unconsciously, by Marxist ideas of history, this has led to their being hardly judged and misunderstood. Their invention of total abstinence and their championship of the temperance cause in its narrowest form have made them unpopular even with many of their fellow Christians.[1] But the spiritual impulse of the preaching of the Wesleys and their hymns is still far from exhausted; if it seems for the moment to have lost power in England, it is still increasing in influence in America, and the Methodist missions are among the finest and most successful in the world.

The critic, while admitting this power of inner renewal, may well ask whether this has been of any advantage to the general body of society, as distinct from the Church itself. I think it can be maintained, without special pleading, that every renewal of life within the Church has been of advantage to society as a whole through the civilization of manners, the spread of education, care for the weak and suffering – in some sphere, that is to say, other than that with which Christianity is primarily concerned, the relationship of man to God.

Almost all that we know of ancient civilization we owe to the monks. When so much was lost, it was the monasteries that became the storehouses for what could be saved from the wreckage. That this service was more than fortuitous, and resulted from something inherent in the nature of the

1. Until the middle of the nineteenth century, the moderate use of alcohol was taken for granted in all classes of society, including the most earnest Christians. The confusion of *temperance* with *total abstinence* is a Victorian innovation.

Christian Church as a society, has recently been maintained by a scholar whose encyclopedic range of knowledge makes him well qualified to judge:

Because the Church in her very essence is holy tradition, she also is the legitimate guardian of all natural and cultural tradition. This function she exerted, though imperfectly, in the epoch of tremendous breakdown, when the Graeco-Roman cultural tradition was about to be lost. She performed the same function of guardianship throughout the Middle Ages, in the Greek Orthodox Churches and in the Churches of the Reformation, passing on the cultural inheritance at a time when respect for the past was already vanishing. ... Humanism kept its cultural vigour only where it remained in contact with Christianity, for the decisive element of tradition, i.e. loyalty to the heritage of the past, does not lie within the principle of Humanism as such, but in the Christian view of history.[1]

The Englishman's traditional dislike of priestcraft makes it perhaps more difficult for him than for others to judge rightly the aims and achievements of the great medieval Popes. In the struggle between Thomas à Becket and Henry II, or between the disreputable King John and Innocent III, our sympathies tend to be with the layman against the priest. Yet, within the limits of human blindness and imperfection, what the Popes were striving after was something noble and necessary in the life of men; it was nothing less than the recognition that the righteous law of God stands above all the laws of human statecraft and above the lawless ambitions of human rulers, and that that law is in all circumstances to be enforced and obeyed. The lesson is one which the human race needs to learn afresh in every generation.

One of the chief criticisms directed by ordinary men against the Church is its callous indifference to the obvious needs and sufferings of men in their temporal situations. For this criticism there is, as we have frankly admitted, all too much justification. Yet it is notable that, whenever spiritual revival has come within the Church, it has been accompanied by a new sensitiveness to the temporal needs of men.

1. Emil Brunner: *Christianity and Civilisation*, Pt. II (London 1949), pp. 31-2.

Perhaps the most remarkable example in history is the campaign for the abolition of slavery in the British Empire. The great men who carried through the campaign of forty years which culminated in 1833 in the final abolition of slavery in every British territory were not, in the ordinary sense of the term, humanitarians; they were evangelicals, who believed passionately that all the concerns of this earth are as nothing in comparison with the eternal destiny of man, and that that destiny depends only and solely upon faith in Jesus Christ; but from those basic convictions they drew the conclusion that, because every man is potentially a son of God, everything that affects him – his bodily health, his freedom, his civil condition – are matters of concern to God no less than his religious edification.

The whole story of the campaign, which the sceptical historian Lecky affirmed to have added some of the very few perfectly virtuous pages to the history of the nations, should be read in detail. The only method followed was the ceaseless revelation of the facts concerning the slave trade; accurate and carefully documented information flowed out year after year in pamphlets, speeches, and sermons. The aim was not to appeal to sentiment but to arouse the conscience of the nation to a great wrong in which far too long it had ignorantly or callously acquiesced. In the end Wilberforce and his friends persuaded the nation not merely to free the slaves but also to pay £20,000,000 in compensation to the slave-owners – a severe test of virtue to a British Parliament – in order that a great act of justice to the oppressed might not be marred by the appearance of injustice to the oppressor. Prof. Coupland, in his standard life of Wilberforce, vividly describes the scene of his greatest triumph in the House of Commons. The year was 1806, the year of disaster and of Austerlitz. Sir Samuel Romilly, comparing Wilberforce with Napoleon, had spoken of Napoleon's repose, banished by the recollection of the blood he had spilled and the oppression he had committed; and then proceeded:

'When I compare with those pangs of remorse the feelings which must accompany my honourable friend from this House to his home, after the vote of this night shall have confirmed the object of his humane and unceasing labours; when he retires into the bosom of his happy and delighted family, when he lays himself down on his bed, reflecting on the innumerable voices that would be raised in every quarter of the world to bless him, how much more pure and perfect felicity must he enjoy, in the consciousness of having preserved so many millions of his fellow-creatures, than . . .'

The startling comparison in that tense atmosphere was a spark on gunpowder. The House was on its feet giving Wilberforce an ovation such as it had given to no other living man. Round after round, they cheered him, . . . It was the supreme moment of his life, but Wilberforce himself was scarcely conscious of it. In the middle of Romilly's noble tribute . . . his emotions overwhelmed him. Insensible, as he afterwards confessed, to all that was passing around him, he sat bent in his seat, his head in his hands, and tears streaming down his face'.[1]

That is what it means to be a Christian. Our Marxist friends tell us that everything is to be interpreted in terms of economic pressures and motives. I have striven hard to fit this episode of the freeing of the slaves into Marxist categories, and I have found it wholly impossible to do so. It seems to me that this, and such enterprises as Lord Shaftesbury's great series of Factory Acts, spring from deeper regions of human experience, the existence of which the Marxist denies, and by denying them fatally distorts his picture of the world and his interpretation of history.

It is necessary to insist a little on the practical contribution of Christian idealism to the well-being of men, since in modern times history is one of the great instruments of propaganda, and a veil of mythological distortion has been spread over all the events of the day before yesterday.

When Elizabeth Fry began her great work for the reform of the prisons, visitors to Newgate were astonished to see the rabble of women prisoners sitting quiet and spellbound as Mrs Fry read to them from the Bible in her wonderful voice.

1. R. Coupland: *Wilberforce* (Oxford 1923), p. 340–1.

It is well that we should remember this picture of the triumph of gentleness and goodness over vice and degradation. But, if this alone were to be remembered, the impression might be given of a merely pietistic attempt at moral reformation. It would be unfair to forget the intensely practical nature of the steps that Elizabeth Fry took for the welfare of her prisoners, while they were in gaol and after. Here is a list of the articles with which she managed to provide every one of the unhappy women sentenced to transportation for life to the Antipodes:

One Bible, one Hessian apron, . . . one small bag containing one piece of tape, one ounce of pins, one hundred needles, four balls of white sewing cotton, one ditto black, one ditto blue, one ditto red [shades of George Fox!], one thimble, one pair of spectacles, where necessary, two pounds of patchwork pieces, one comb, one small ditto, knife and fork and a ball of string.

Those who are familiar only with the portrait of Elizabeth Fry in later life, portly and a little formidable, might imagine her to have been one of those bold, managing women from whom the mere male flees in terror; it is strange to learn from her biography that she was in fact a timid, shrinking woman, full of what in our day we have learned to call phobias, and that she was driven to carry out her incomparable work only by the compelling power of the love of Christ.

One of the spheres in which the great service rendered by the Church is to-day most readily forgotten or denied is education. The first general Education Act for England was passed only in 1870. Up till that date education had been wholly in the hands of voluntary bodies, among which the Churches were vastly the most considerable. There is a tendency on the part of people who ought to know better to imagine that 1870 marked the beginning of the first serious attempt to educate the nation. For instance, Messrs B. Seebohm Rowntree and G. R. Lavers, in their book *English Life and Leisure, A Social Study*, published in 1951, assert categorically of the nineteenth century that 'it was mainly a century of illiteracy, with the real assault on that evil not beginning until 1870'.[1] This statement will not bear comparison with the facts.

The Reformation in England resulted in a great increase in educational activity.[2] Nevertheless, until the end of the eighteenth century, illiteracy was general among the poorest classes of the population. The real educational charter of the poor was the foundation of the Sunday school. To-day, Sunday school is so inseparably connected in the minds of many with rather inferior hymns and rather dull Bible lessons, that it is not generally realized that, in its beginning, the Sunday school was an immense enterprise of secular as well as of religious education. In days when poor children worked anything up to fourteen hours a day on weekdays – on the farms as well as in the factories – Sunday was the only day on which they could learn anything. In many schools reading only was taught, as it was felt that writing and arithmetic were too secular to be handled on the Sabbath; but the real assault on illiteracy had begun long before 1870.

The nineteenth century was the great period of the development of the elementary day school. The year 1825 saw the formation of a society with the characteristically cumbrous title, 'The National Society for promoting the education of the poor in the principles of the established Church throughout England and Wales'. The Free Churchmen took a hand with the 'British School Society'. In the period before 1870, while activity on the part of the State was limited to some rather niggardly financial grants, private enterprise, and in this case the phrase means almost exclusively Christian enterprise, had built, equipped, and staffed 9,000 schools, with 2,000,000 places. If the children of school-going age are reckoned at 9 per cent of the population, the number of children due to be in school in 1870 was 2,246,566; if the higher figure of 12 per cent is taken the number was 2,839,000. This indicates that there was still much to be done, and that with the rapid growth of popula-

1. *Op. cit.* p. 368.
2. See A. L. Rowse: *The England of Elizabeth* (London 1950), pp. 489–509.

tion, the education of the people was becoming a task too heavy for the Churches alone. But this great Christian achievement is one that ought not to be forgotten; especially if it is true, as is affirmed, that in Britain in 1951 more than 2,000,000 persons over the age of sixteen are either illiterate or semi-literate. Some people would maintain that the old-fashioned education based on the Bible was far more valid as education than the shapeless, synthetic product to which the young of to-day are exposed.

It is sometimes supposed that missionaries in non-Christian countries are entirely occupied with preaching, and are neglectful of physical and social conditions. In the part of India which I knew best the Churches were first in the field with education for women and girls, with hospitals for women and children, with clinics and asylums for the victims of leprosy and tuberculosis, and with schools for the blind and the deaf – surely a memorable achievement, especially in view of the miserably straitened conditions in personnel and finance with which Christian missions have had to contend since the beginning of time.

The necessity and the divine character of the Christian Church are not proved by its philanthropic activities. But its Founder did say that 'by their fruits ye shall know them', and Himself had testimony borne to Him that He went about doing good. The non-Christian has every right to ask what visible results have been produced by those who call themselves Christians, apart from an alleged and invisible inner holiness; and Christians have no right to object if they are bidden to stand and deliver. If they know the facts, they need have little fear. The Christian Church does not exist for the provision of loaves and fishes; but whenever and wherever it has been true to the spirit of its Master, it can afford to challenge comparison with any other agency devoted to the well-being of men and women.

It may be, however, that what keeps those who love Jesus faithful also to His Church is something much more prosaic than the attractive power of heroic saintliness, or a careful balancing of the good and evil that the Church has done.

E.P.E. College Library
1100 Glendale Blvd.
Los Angeles, Calif. 90026

In all the life of men, use and wont, mere routine, plays a larger part than we sometimes suspect. If every act of the day had to be carried out with deliberate care and foresight, by the end of the day we should be utterly exhausted. It is just because, through practice and habit, we can do so many things, even things which require a good deal of manual dexterity like shaving, literally without thinking, that we are able to reserve strength and the power of thought for those things that lie outside routine, and can be handled only by the application of special care and attention.

In the world of religion, the ordered life of the Church plays the same part as routine in the life of the individual. Whatever happens, Holy Communion will be celebrated day by day, with the repetition of the same ancient prayers, heavy with the intercessions of many generations. Throughout the Church of England, Matins and Evensong will be sung Sunday by Sunday, with the same lovely cadences that no one since the time of Cranmer has ever quite been able to equal. The timelessness and continuity of this almost impersonal life form the quiet background, against which the individual can make the personal efforts, without which no effective Christian living is possible.

Young people on the whole are so far from valuing this sameness in the life of the Church that they not infrequently make it their first ground of complaint: Church service is so boring, there is nothing fresh and lively about it. Experience sometimes changes the point of view. Some have come for the first time to understand the value of continuity when lying desperately ill in hospital. If the bell is rung at the moment of consecration in the Holy Communon and sounds throughout the hospital, even those who are so ill that they can hardly remember their own name will know that the death of Jesus Christ for sinners is being remembered, as it has been by Christians every single day since Pentecost, and as it will be every day until the end of the world; and even if they are unable to make any effort, even to pray, they may realize that that life of the Church is a flowing river, which, if they will yield themselves to it, will carry them onwards, until they are again able consciously to respond to what is offered them in the Gospel of Jesus Christ.

All the reasons here suggested, as having helped men of wisdom and intelligence to hold faithfully to the Church, while reserving their liberty to criticize it, may sound very dull and pragmatic. This picture of the Church seems to have little to do with the glorious visions and expectations of the New Testament. There the Church is the body of Christ, 'the fulness of him that filleth all in all';[1] it is 'a glorious church, not having spot or wrinkle or any such thing, holy and without blemish'.[2] It is the woman of the Apocalypse, 'arrayed with the sun and the moon under her feet, and upon her head a crown of twelve stars'.[3] What have such laborious defences to do with a Church which is God's own creation and the bearer of His eternal purpose? We may answer that almost the whole of this study has been concerned with the pragmatic and the prosaic, since that is the kind of world in which the life of most men has to be lived; we have tried to deal faithfully with the obvious facts, while not denying any splendour which under the pragmatic and the prosaic may be concealed.

The contrast between the Church as ideally depicted in the New Testament, and as actually seen by the eyes of men, becomes less disturbing, if we note that something of the same contrast is to be found between Jesus as interpreted in the light of Christian faith, and Jesus as seen by the eyes of His contemporaries. Here is the description of faith: 'His Son, whom he appointed heir of all things, through whom also he made the worlds; who being the effulgence of his glory, and the very image of his substance, and upholding all things by the word of his power, when he had made purification of sins, sat down on the right hand of the Majesty on high; having become by so much better than the angels, as he hath inherited a more excellent name than they.'[4] Here

---

1. Ephesians i: 23.
2. Ephesians v: 27.
3. Revelation xii: 1.
4. Hebrews i: 2–4.

is the description in the words of those who had known Him as the carpenter of Nazareth: 'Is not this the carpenter? . . . a gluttonous man and a winebibber . . . a friend of publicans and sinners . . . how knoweth this man letters, never having learned? . . . can any good thing come out of Nazareth? . . . he saved others, himself he cannot save.'

To one who has considered the nature and purpose of this contrast, the present condition and appearance of the Church will present hardly any surprises. It is both divine and all too human. It is an assemblage of sinful and very imperfect human beings. It is often in error, though not irreparably. It is often corrupt, though not incurably. It is often asleep, though not beyond the power of waking. It is often neglectful of its duty, though not to the point of utter dereliction.

In both cases, that of the Lord and that of the Church, one part of the contrast cannot be held without the other. No one can truly worship the glorified Lord of Christian faith unless he has first accepted from the heart the scandal of the Jewish carpenter who was crucified. No one can be a participant in the heavenly kingdom who has not first taken the cross of Jesus as His portion. No one can claim membership in the ideal Church unless he is prepared to accept the scandal of a divided, imperfect, unfaithful Church, and unless he is prepared to take his place with the least, and the least lovable, of those who are called by the name of Christ.

This is the lesson of Robert Browning's poem *Christmas Eve*:

> I very soon had enough of it.
> > The hot smell and the human noises,
> And my neighbour's coat, the greasy cuff of it,
> > Were a pebble stone that a child's hand poises,
> Compared with the pig-of-lead like pressure
> > Of the preaching man's immense stupidity.
>
> . . . . . .
>
> I flung out of the little chapel.

Bad singing, crude theology, an ugly building, and a poor bedraggled congregation had proved too much for the refined susceptibilities of the poet. But, as in the majestic arc of the great moon rainbow he sees the glory of the vision of Christ, he realizes with awe that only out of the little chapel can Christ have come; and, as his strange pilgrimage proceeds, he learns that he can have Christ only as he is willing to have Him with those who love Him; he can hold Him fast only as He is willing to go with Him again into the little chapel. Many have had to learn the same lesson as Browning. They have thought to worship Christ in the solitary cell of their own highest aspirations, only to find that He will not meet them there, but only where His feet stand, amidst the poorest, the loneliest, and the lost.

8

THE CHRISTIAN WORLD COMMUNITY

Is a world-wide religion, a religious world community, possible?

Until the beginning of the twentieth century that question could be answered only hypothetically. There were missionary religions in the world, but none had succeeded in spreading itself over more than a very limited part of the world's surface. Buddhism had died out completely in India, the country of its origin, and had undergone strange transformations in Tibet and Mongolia; though strongly established in Burma, Ceylon, and Siam, less strongly in China and Japan, it gave no evidence of power either to recover the lost regions or to extend itself to other regions where Buddhist influence had not yet been felt. Hinduism had been submerged in south-east Asia, except in the island of Bali, and was no more than the religion of a part of the Indian sub-continent. Islam, spreading out like an octopus from its four great centres, Mecca, Damascus, Baghdad, and Cairo, extended over a vast area from Morocco to Indonesia, from western China to the heart of Africa, and was still gaining ground among primitive African races; but it had lost ground in Europe, and had failed either to make a deep impression on the western peoples or to win more than a handful of converts among them. Christianity was overwhelmingly the religion of the white races, closely bound up with the culture and traditions of Europe, supporting a number of rather insignificant missions – 'colonies' largely dependent upon western political and economic power – in regions dominated by other religions and cultures of their own.

In 1955 the situation is remarkably different, and the answer to the question is no longer hypothetical. To-day, for the first time in history, the religion of Jesus is actually what it has always been potentially, a world-wide religion. There are few facts or situations of which it can be said that they are wholly new; but this is one; never before in the history of the world has there existed a religious faith of which it could be said, in any sense of the word, that it was world-wide.

In relation to the Christian faith, the expression 'world-wide' needs some explanation and some qualification.

Obviously it is not the case that everyone in the world is Christian. Less than one-third of the men and women now living are even nominally Christian. It does not even mean that everyone now living has heard the name of Christ.

If the use of the term is defensible at all, the defence must be established along the lines of the following incontestable affirmations:

1. There is now no major region in the world in which the Gospel of Jesus Christ has not been preached, and in which Christian propaganda is not regularly carried on.

2. The New Testament has been translated into more than 400 languages, and one Gospel or more into at least another 600. As a result of this great achievement, of the people in the world who are literate considerably more than 90 per cent have available to them, if they wish, at least the elements of the Christian message in a language that they can understand.

3. In every area in which the Gospel has been preached for a considerable time, some converts have been won, and in most cases have given evidence of the sincerity of their faith by the endurance of persecution. In almost all these areas indigenous Churches have come into being. At present all the Christians in Afghanistan are foreigners, no Afghan Christians having been able to remain within the country. It is uncertain whether there are any Christians in Tibet proper; though in the adjoining territories there are Christians who are Tibetan in racial type, in language, in religious and sociological background, in everything, in fact, except political allegiance. Nepal remained till 1951 closed to all missionary effort. With these three exceptions, it is believed

that there is no country or large island in which there are not indigenous groups of Christians.

4. There is no religion in the world from which Christianity has not won some adherents. The number of converts from Islam, and from among the Sikhs, the Parsees, and the Jains has never been large, but it is much larger than is sometimes imagined by those who have not taken the trouble to ascertain the facts.

5. The Gospel has made its appeal on every level of culture, from the highest to the lowest. At one end of the scale, it has won the allegiance of Brahman priests and Chinese literati; at the other end it has been understood and accepted by peoples like the Australian aborigines, who stand so low in the cultural scale that some observers have judged them incapable of grasping any religious idea at all.

If these five aspects of universality are taken together, they constitute reasonable support for the claim that the Christian faith is universal, in a sense in which that term cannot be applied to any other existing religion or to any other religion that ever has existed in the world.

To many people the missionary activity of the Christian Church is an offence. What right has one man to interfere with another's religion? When people have religions of their own which suit them, is it not both impertinent and harmful to bring pressure to bear on them to change their ideas?

Sometimes Christians, more deeply moved by these objections than they should be, try to erect a defence of Christian missions on humanitarian or philanthropic grounds. It is true, as has already been stated, that the Christian missionary enterprise includes a great amount of useful humanitarian work, ranging from colleges of the highest academic standard to orphanages for unwanted children. But a defence based on such grounds as these evades the main issue, which is the issue of truth.

The claim of the Gospel to universal allegiance is plain in the earliest records, as well as in the later. The ministry of Jesus Himself was confined to Israel; yet, seeing the faith of one individual Gentile, He said to those by whom he was surrounded: 'I say unto you, that many shall come from the east and the west, and shall sit down with Abraham, and Isaac, and Jacob, in the kingdom of heaven.'[1] This is one of the sayings of Jesus, of which we have good reason to think that it has come down to us in exactly the form in which it was spoken by Him. Paul was impelled to his restless missionary activity by the same conviction that this Gospel must be preached in all the world. The great vision that had come to him, as he believed by revelation, was that there was now no more distinction between Jew and Gentile, but one universal salvation, equally valid for all, since 'all have sinned, and come short of the glory of God; being justified freely by his grace through the redemption that is in Christ Jesus'.[2] In that faith the Christian Church has lived ever since his day.

This faith was simply set forth by Archbishop William Temple, with characteristic common sense, when he remarked that, if the Gospel is true for anyone anywhere, it is true for all men everywhere. No one imagines that there is one scientific truth for the African and another for the European; one historical truth for the Englishman and another for the American. Governments object very strongly to Marxist propaganda, because it is politically subversive and dangerous; but few educated men would question the right of the Marxists to spread their ideas by every means within their power, provided that coercion and incitement to violence are not added to legitimate methods of persuasion. Why should what is granted to the Marxists be grudged to the Christians?

Now it is perfectly evident that, when a new doctrine is launched upon the world, the result is a conflict of ideas. The whole history of the world can be viewed as that of the continuous and internecine battle of ideas, which, though invisible, is no less violent, and in its consequences much more far-reaching, than those other wars which have left visible scars on all the inhabited regions of the earth.

This is true in science. The Copernican theory of the solar

1. Matthew viii: 11.   2. Romans iii: 23-4.

system introduced a revolution into men's views of the world they lived in. It was denounced, opposed, persecuted. It was accepted provisionally. Even in the eighteenth century both the rival systems of astronomy, the Ptolemaic and the Copernican, were taught at Harvard University in the United States of America. But eventually victory rested with Copernicus; and that victory was decisive, final, and irrevocable. More recent investigation has introduced many modifications into the theory as originally set forth by Copernicus; but no one in his senses today would suggest going back to the geocentric view of the solar system, and the Ptolemaic astronomy that was based on it.

The scientist is fully aware of this conflict. When he launches a new hypothesis, he knows that it will be subjected to every kind of adverse criticism. Sometimes he is intemperate in the defence of his hypothesis, just as sometimes others are intemperate in their assaults upon it. But both alike, if they are true scientists and not influenced by ideological considerations, are marked by the same austere devotion to truth, and to the conviction that *magna est veritas et praevalet.*

What is true in the sphere of science is equally true in the world of religion. It is generally held in the West, though not always so firmly in the East, that things which are contradictory to one another cannot both be true. The leading ideas of the Gospel are directly contradictory to the leading ideas of a number of other philosophies and systems of religion. If separate territories could be neatly marked out for each, conflict would be avoided by a neutral policy of live and let live. But if Christianity is true to its own aggressive and missionary nature, then the conflict of ideas cannot be avoided, and must continue till the victory of one idea over the other is as complete as the victory of Copernicus over Ptolemy, or the victory of Jesus Christ over Zeus and Hera and Odin and Thor.

Islam denies all the principal doctrines which Christianity affirms. It denies that Jesus was the Son of God. It denies that He was crucified – the Jews were deceived by a false appearance at the moment of the Crucifixion. Consequently it denies that forgiveness and reconciliation were achieved by His death. *Christians* and *Moslems* can and should learn to live in amity, as to a large extent they do in Egypt. But in the world of ideas there can be no truce; if Islam is true Christianity is false and ought to perish, and conversely.

Christianity maintains that spirit is prior to matter, that man cannot be understood at all unless he is regarded as a spiritual being, whose destiny is to be fulfilled in an eternal world beyond space and time. The system of Marx, Lenin, and Engels is based on the categorical denial of these ideas. There is no possibility of reconciliation. If orthodox Marxism prevails, Christianity will disappear from the earth; if Christianity prevails, some of the economic doctrines of Marx and their social applications may well continue to be influential; but his philosophic doctrines will be no more than a memory.

Nothing is to be gained by refusing to face the stark realities of the situation. Jesus Himself said that he came to bring not peace but a sword, and that His doctrine would prove a source of bitter division, even among families and friends. He said that He came to fulfil the law and the prophets; but in fact He fulfilled them only by revealing that the old law was becoming old and was nigh unto vanishing away,[1] and by establishing a new covenant, by which the old was made obsolete. The Gospel cannot build until it has destroyed; everything that is good and of value in the old will be taken up into the new building; but there are times and areas in which the Gospel will appear first in the character of a destroyer.

This destructive character of the Gospel is often used as one of the strongest arguments against Christian missionary work.

Though Christianity may be a suitable religion for peoples at a certain level of civilization and social and economic development, has it not now been clearly proved that it is wholly unsuited to primitive peoples, that its effects have

1. Hebrews ix: 13.

been harmful in disrupting the social patterns to which they have been accustomed, and that the disappearance of some interesting and attractive peoples has been due to the well-intentioned but mistaken efforts of missionaries to Christianize them?

The problems of the interaction between Western civilization and primitive man are far too complicated to be summarized in a sentence or a paragraph.

The disappearance of many simple races has been due to deliberate policy and wanton wickedness on the part of the white man. The evidence is overwhelming that British, French, and Dutch were equally concerned in the selling of strong spirits to the Indians in America, long after it was known that the traffic was likely to lead in the long run to the extermination of the race. The difference between West and East Africa has been expressed in the saying that, whereas in East Africa the first representatives of the white race with whom the Africans came into contact were men whose one aim was to deliver them from the agonies of the slave trade, on the west coast the white men most in evidence were those whose chief concern was with the sale of gin.

Undoubtedly some of the actions and policies of missionaries among primitive peoples have been unwise. The insistence on the wearing of clothes, often of most unsuitable and ungainly European clothes, was certainly a mistake and harmful to the health of the people; though it must be remembered that often it was the missionaries who tried to check the enthusiasm of the people for imitating everything that was done by their European friends, and to slow up the speed with which they rushed into so great a change from all the habits of life to which they had been accustomed.[1]

But it is clear that over and over again missionaries and governments alike have been faced by a problem that defies precise analysis – the inability of primitive man to adapt

1. It is interesting to note that James Chalmers of New Guinea, the most original and independent of the missionaries in the Pacific, did not expect his converts to take to the wearing of Western clothes.

himself to the shocks and complexities introduced by contact with a higher civilization. Even where there has been no violent oppression, even where governments have taken steps to protect simpler peoples and to maintain them as far as possible in their own way of life, apathy and decay have set in: the primitive people have failed to reproduce their kind in sufficient numbers to maintain the stock, and have begun to disappear through a process of sheer inanition. In these circumstances it may be maintained, with considerable evidence to support the contention, that the preaching of the Gospel, so far from hastening this decay, acts as a powerful counteracting force; by giving to a failing race new interests and a new impulse to live, it may initiate something like a resurrection from the dead. In most cases the factors involved are so complicated, and control so difficult to establish, that no serious student would dare to make more than the most cautious affirmations about the part played by Christian influences in either the decline or the rejuvenescence of a people. There is, however, one instance where the numbers involved are so small, and the figures so striking, and concerning which precise information is nowhere available in print, that it may be well to set out the facts in some detail.[1]

The Todas are a very primitive pastoral people, living in the Nilgiri Hills in South India. Until 1830 they dwelt in the remote seclusion of the hills, following their buffaloes, which wandered over the wide grassy downs more than 7,000 ft above the sea. They retained the very ancient Indian custom of polyandry, and it is almost certain that their numbers were kept down by the practice of female infanticide. When the tribe first came under European observation it seems to have consisted of about 1,000 people.[2]

In the 1830s the Nilgiri Hills were opened up as a sana-

1. I have briefly alluded to this situation in my book *The Christian Society* (London 1952), pp. 233-4.
2. The Todas have been the object of very careful anthropological research by W.H.R.Rivers, the results of whose studies were published at Cambridge in his book *The Todas* (London, 1906).

torium for Europeans. Ootacamund became the summer seat of the Government of Madras, Wellington the head-quarters of the Madras Army. The Todas were suddenly drawn out of their isolation, and exposed to all the disinte-grating influences of Western civilization. Syphilis was intro-duced among them, and, owing to their peculiar marriage customs, spread with frightful rapidity to every settlement. To this were added the harmful consequences of strong drink. The race began to die out. The census figures are most revealing. In 1871 the number was given as 681; by 1921 this had dropped to 640, and 1931 to 597. By this time the government was alarmed, and remedial measures were undertaken; the sale of alcoholic liquor to the Todas was strictly forbidden, and medical clinics were established. By 1941 the number had risen to 630; but it was reported that the majority of marriages was still barren, and that infant mortality was still very high.

In the meantime, however, a wholly new factor had entered in. The Todas had begun to be influenced by Chris-tianity. The first convert was baptized about the beginning of this century. In 1948 there were 142 Christian Todas, in twenty-six families. If allowance is made for barren mar-riages among the older converts, it is clear that the average number of children among the younger Todas Christians is more than four per family. Some Todas Christians have married outside the tribe; but no difference is observable between mixed marriages and pure Todas marriages; one mixed marriage has produced seven healthy children, one pure Toda marriage eight. Among the non-Christian Todas, it appears that remedial measures have just succeeded in arresting the decay; but evidently there is no danger of the Christian Todas dying out. Purer standards of morality, often unfortunately disregarded in practice, a new sense of value, the determination to master the problems of modern civilization instead of yielding to despair, have rescued this ancient and interesting race from what fifty years ago seemed to be inevitable annihilation.

If the Gospel is life, as well as way and truth, this is precisely what we should expect. It is in fact doubtful whether there is any area in the world in which it can be shown that the adoption of Christianity has hastened the decay or disappearance of a primitive people.

It has to be admitted that the main triumphs of the Christian faith, in its pilgrimage through the world, have so far mostly been won in areas and among peoples where there was no strongly established culture or religious system to resist the incursion of the new religion.

Greece and Rome were already long past their best when the Christian assault was launched upon them. The Christian Church managed to attract into itself a great deal of the best talent of the day. The Christians survived because they not merely out-lived and out-died, but also out-thought the pagans. With the single exception of Plotinus (and perhaps we should add the Roman historian Ammianus Marcellinus), there is no pagan Latin or Greek writer who can compare in interest or power with Origen or Tertullian or Augustine. What survived from the culture of the ancient world survived within the Church; the Christians were the heirs of Greece and Rome, just as they were the heirs of ancient Israel.

For more than 1,000 years the Church lived almost entirely within the world of Greek and Roman culture, and it was its cultural, as well as its religious eminence, which enabled it to win its way among the non-Christian nations. To this generalization there is one marked exception. The missionary enterprise of the Nestorian Churches, on the eastern fringe of the Roman Empire, penetrated in the eighth century as far as China. But Christianity, though it maintained itself in China for two centuries, failed to take deep root and eventually disappeared. Nor must it be forgotten that the conquests of Alexander had spread Greek influence far into the heart of Central Asia, and even to the frontiers of India; and that the Nestorian culture, though it expressed itself in Syriac, was not so much original as derivative from the Greek.

Among the barbarian nations – Goths and Vandals and

Franks, who poured into the Empire from the north and east – the Church found little in the way of culture or of organized religion that could resist the steady pressure of Christian missionary work. Some of the barbarians had become Christians even before the days of the great invasions. All were profoundly under the influence of the majesty of the Roman name, and readily susceptible to influences which derived from the great past of Rome. The difficulty which the Church then experienced, as it has again in later times, was not so much in convincing the barbarians that they ought to become Christians, as in persuading them to accept even the minimum of the moral demands which the Gospel is bound to make.

Christianity is a pervasive, and in some respects a levelling, influence. But it does not obliterate the characteristic marks of racial and national traditions. Even when the whole area of the old Roman Empire was Christian, there were marked differences in the form of the Church and the expression of the faith in the various cultural and racial zones of which it had taken possession; as between, for instance, the Levantine with its great centre in Byzantium; the genuinely Latin, which maintained its centre in Rome but presented some of its most characteristic manifestations in southern France and Spain; the Celtic, found in its purest form in Ireland; and the Teutonic, among the German tribes, which from the time of Charlemagne onwards began to be brought into the Church by a mixed process of persuasion and violence.

The case of the Scandinavian nations was rather different from that of the earlier invaders. They came under the influence of the Gospel only after the general medieval pattern had settled itself in southern and western Europe. 'The conversion of the northern peoples did not mean the victory of an alien culture and the loss of national independence, as happened to the continental Saxons or the Slavs of eastern Germany. The pagan North entered the society of Western Christendom at the very time when its social vitality was greatest, and its culture most creative. It was the work of the greatest of their own rulers, kings like St Vladimir in Russia, Canute the Mighty in Denmark, and Olaf Tryg-vason and Olaf the Saint in Norway.'[1]

This greater independence of the North, however, was only relative and not absolute. Latin became the learned language of Scandinavia, no less than of the rest of Western Europe, and only in Iceland was an authentic vernacular tradition preserved unbroken. Similarly in the East, Russian culture, of which, with an exclusiveness unknown in most of the other Christian countries, the Church was the cradle and the vehicle, bears the deep imprint of its origin in Byzantium. Until the twentieth century the word *Europe* has had a real meaning, though the exact geographical and cultural significance of the word might be hard to define. It has meant that part of the world in which thought, social life, and worship have been determined, imperfectly as all human things must be, by Christian norms, mediated through the Greek and Latin understanding of them, as those were developed in the life of the early Church.

In more modern times, as in the centuries of the Church's expansion in Europe, Christian propaganda has won its most conspicuous successes among peoples which, though not devoid of culture, had no developed systems of religious thought capable of standing against the new influences from without. The overwhelming impact of Western technical skill has sometimes to a dangerous extent seemed to commend to primitive man the effectiveness of the European God.

The great mission field of the present day is tropical Africa. In countries where, within the memory of living man, there was not a single Christian, there are to-day great Churches, with African priests and bishops and elders of their own. Progress has been so rapid that in many areas the Christian enterprise is borne down under the weight of its success, and the leaders are troubled that so superficial a Christian education is all that can be given to the multitudes

1. Christopher Dawson: *Religion and the Rise of Western Culture* (London 1950), p. 109.

who are pressing into the Christian fellowship. It is probable that there are in tropical Africa to-day more Christians than there were in the Roman Empire when Constantine made his historic decision to accept Christianity as the religion of the state.

What is true of Africa is true also of the islands of the Pacific. Almost half the population is now Christian; without any sensational or startling movement, between 1930 and 1947 the Christians increased from 30 to 44 per cent of the total population.

In India the great majority of converts has been drawn either from the depressed classes – the 60,000,000 people whom the Hindu religion excludes from all social privilege and recognition – or from the mountain and forest folk, whom the pressure of stronger races has gradually driven back from the more fertile lands and who have never been incorporated within the Hindu system. Although in a sense these groups may be classed among Hindus, since their ideas and way of life have been influenced by their Hindu neighbours and overlords, their religion is almost pure animism – and it is animism, with its lack of clear intelligible religious ideas, that has always found it hardest to stand against a determined and persistent presentation of the Christian Gospel.

There is nothing discreditable to Christianity in its success among the less cultured peoples of the world. From the beginning it was noted that not many wise, not many mighty, not many noble, were called into the fellowship. Many among the earliest Christians were slaves. The Gospel does come with a message of deliverance, hope, and manhood to those who are perplexed and oppressed; if they turn to it with expectations and hopes which are not wholly disinterested, this is no more than to say that Christ must create His own climate of thought, and that it is only in the light which He Himself gives that His message can be understood in its purity, and as it ought in sincerity to be received.

But even if the Christian Church were to win to itself all

the simpler and less privileged peoples in the world, it would still only be at the beginning of its task. What makes the contemporary Christian situation so intensely interesting is that, during the past century, the confrontation of the Gospel with all the other great religious systems of the world has become inescapable and the warfare of ideas has begun.

There are in the world to-day three great non-Christian religious systems, each reflected in a culture and order of society, which is penetrated through and through by the influence of its religious origins. One of these systems is the apotheosis of the priest, one of the wise man, and one of the prophet. To the Christian it is evident that the partial aspirations and insights of these systems can find their fulfilment only in one who combines in Himself the offices of prophet, priest, and king.

Hinduism is the religion of the priest. From a date anterior to the composition of the first books of the Old Testament, the Brahman was the man who knew; and what he knew originally was the ritual of the sacrifice, the tending of Agni the sacred fire, to whose ministrations kings and people looked for the satisfaction of their not very spiritual desires. In time the ritual became immensely complicated. Such importance came to be attached to the sacrifice, and in particular to the sacred formulas by which it was accompanied, that even the gods were regarded as being in some sense dependent on the due performance of the rites, and therefore the Brahman could be esteemed as even greater than the gods. The first beginning of philosophical speculation, as we find them in the earlier Upanishads, seems to have been a lay movement, and to represent an attempt on the part of the Kshatriyas, the warrior class, to break away from the priestly domination. Within a very short time the Brahmans had succeeded in acquiring the new technique, and in establishing themselves as the holders of the key of the new knowledge as of the old. In the ritual worship of the great temples, in the domestic rites which retain their importance in a land where, far more than in Europe, the family is the centre of existence, and in the Mutts, the monasteries in which deliverance through the way of wisdom is pursued, the Brahman is supreme.

Buddhism arose in India in the sixth century B.C. as an offshoot of Hinduism, and in part as a reaction against it. It has undergone the strange destiny of totally disappearing in the land of its origin, while extending and maintaining its hold on the neighbouring countries to south and east and north. In spite of the manifold differences in the later developments of the two systems, classical Buddhism, as one of the great world-denying religions, belongs to the same general type as Hinduism, and for our purposes can be treated in close connexion with it. Here the denial of the world is even more radical than in Hinduism. Everything is reduced to flux and illusion. There is no stability or continuity anywhere, even in the human personality, which is regarded as a succession of momentary states without any connexion between that which comes before and that which follows after. What holds man bound to this perpetual phantasmagoria is desire; with the renunciation and elimination of desire man can become free; in tranquillity he can establish his freedom from the world by rising superior to it. Here there is no question of God or grace or worship; the self can be saved by the self and by nothing else. It is not surprising that some observers have doubted whether the term religion can rightly be applied to such a system: 'We are in the presence of a system of thought and conduct which, whatever it may have developed into later, fundamentally has little, if any, of living, substantive religion in it. . . . It is small wonder, therefore, that many have denied that original Buddhism is religion at all, and, so far as my knowledge carries me, I would agree with this. Quite certainly its religious quality is highly obscure and problematical.'[1] Yet inner and outer peace are among the most clamant of the spiritual needs of mankind; and, since Buddhism claims to show the way to peace, it can hardly be denied that it has for those who follow it the significance of a religion.

Since Buddhism, in its older forms, dispenses with God

1. H.H.Farmer: *Revelation and Religion* (London, 1954), p. 201.

and with worship, here the place of the priest is taken by the monk. In a Buddhist country the monk is everywhere – the standing reminder to men that only by total renunciation of the world can peace and salvation be found. In Burma almost every boy passes some part of his earlier years in a monastery, thus being introduced at once to the practice and to the understanding of his religion. The monastery, by its maintenance of a learned tradition, and of a complex ritual in which readings from the sacred books play the major part, and by the services which it renders to religious instruction, plays a part not dissimilar to that of the Brahman priesthood and the Mutt in the Hindu system.

In the classical tradition of China, social ethics have almost taken the place of religion. This is the world in which the wise man rules supreme. It is no accident that Confucius is taken as the representative, *par excellence*, of the Chinese civilization, and of the values which it strives to incorporate. It would be wrong to regard the Confucian tradition as unreligious; behind its concern for the correct behaviour of the well-regulated man, there is a sense of the dependence of all earthly order on the sacred decrees of heaven; its aim was to establish a correspondence between the life of society and the sacred order, which had been handed down by tradition from the founders of Chinese civilization. The most notable expression of the Confucian spirit is filial piety – not merely respect for the elders, but an attitude of veneration towards the whole of the order that has come down from the past, and a self-subordination of the individual to the continuity and well-being of the family. It is a natural consequence of this attitude that worship of the ancestors has been to the present time the most living part of Chinese religion.

Islam is the religion of the prophet. This it is historically. It owes everything to the strange, passionate man, who in the seventh century welded some of the warring tribes of Arabia into a political and spiritual unity and launched them on a career of world conquest. Islam has no scripture other than the Koran, the whole of which was composed by the prophet – or, as the devout Moslem would say, was received by him through direct dictation as the very word of God, perfect and unalterable. The breath of the desert is in it – an immense simplification of creed and thought, under the impact of the felt presence of God in the wilderness; total submission to the will of God, accepted as absolutely supreme and inscrutable; a contempt for the gentler virtues, with a certain hardness and insensitivity of mind; above all a proud sense of being the bearer of the last and final revelation of the will of God to men. However far Islam may wander, it always turns back to Mecca, and always finds its renewal in a return to the austerity of its desert origins.

Each of these systems has in it a characteristic and immensely strong element of resistance to change.

Hinduism, in the realm of thought, is pliable, receptive, and resilient. It has absorbed materials from many quarters. One of the Vedas, the Atharva, is a collection of magical spells, some of them very ancient, some certainly of non-Aryan origin. But in structure the Hindu system is the most rigid in the world. At a very early date it evolved the organization of caste, which, though modified by the inclusion of new non-Aryan groups, has remained essentially unchanged for 2,000 years. The origins of the system are still, and perhaps always will be, obscure. The nature of it is simple; in whatsoever caste a man is born, in that he remains, and there is no power in heaven or on earth which can set him free from the obligations of that position: 'better thine own caste duty ill done', says the Bhagavad Gita, 'than another's caste duty well done'. The Western mind is quickly sensitive to the evils of the system – the paralysis of effort which results from it, the suppression of millions of people in the excluded groups, and so forth. The excellences of the system are not always so clearly recognized. It assigns to every one a place in society, with certain privileges which, though they may be very limited, are assured; it provides him with a brotherhood, in which, if the system is working properly, he is guarded against the hazards of unemployment and old age. He is separated from those of other castes; but he is assured of the support of those of his own caste, in a solidarity which, to give only one instance, often hopelessly baffles and frustrates the police in the investigation of crime. The caste-system is far older than any social order now prevailing in Europe. It may be taken as certain that there must be some solid merits in a system which has maintained a large society in a balanced stability for more than 2,000 years.

Of the Chinese order, it has been well said that it is the Gospel of unchangeableness. The rigid rules, which govern the actions of the well-educated gentleman in every circumstance of life, cannot be improved upon, and therefore there can be no need for change. The recent incursion of Marxism has subjected the Confucian order, inevitably feudal in many of its ideas, to more violent shocks than any which it has previously undergone; but China in the past has gone through periods of disorder lasting through centuries, and has emerged with its essential order unchanged: it may be that the Marxist period will be no more than another of these recurrent times of threat and disorder, and that the unchanging Chinese spirit will in course of time digest and absorb the Marxist foreign bodies, without radical modification of its own age-long character.

The unchanging stability of Islam is found not in the realm of social order or of ethical principle, but in that of religious practice. Unlike Jesus Christ, Muhammad laid down many detailed regulations for his followers; these have had the inevitable effect of to some extent ossifying Islam, of fixing it in the conditions of Arabia in the seventh century A.D., and of preventing it from being a progressive force in the affairs of men. On the other hand, the external signs of the five daily prayers, the fast of Ramadan and the pilgrimage to Mecca, create a felt unity among Moslems, which makes Islam in some ways the most effective world brotherhood that the world has yet seen. The changelessness of the prayers, their limited scope, and the sufficiency of external observance for the fulfilment of all Moslem obligation, tend to dry up the springs of spiritual feeling, and to produce an aridity against which the movements of the Sufis and other mystics are a continual protest. Nevertheless the devotion with which the commands of Muhammad are observed throughout the Moslem world are an example which may well put the adherents of other religions to shame.

How has Christianity fared in its confrontation with these other faiths and systems of ideas?

In the first place, it must be noted that the non-Christian systems, which at the beginning of the twentieth century seemed to show signs of senescence, have in the course of fifty years begun to give evidence of renaissance and new vigour.

It was often supposed by Christian propagandists in the nineteenth century that the ancient religious systems would not be able to stand against the undermining power of Western knowledge and science, and that into the vacuum created by the decay of age-long superstition Christianity would naturally enter. To a small extent, but only to a small extent, this expectation has been fulfilled. Many members of the new Western educated class in Asia and Africa have become detached from their old faiths; but very few of them have shown any desire to become Christians, and the gap left by the disappearance of the old faith is more often filled by secularism than by anything else. And the traditional religious systems, which for a short time seemed to have been severely shaken by the new contacts, have on the whole successfully rallied their forces and maintained their position.

In part, the renaissance of the old faiths has been an accompaniment of the political emancipation of Asia from the dominance of the West. One of the most important consequences of the first World War was the emergence in a new form of Arab nationalism, incorporated in a number of independent countries, strongly, even fanatically, Moslem in principle and united, though not very effectively, in the Arab League. Though India has been proclaimed a secular democratic republic, and both professes and practises religious neutrality, there are not wanting voices to proclaim that the destiny of India is to become Hinduraj, a polity based on the supreme authority of the ancient Hindu scriptures. Similar movements can be observed in Burma and Ceylon, where some nationalists would be pleased to see nationalism interpreted directly in terms of the Buddhist tradition, and political loyalty identified with loyalty to one particular form of religious faith.

It must be admitted that so far Christian propaganda has made little impression on the central citadel of these ancient faiths. Some outstanding individuals have been detached from the mass and have become Christians. Mr M. K. Gandhi's movement for the abolition of untouchability in India, though represented as a return to a purer form of the Hindu tradition, in reality owed almost everything to the teaching of the New Testament. But, in general, those who hold to the old ways are convinced of their superiority to any other, and are a little contemptuous both of the Western propagandist whose aim is to unsettle them, and of the form of civilization with which Christianity seems to have become inseparably associated. The Hindu despises the philosophical naïveté of the average European or American, and contrasts the simplicity of the West with the subtlety of the East, greatly to the advantage of the latter. The Chinese look down upon the bad manners of the West, its utilitarianism, and its ignorance of the art of living. The Moslem, secure in the possession of the last and final word of God to man, has nothing but contempt for 'idolaters', who every time they profess the Christian Creed commit the unpardonable sin of *shirk*, the attribution of a partner to God.

Christianity cannot successfully establish its position as a world religion unless it can meet the other great religions in fair fight, intellectual and spiritual, and decisively show its own superiority. It can do this only if it can demonstrate not merely its excellence as a historical way of life, but also that it has the answer to new questions, which are outside the range of the old religions, and is at home in new situations, for which the old religions have no message. There is already evidence that the Christian faith, if it is true to itself, has to its hand the material for victory in the inescapable warfare of ideas.

Hinduism is a great world-renouncing religion. Its ideal is the *Sannyāsi*, who has turned his back on every worldly attachment or responsibility. It can give significance neither to history, nor to human action in this world, which is always the world of *Māyā*, unreality. But the new India is conscious of a destiny in history. Its peoples recognize the duty to remake the whole life of their country; the very last thing that they propose to do to-day is to sit still and passive under the tyranny of fate. They are conscious of a vocation to play a part in the fashioning of history on the stage of the world. For this new attitude to life, Hinduism fails to supply either a rational guide or a spiritual principle. Christianity, if true to itself, can offer both. Alone among the great religions it is both world-denying and world-affirming. Jesus, to borrow a useful phrase from Mr Arthur Koestler, stands exactly midway between the Yogi and the Commissar.[1] He teaches that the fashion of the world passes away, and that all man's treasure must be in the unseen world. But, just because time is short and eternity is long, He is passionately concerned about the deliverance, in this life, of those whom Satan has bound. History becomes of immense significance. Christian faith is a fully adequate justification for every effort of man to master his environment, and to make life civilized, dignified, and beautiful for every human creature born into the world.

The Confucian tradition has given to China for millenniums stability, and an ideal of dignity and decorum in social life. But at two points the system is weak. In the first place, like the Jewish law, though it can point the way to right conduct, it knows no power outside man himself that can effect the transformation of human nature according to the ideal which it sets forth. This failure was savagely expressed as early as the third century B.C. by the Taoist critic

1. See *The Yogi and the Commissar* (London 1945), pp. 9–12, esp. p. 10: 'It is easy to say that all that is wanted is a synthesis – the synthesis between saint and revolutionary; but so far this has never been achieved.' Mr Koestler is not a Christian, and it is exactly at this point that the Christian would be prepared to take issue with him.

of the Confucianists, Chang Tzu: 'How extreme is the obduracy of these men, how boundless is their impudence. Does the cangue sum up the wisdom of the sages? Are the handcuffs, shackles, and tortures the expression of their benevolence and equity? Are not these statesmen more maleficent than the most infamous tyrants in history? There is truth in the proverb which says, 'Exterminate wisdom, destroy science, and the empire will return to order of its own accord.'[1] In the second place, Confucianism discounts emotion, and fails to recognize its importance both for social life and for the satisfaction of the religious needs of men. In China, as elsewhere, where emotion is suppressed or denied, it tends to find its outlet in aberrant and tangential ways. A truly balanced Christianity allows full scope for emotion, but for emotion disciplined by the will and directed towards practical service in the world. And the Gospel, rightly understood, provides the spiritual dynamic which no system of law can offer. After the troublous period of the Boxer rising at the beginning of this century, hundreds of young Chinese accepted Christian baptism; even those who still accepted much of the Confucian tradition recognized that the Gospel alone could give the moral and spiritual power needed for the regeneration of their country. Whether the same thing will happen again when the Communist waves recede, time alone will show; but one thoughtful Chinese Christian has already expressed the view that at that time the Church must be there, ready to make welcome numbers of 'disappointed revolutionaries'.

The weakness of Islam is in the character of its founder. Until the beginning of the nineteenth century, Christians were on the whole content to speak of 'the false prophet'. With the nineteenth century a reaction came, and such idealizations as are to be found in Carlyle's *Heroes and Hero Worship* became popular. Through the immense labours of critical scholarship both prejudice and legend have been dissipated, and the man Muhammad has begun to emerge –

1. Quoted in Christopher Dawson: *Religion and Culture* (London, 1948), pp. 168–9.

as one of the most remarkable men in history, as an ideal leader for the Arabs of the seventh century; but also with such grave defects of character as make it impossible that he should ever be the ideal and leader for the whole of mankind. The great Christian weapon in the controversy with Islam is the human character of Jesus Christ. Some few converts have been won from Islam by dialectical argument; the great majority have been drawn, almost unawares, by the character of Jesus Christ, and have found, almost to their dismay, that no one who has accepted Jesus as the ideal of human life can continue to be a Moslem. Evidence of a certain discomfort in the Islamic world is to found in modern lives of Muhammad by Moslems: there is a tendency for the less agreeable traits to be suppressed, and for a subtle process of transformation to take place, by which the picture of Muhammad is redrawn a little after the likeness of Jesus of Nazareth. If imitation is the sincerest flattery, this process may give the Christian stronger ground for hope in the ultimate triumph of the Christian idea than is afforded by the disappointingly slow growth of the Christian Church itself in Moslem lands.

In the nineteenth century Christianity emerged as a world religion, and became involved in its great debate with all the non-Christian religions of the world. At the same time, it was subjected to such severe assaults in the West as to make it seem at least possible that it might suffer in Europe and America the same fate as befell it, under the shock of the Moslem invasions, in its original homelands in the Levant.

The most evident and virulent assaults are those of Marxism, incorporated in the Communist system in Russia and its satellite countries. But it would be a grave mistake to regard Marxism as the enemy *par excellence*, and to identify the rest of the West with the cause of Christ and Christian civilization. The real enemy is materialism. From the point of view of, for example, an orthodox Hindu, there is little to choose between the Russian and the American ways of life. Both are products of Western materialism; both are alike in their extravagant emphasis on material things, and on the accumulation of possessions in this world; and in their failure to take account of the balancing factor of renunciation and denial of the world. Ever since man became man, his immediate concern has been with material things; he has had to live, and living has been for most men an exhausting and dangerous affair. But the contemporary materialism, which theoretically or in practice denies all importance to the spiritual, and shuts out from the perspectives of man's mind the mysterious and the eternal, is a new phenomenon; and one which, whatever compromises it may succeed in making with the organized Churches, is more dangerous to real Christian faith than any force of non-Christian or anti-Christian religion.

Schleiermacher defined religion as 'the feeling of absolute dependence'. The definition is open to certain criticisms, especially if the term *feeling* is interpreted as *emotion*, and not, as Schleiermacher intended it to mean, as *intuitive awareness* of an unconditioned reality beyond the immediate objects of our consciousness. Imperfect as his expression of his own intuitions may have been, Schleiermacher had correctly discerned something that has been central in man's experience and in his attitude to the world around him; he is dependent on the world and the mysterious powers that are hidden within or beyond it for his very existence; every part of his social and economic life has been shot through with that religious awe, which has been the expression of this sense of dependence on powers that are beyond man's control.

But now we have changed all that. The wonderful increase in technological skill has immensely increased man's control over his environment, and lessened his sense of dependence on it. The value of this achievement can be appreciated only by those who have lived for a time beyond the technological frontier – as, for instance, in an Indian village, where every drop of water must be drawn by hand from a well 20 ft to 40 ft deep, where light is supplied by a twist of tow floating in a saucer of castor oil, and transport is represented by the bullock cart, with a maximum speed of three miles an hour. It is not surprising that man, whether Marxist or American, has come to look forward to a time when his control over his world will be complete, and when he will have entered into the empire of his own achievement. It is true that neither Marxist nor American man has been able to master the last enemy – death, though modern science has made it much easier and less painful to die – and that too is a service by no means to be despised. Yet it is clear that, in so far as religion is dependence on unseen powers, its existence is threatened by man's new claim to independence.

The first and most evident consequence of the new materialism, both Marxist and Western, is the loss of the element of depth in human life. We are under the tyranny of that which can be numbered or measured or weighed. Pictorial art has become so concerned about form as to have little regard for content. Poetry seems to be rather the expression of the poet's own neuroses than the result of his wrestlings with the ultimate problems of human life. The garish, the vapid, the sensational glare continuously on men's minds, as brightly and remorselessly as neon street signs. Superficiality is the greatest of all threats to Christian faith. Religion can flourish only when the element of depth in human life is recognized and honoured.

This quality of depth is so important, and so little recognized in the modern world, that it may be well to quote here a description of it which, though difficult in style, sets forth in the briefest possible form all the essential elements of the problem:

In the cognitive realm the depth of reason is its quality of pointing to 'truth – itself', namely to the infinite power of being and the ultimately real, through the relative truths in every field of knowledge. In the aesthetic realm the depth of reason is its quality of pointing to 'beauty – itself', namely, to an infinite meaning and an ultimate significance, through the creations in every field of aesthetic intuition. In the legal realm the depth of reason is its quality of pointing to 'justice – itself', namely, to an infinite seriousness and an ultimate dignity, through every structure of actualized justice. In the communal realm, the depth of reason is its quality of pointing to 'love – itself', namely, to an infinite richness and an ultimate unity, through every form of actualized love. This dimension of reason, the dimension of depth, is an essential quality of all rational functions.[1]

Modern life does not yield many impressions of infinite meaning, infinite seriousness, and infinite richness. It rather suggests meaninglessness, triviality, and poverty. If contemporary Western society continues to lose the element of depth, it may yet become a soil in which no religion, no art, no dignity, no genuinely human life at all, can grow. And that would, naturally, be the end of Christianity in the West. But if a vacuum is created in the souls of men it will not long remain empty; other, and much less desirable forces may rush in: 'Under the guidance of technical reason autonomy conquered all reactions but completely lost the dimension of depth. It became shallow, empty, without ultimate meaning, and produced conscious or unconscious despair. In this situation powerful heteronomies of a quasi-political character entered the vacuum created by an autonomy which lacked the dimension of depth.[2]

Christianity has survived all the storms of nineteen centuries; but that does not mean that its survival in the future is self-evident or assured. There have not been lacking prophets who have foretold, either with jubilation or with dismay, the total disappearance of the Christian Church within a measurable span of time.

Our present study is factual and empirical, not prophetic; it cannot, therefore, include any confident predictions as to the future. But certain grounds can be stated for a sober expectation that the Christian faith will not disappear, but will continue to exercise a great and increasing influence in the affairs of men.[3]

1. Paul Tillich: *Systematic Theology*, Vol. I (London, 1953), pp. 85–6.
2. Paul Tillich: *op. cit.* p. 95.
3. The Christian assurance that 'the gates of hell shall not prevail against the Church' is clearly an affair of convinced Christians, and cannot, at the present stage of our argument, be used as a presupposition from which other conclusions can be deduced.

In the first place history bears witness to the extraordinary toughness of Christianity in the face of hostility and persecution. Like any other faith it can be destroyed in any given part of the earth's surface, but only by the process of total annihilation. Short of that, it has survived. The Reformation movement was brought to an end in Spain and Italy by the extermination of its adherents. In modern times, it appears that the small Christian movement in Central Asia was completely obliterated by the arrival of Bolshevism and Russian influence. Elsewhere the Church has survived. The Marxist attitude remains unchanged: religion is a superstition, natural to a childish stage in the development of the human race, but bound to disappear as people become enlightened and educated. But in Russia, in Bulgaria, in Yugoslavia, the homelands of Communism, the Church has not disappeared. It is difficult to judge how far it retains spiritual independence and freedom of action; but all reports indicate that such churches as remain open are crowded by people, and not by old people only, whose devotion is proof against the criticism and suspicion which in those countries attendance at church is bound to excite.

Secondly, the Christian faith, when it is true to itself, seems to hold more than any other faith, political or religious, the secret of the balance between tradition and renewal, between conservatism and adventure, between reverence for the old and joyful acceptance of the new. The conservative is timid in the face of change. The revolutionary despises the old, and therefore tends to produce a rootless and uneasy order of society. Both stability and change in due proportion are necessary to human welfare. It must be admitted that in general Christians and Churches have been among the most timid conservatives, not to say reactionaries, in the world. But this is contrary to the true nature of the Church. The promise of its Founder was that the Holy Spirit would lead the disciples into all truth; its concept of truth is dynamic, not static. To the Christian, all discovery is a form of the service of God. All new truth is truth from God, which may be joyfully, though not precipitately, welcomed, even though its effect may be to modify some existing ideas, and to put out of currency some venerable formulations of truth.

Thirdly, the Christian Church in the present day has shown itself in certain respects most adaptable and flexible.

When the Church is founded in a non-Christian country, it is at the start wholly dependent, spiritually and often financially, on its foreign founders. This undeniable fact is the basis for the charge that Christian missionary expansion has been no more than a part, and sometimes a tool, of Western imperialism. 'First the missionaries, then the traders, then the gunboats.' There is just enough truth in this assertion to make it worthy of passing mention. Whatever may have taken place in the past, no such allegations can be made in the changed situation of the twentieth century. The new Churches in Asia and Africa and elsewhere are no longer colonies of the West. They are independent Churches, responsible for their own life and providing their own leadership. During the war years many Churches in the Pacific and elsewhere were completely severed from Western aid and Western leadership; none of them collapsed. Since the Communist invasion the Churches in China have gradually been cut off from all participation in the world-wide Christian fellowship; but at present there is every indication that they will be able to survive and to grow, under the grave disadvantages of isolation.

The Christianity of these younger Churches still tends to be imitative, and too much dependent on Western ideas and categories of thought. But there are heartening and increasing signs that the Churches in each of the great regions of the world are becoming genuinely indigenous, and learning to impart to their understanding of the Christian faith a character of their own not derivative from the experience of the West. This process, as it goes forward, should both enable each particular Church to become genuinely at home in the country of which it is called to be the soul, and should make of the universal Church a treasury which all the nations can enrich by bringing into it the varied richness of their own inheritance.

Fourthly, the Christian Church is showing increasingly a capacity to be the one genuinely world-wide society, and to seek again that unity for which it has always prayed, and which it has always recognized to be an essential constituent of its life.

During the second World War almost the only links between the warring nations which were not broken were the spiritual links maintained between Christians on opposite sides of the fighting front. When the war ended, it was found possible to restore at once the previously existing fellowship, even though the nations continued to be technically in a state of war. The separation in thought and outlook between the Western countries and those in which Communist control has been established is now almost complete; yet the Christian community in East and West is still conscious of its unity. Communication becomes increasingly difficult, and that unity is at times grievously strained. Christians on both sides of the barrier are influenced by the politics and the propaganda of their own countries, and at times find it hard to understand one another. But a time may come in which Christian faith is the only bridge left to unite two warring worlds which have lost every other instrument of mutual understanding.

The separate parts of the world-wide Church are becoming much more conscious of one another than they were. The most representative Christian assembly, geographically, ever to be held, was the meeting of the International Missionary Council held at Tambaram near Madras in 1938; there representatives from sixty-four countries in all parts of the world were present, and were immediately conscious of a unity in Christ that transcended differences of race, language, cultural background, and confessional tradition. The most representative gathering, ecclesiastically, was the second Assembly of the World Council of Churches at Evanston in 1954; in this delegates from each of the main sections of Christendom, except the Roman Catholic Church, participated. These are only specially notable indications of a process of co-operation and closer integration which is perhaps the great new feature of the life of the Church in the twentieth century.

To the outside observer, the movement towards integration is much less evident than the divisions of the Christian world. Almost every village in England gives evidence of those divisions; a weakness in predominantly Christian countries, they are a disaster in lands where Christians are still a small minority of the population.

Yet this appearance, and this reality of division, should not be allowed to obscure the measure of unity which does actually exist in the Christian world. On the central doctrines of the faith, almost all Churches and almost all Christians are agreed. If the Nicene Creed is taken as the basis of comparison, that acute observer Dr Edwyn Bevan has reckoned that the area of agreement is not less than 85 per cent of the whole. If Christians are compared with one another, the differences may be startling. If they are compared with, for example, either Hindus or Moslems, the differences seem almost insignificant in comparison with those matters in which all agree.

But the Christian world has moved far beyond this general agreement in doctrine. It has created immense interdenominational fellowships, through which Christians, without fusion of Church organization, can act and express themselves in common. And, in the twentieth century, it has set itself, with greater seriousness than ever before, to overcome the barriers of sectarian division, and to work towards complete fellowship in a single body. Since 1910 more than thirty united Churches have come into existence. Every kind of barrier has been surmounted – that between episcopacy and non-episcopal organizations, those arising from relations with the state, or from differences in liturgical tradition and doctrinal emphasis. In a few cases union has been marred by fresh division, some part of one or more of the uniting Churches remaining still in separation. But none of the united Churches, which have come into existence through these movements for reunion, has broken up into its constituent parts or has failed to maintain itself. And the interest in Christian union has spread far beyond those Christian bodies which are immediately concerned with it. Even in the Roman Catholic Church, which has not abated one jot of its claim to be *the Church* in a sense which denies the right of every other Christian body to claim that title, the most devout spirits long intensely for union with those whom they are happy to call their separated brethren.

A fully united Church is a dream which belongs to a very distant future; but every movement towards Christian union is likely to increase the effectiveness of the Christian bodies in the affairs of men.

Fifthly, if there is ever to be a reintegration of religion and culture, there is no candidate but Christianity for the role of that religion, in which the culture of the modern world might find again its focus, its inspiration, and its vital principle.

Many scholars have demonstrated in recent years that there has never been a great culture in history which has not had a religious basis. One of the reasons why 'to-day man experiences his present situation in terms of disruption, conflict, self-destruction, meaninglessness, and despair in all realms of life' (Tillich) is that religion and life have become separate, to the disastrous distortion of both. 'Thus we have a secularized scientific world-culture, which is a body without a soul; while on the other hand religion maintains its separate existence as a spirit without a body.'[1]

Whether religion, and in particular the Christian religion, will ever re-establish itself as the point of unity and balance for all the diverse activities of man, it is impossible now to predict. Already there are signs that the question is being seriously faced from both sides. Churchmen are more aware than they were that the abdication of the Church in the field of culture has been in part responsible for the moral chaos of today. Some poets and artists have begun to abhor the vacuum which they have found their world to be, and

1. C.Dawson: *Religion and Culture* (London, 1950), p. 216.

are turning back to the mysteries of man's being and the problems of ultimate existence. It may be that our present discouraging and untranquil age is suffering from the birth-pangs of a better age that is to be.

But even if we reach agreement as to the possibility that all these things may come to pass, we have still not begun to consider the essential questions posed by the Christian message and the existence of the Christian Church.

We may see good reasons for moderate hope that the Church will survive, and will continue to display its marked capacity for self-adaptation to changed conditions. Its present expansion to the uttermost parts of the earth may continue, until the Gospel has really been preached to every nation upon earth. The number of its adherents and its influence on all the affairs of men may increase. A reintegration of the separate elements of spiritual life may be achieved, and Christian faith may become the basis for a new world-wide culture.

But all these things would be achievements in time; and, though the Gospel rests on events which took place in time, and though it is greatly concerned with the life of men in time, its chief concern is not with time but with eternity.

The ambiguous and erratic career of the Christian Church in history should not be surprising to anyone who has read the Gospels. Christ plainly told His disciples that their life would always be like His – marked by weakness, suffering, and persecution. The Church would be (and this in sharp contrast to its Founder) a body of sinful men, like the first disciples, called by Christ and in process of being perfected, but very far as yet from perfection. Evil in the world would not grow less, but would grow with the growth of the Church; and the bitterest conflicts would be at the end. There is no suggestion in the New Testament that the course of the Church will be marked by steady growth and development until it triumphantly fills the earth. The triumph will come not by the working out of some inner principle of growth, but by a new act of God.

The Church is by its very nature transitory and provisional. The Kingdom of God was visibly manifest in Jesus Christ. It will be visibly manifest again in power, at the end of the ages, when God, by a new act now inconceivable to the minds of men, winds up all the processes of history and brings in the hidden consummation. 'For this corruptible must put on incorruption, and this mortal must put on immortality. But when this corruptible shall have put on incorruption, and this mortal shall have put on immortality, then shall come to pass the saying that is written, Death is swallowed up in victory.'[1]

The Church belongs to the period 'between the turning-points'. It is appointed to bear witness to something beyond itself. All that is promised is that the gates of hell shall not prevail against it, and that when the end comes, the Church will still be found existing as the witness to the new age, and as the nucleus of the new humanity which has been brought into being through the redemption wrought by Jesus Christ.

The purpose of God is affirmed, in the Bible and in the Christian creeds, to be a purpose that is working itself out in time, but of which the fulfilment can be known only in eternity. Is it possible for us, even now, in some measure to grasp the nature of the consummation to which Christian faith looks forward, and to understand, however dimly, the eternal purpose which, if the Gospel is true, God has purposed in Christ? To that subject we must now turn, and that shall be the end of our enquiry.

1. 1 Corinthians xv: 53–4.

9

BEYOND TIME AND SPACE

EVEN if the Christian Church were to spread to every corner
of the earth and eventually to include within itself every
single living human being, its success in the realm of time
and space would not necessarily guarantee the truth of its
claims, and might leave unanswered one of man's most
anxious questions – is this life all that there is, or is there
something beyond?

The question is of importance both for the individual and
for the race.

Sooner or later human life on this planet will come to an
end. The end might come suddenly and unpredictably,
through erratic movement on the part of one of the heavenly
bodies, like that of the asteroid Hermes to which reference
was made in our first chapter. It might come in the way
brilliantly and grimly depicted by Mr H. G. Wells in *The
Time Machine*, through the gradual cooling of the planet
until life in any form in which we know it now is no longer
possible upon it. But, whatever the manner, the fact is certain. Man's tenure upon earth is not freehold but leasehold;
whether the lease has many years to run or few, we are not
in a position even to guess; we know, without a shadow of
doubt, that one day it will run out.

Then, if the materialists are right, everything is at an end;
the striving, the aspiration, the nobility, the baseness of
human life, all end in a handful of dust:

> To-day the Roman and his trouble
> Are ashes under Uricon.

Even if the materialists are right, the Gospel of Jesus
Christ is still the best news that has ever broken in upon the
history of the world. If there is nothing but time, if the life
of mortals, of the whole human race, is evanescent, and no
more than a bubble in the universe –

Like the bubbles on a river,
Sparkling, bursting, borne away –

if no more is given to us than a moment, we can at least make that moment noble, and as comfortable as may be for others like ourselves. And nothing in the world has yet equalled the power of the Gospel to make men forget themselves, giving themselves in devoted service to others, and to make life endurable, where it cannot be happy.

But, in fact, Christianity like almost all other great religions, affirms the polarity of time and eternity. For Plato, time is simply the moving image of eternity. For the Hindu, it belongs to the world of illusion and unreality. For the Christian, time is that sphere in which a purpose of God is being worked out; but the consummation of the purpose cannot be realized in time; the fulness of its meaning must be made manifest elsewhere. Time is the loom on which the garment is being woven, the wheel on which the pot is being shaped. When the work is done, the loom is abandoned, the wheel is broken; what has been woven, what has been shaped endures:

Time's wheel runs back and stops,
God and thy soul endure.

At a much earlier stage of our study, we set out, quite provisionally, the Christian conviction that history is the scene of a divine purpose in which the whole of history is included, and that Jesus of Nazareth is the centre of that purpose, both as revelation and as achievement, as the fulfilment of all that was past, and the promise of all that was to come. The nature of that purpose was then left vague, on the understanding that an attempt would be made at a later stage of the argument to define it. If God is God, and if He made all these things, why did He do it? Is it possible to discern any pattern in His weaving? If our long argument has suggested any answer, this is the point at which that answer must be set forth. Here is the answer:

God created a universe, bounded by the categories of time, space, matter, and causality, because He desired to enjoy for ever the society of a fellowship of finite and redeemed spirits, which have made to His love the response of free and voluntary love and service.

The Biblical revelation begins with the simple affirmation that 'In the beginning God created the heavens and the earth'. It ends with the promise that 'his servants shall do him service: and they shall see his face; . . . and they shall reign for ever and ever'.[1]

This tension between time and eternity is characteristic of every part of the New Testament.

St Paul says, 'If in this life only we have hoped in Christ, we are of all men most pitiable'.[2] Belief in Christ has enlarged men's views of the dignity of man and of the destiny that God has appointed for him; it has offered in His resurrection a guarantee that hope and aspiration are not ultimately frustrated, that immortal longings are given to man just because he is potentially immortal, and that what on earth can never be more than the broken lights of the spectrum will eventually coalesce in the white radiance of eternity. If all this could be shown to be false, just because of the brightness and apparent reasonableness of the hopes that men had set on Christ the bitterness of the disappointment would be unbearably keen.

But the New Testament is full of the joyous and confident affirmation that now there is no doubt at all. The resurrection of Jesus Christ is not regarded as an isolated event; He is the firstfruits, the one in whom has been for the first time revealed the glory that God has laid up in store for all those who through faith share in the new and triumphant life of Christ. 'Now hath Christ been raised from the dead, the firstfruits of them that are asleep.' 'Our Saviour Christ Jesus, who abolished death, and brought life and incorruption to light through the gospel.' 'Blessed be the God and Father of our Lord Jesus Christ, who according to his great mercy begat us again unto a living hope by the resurrection of Jesus Christ from the dead.'[3] It would be tedious to

1. Genesis i: 1; Revelation xxii: 5–6.
2. 1 Corinthians xv: 19.
3. 1 Corinthians xv: 20; 2 Timothy i: 10; 1 Peter i: 3.

multiply examples. The Christian Gospel is otherworldly through and through; it adds to time the dimension of eternity, as that without which time cannot be understood.

In view of constant misuse of the word, the nature of Christian otherworldliness requires to be rather carefully set forth.

To the Christian, time and eternity are not consecutive phenomena – as though in this life we were entirely bounded by time but immediately after death would enter on an unconditioned state of eternity. Nor are the two concepts to be understood spatially, as though time were below and eternity above. They are different dimensions of existence, which can coexist and for the Christian actually do coexist, since through faith in the resurrection of Jesus Christ he already participates in eternal life. 'Verily, verily, I say unto you, He that heareth my word, and believeth him that sent me, hath eternal life, and cometh not into judgement, but hath passed out of death into life.' 'For the wages of sin is death; but the free gift of God is eternal life in Christ Jesus our Lord.'[1]

This participation in eternal life here and now is affirmed to be possible because in Jesus Christ God has already acted, and brought in the new age of deliverance and fulfilment. Two aeons, two epochs, of world history coexist. There is the old epoch of frustration and decay, to which we all by nature belong. This is the stream of time, that wears away even the strong mountains and carries away all that can be destroyed. The characteristic form of this aeon is law, as exemplified in the pitiless and unchanging uniformity of nature. Since all mankind is marked by the stigma of aggressiveness, inordinate desire and self-assertion, law issues in that just judgement of God, under which the whole of the old dispensation stands. The new aeon is the realm of light, life, victory, deliverance, and fulfilment. Its

1. John v: 24; Romans vi: 23. The 'free gift' is that which has already been given in Christ, not that which will be given 'at the end of the world'.

ruling principle is love, which issues in forgiveness and self-forgetful service. The cross and resurrection of Jesus Christ proved once for all that love is stronger than hate, and that the pillars of the universe are truth, loyalty, and justice. Through the perfect obedience of Jesus as man to the will of God, the new aeon is an already present actuality in the world, and the way into it is open to all men through faith in Christ.

The peculiar tension in the life of the Christian is that he belongs simultaneously to both aeons, the old and the new. His perplexity is that he is bound, by his loyalty to Christ, to allow his life to be shaped wholly by the principles of the Kingdom of love, of which he is now a citizen; yet he may not deny the continuing reality of the old order of law and decay of which, as a man, he is still a part. The dilemma is perfectly expressed by St Paul: 'And be not fashioned according to this world: but be ye transformed by the renewing of your mind, that ye may prove what is the good and acceptable and perfect will of God.'[1] The Christian continues to live and move in the old order; yet his life is not to be determined by its principles or practice, but by those of the new invisible order, which, in so far as it can become concrete in time and space, finds, or should find, its visible expression in the Church.

Many of the failures and imperfections of the Church and of Christians can be traced to confusion as to the relationship between the old aeon and the new.

Some Christians have been tempted to deny the reality of their continued participation in the old, and have believed that they could live a purely 'spiritual' life. The history of all perfectionist movements shows that, if the reality of the old is denied, it will reassert itself in brutal, violent, and most disturbing forms.

Others have lived in a kind of perpetual schizophrenia, cultivating an intensive inner spiritual life, but admitting in their daily life and business principles which they know to

1. Romans xii: 2. The word translated *world* is the Greek word *Aeon* or world order.

be contradictory of everything that they profess in the sphere that they have reserved for religion.

Yet others have divided the world between God and the devil. Denying any responsibility of the Christian as Christian for the world of politics, of social or economic life, they have left all those great spheres of human life to be directed by autonomous principles of their own, without challenge from the Christian ethic, and without demand that in those spheres also the law of God shall be acknowledged and obeyed. The results have been seen in the recrudescence of the law of the jungle in our civilization. The daily life of men is corrupted and impoverished, because it is cut off from its spiritual roots; the life of the Church becomes as frail and artificial as that of cut flowers in a vase, because it has abandoned the basic doctrine of the concern of God with the whole of man's life.

It is indeed most difficult for the Church and for the Christian to do justice, in due proportion, to the claims of both the aeons with which they are concerned; to avoid on the one hand a spirituality which is content to enjoy the jam of life without due concern for its bread and butter; and on the other an optimistic social activism, which fails to take seriously the radical contradiction between the two aeons and the principles by which they are governed. But this is no more than to say that the life of the Church is lived under conditions of tension; and this is a mark of its provisional, interim character.

When the Church is true to its own nature, it recognizes the difference between the aeons, and finds an experimental balance between the service which it owes to each.

The Church itself should be governed wholly by the principles of the new aeon. It is the place of forgiveness, of love and unconstrained mutual service, in which any element of coercion is wholly out of place. It is to be a colony of heaven, the members of which already have their citizenship elsewhere and not here.[1] This being so, it cannot regard anything within the sphere of time and space as of ultimate

1. Philippians iii: 20.

importance; it lives in perpetual expectation of a deliverance and a consummation, which cannot come through man's effort and striving, and yet, by another of those apparent contradictions which meet us in many contexts in the Christian faith, depends also on man's faithfulness in his appointed task.

In so far as the Church is faithful to its own nature, it ought to appear visibly as a society different in kind from any other that exists on the earth. The charity by which all its members are supposed to be bound together should be a perpetual challenge to other societies held together by different bonds of union. The principles by which it lives should be a continuous judgement on the motives by which other men and societies are generally impelled.

But the Church is concerned with much more than its own interior life, and has much more to occupy it than the functions of critic and judge. It professes faith in One of whom it is written that He took upon Himself the form of a servant; the Church is not the Church of Jesus Christ unless it makes itself the servant of the world.

The Christian who pays attention to the New Testament records is not likely to be deluded by utopian expectations of the future. He knows that good and evil grow together, and will do so until the time of the end. He knows that evil, cast forth in one form, displays the utmost ingenuity in transforming itself and finding its way back in another. He knows that the Kingdom of God will not come upon earth until God Himself is pleased to bring it in by a new act of His sovereign power. But he also recognizes that, though no human society can ever correspond exactly to the will of God for men, some societies are much further away from that will than others. Cruelty, oppression, and exploitation are always directly contrary to the will of God; the elimination of them is always a form of service to Him. This is the charter for the social activity of the Christian and the Christian Church.

Social and philanthropic service of others is the necessary and unforced expression of something at the very heart of

Christian life. The many enterprises in which it takes form stand as signs, to those who can see, that the powers of the age to come, the new aeon, have already broken in on the old world that is passing away.

But the Church has a wider function than the merely philanthropic to perform. It is called to serve as the conscience of the nations. Its task is so to educate national conscience that what once seemed tolerable becomes intolerable, and that the nations will no longer endure wrongs which have been taken for granted as incurable. No politician to-day would dare to defend slavery, as less than two centuries ago it was defended in the House of Lords by the Duke of Clarence, later King William IV, and by the Bishop of Llandaff. The doctrine of Rousseau and new ideas concerning the rights of man may have had something to do with the change in national feeling. Historically there is no doubt that it was the doctrines of Jesus Christ, as set forth by Wilberforce and his friends, that brought about a late but far-reaching change in human ideas of the dignity of man as man. When the education of national conscience has reached a certain point, the new conviction will find its expression in legislation, by which indurated wrong is exposed, condemned, and for ever abolished. In the constitution of the new Indian Republic, untouchability has been legally abolished. Western ideas of equality may have had something to do with the change; but it was Christian missionaries, first and almost alone, who had prepared the way by showing what the despised untouchable can do if he is treated as a man, loved, educated, and given a chance to develop the God-given powers that are latent in him.

In its three-fold task of strengthening its own inner life, of preaching the Gospel to every creature, and of witnessing to the righteousness of God in every sphere of human life, the Church has more than enough to occupy it until the end of the age. But what happens then? What happens when time finally runs down, and eternity takes its place? At present the Christian lives in a perpetual tension, because of his relationship to the two aeons which are in radical contradiction to one another. But this state of tension will not last for ever. The old aeon will come to its appointed term; to quote another Biblical expression: 'This word, Yet once more, signifieth the removing of those things that are shaken, as of things that have been made, that those things which are not shaken may remain.'[1] When all those things that can perish have perished, then only that which can partake in eternity will remain.

Let it be made plain at the outset that, placed as we now are within the limitations of humanity, we can speak only hesitantly and symbolically of eternity.

All our thought is conditioned by the categories of time, space, and matter. As long as we are in the body we can never escape from them, and it is no use imagining that we can. True, the recognition of the limiting factor itself demands, as a necessity of thought, that we should posit the existence or at least the possible existence of the unconditioned; the recognition of the idea of time itself gives birth to the corresponding idea of timelessness. But it is impossible for us to give any positive content to the idea of timelessness. There are occasions on which we cease to be *conscious* of the passage of time. There is a famous passage in the *Confessions* of St Augustine, in which he describes how, as he sat with his mother Monica at the port of Ostia shortly before her death and conversed with her of divine things, their minds were led up step by step to such rapt contemplation that for a moment time and change had ceased to be; and he suggests that, if such a moment could be prolonged and never cease, that would give a picture of the unitive intuition of God and of reality such as we may hope to have in the eternal world. But, though for the moment we may cease to be conscious of time, time has still proceeded at his even pace; the fire has burned down in the grate, the shadow has gone down on the dial; and nothing that we can do or experience here can stay his course, or give us more than a faint indication of what a timeless existence might be.

Our inability to speak positively of eternity does not mean

1. Hebrews xii: 27.

that we can say nothing positive as to the being of the eternal God. Mysticism has always made use of the *via negativa*, the way of denial – whatever is affirmed of God must be immediately denied, since no human word can be adequate to what He is, and every human affirmation implies limitation in Him who by definition is illimitable. This way ends with the *Neti, Neti*[1] of Brahmanism – whatever you say of God, that He is not. This is directly contrary to the realism of the Biblical revelation. It is true that God must always remain *mysterium tremendum*; if He were not mysterious, He would no longer be God. Christian hope recognizes that, even in eternity, there will be infinite depths in the being of God which no finite creature can ever penetrate or apprehend. The finite can never become *capax infiniti*, able to comprehend the infinite; if it could, it would have ceased to be finite. But, if the Christian Gospel is true, we are not so much concerned with God as He is in Himself, as with the God who has been pleased to make Himself known, who has bound Himself by chains of unchangeable faithfulness to His creation, and who is known, as we are, in the experience of relatedness. Concerning the God who participates in the life of His creation, and who speaks in revelation, the New Testament makes the three tremendous affirmations that God is Light, God is Love, and God is Spirit; in these three phases, the whole of Christian theology is implicitly contained.

Similarly, though we cannot form any precise intellectual concepts of eternity, we can make a number of positive affirmations about it; and though these must necessarily be symbolic in form, that does not mean that they are not genuinely significant.

The classical passage on this subject in the New Testament is in the First Epistle of St John: 'Behold what manner of love the Father hath bestowed upon us, that we should be called children of God: and such we are. . . . Beloved, now are we children of God, and it is not yet made manifest what we shall be. We know that, if he shall be manifested,

1. The Sanskrit words mean literally 'saying No, saying No'.

we shall be like him; for we shall see him even as he is.'[1]

The vision of God is the end of all Christian hope and aspiring. What that vision may be is now inconceivable and beyond description. But if God is such as Christian faith, basing itself on the words of Jesus Christ, has affirmed Him to be, three convictions as to the nature of eternal fellowship with Him may be put forward tentatively but with a certain measure of confidence.

The first is that, in eternity, the human will will be unshakably set upon God. The trial and the tragedy of existence in time and space is the indeterminacy of the will. The will is ever and always the battlefield of human life. To the believer, God is the source of all good; only in fellowship with Him can the human spirit find its peace, only in His service can the human will find its satisfaction. Yet even those who have most earnestly set their wills towards Him know well how easily they are distracted and turned aside, how their best intentions are frustrated by a will which still tends to turn as a weathercock in the wind. 'From his hands who fondly loves her ere she is in being, there issues, after the fashion of a little child that sports, now weeping and now laughing, the simple tender soul, who knoweth naught save that, sprung from a joyous maker, willingly she turneth to that which delights her. First she tastes the savour of a trifling good; then she is beguiled and runneth after it, if guide or curb turn not her love aside.'[2] The best that can be hoped of in this life is the *beata potestas non peccandi*, the happy power of not sinning, which comes through constant dependence on the grace of God and constantly renewed fellowship with Him. But this is not given in perpetuity; it is maintained only in conflict and tension. Eternity offers the *non posse peccare*, the impossibility of sinning, when the will is no longer variable, but unalterably fixed on God. All this is summed up superbly by Dante's Piccarda in a single line:

E la sua volontate è nostra pace.[3]

1. I John iii: 1–2.
2. Dante: *Purgatorio* xvi: 85–93.
3. *Paradiso* iii: 85. 'And His will is our peace.'

Secondly, spirits will be perfectly translucent to one another, because they will be seen as they are in God. Here we are opaque to one another. Even the closest friendship has its disappointments, the deepest love its frustrations. When God is all and in all, the barriers to fellowship will be taken away, and we shall know one another as we are in the fellowship of perfect love.

Thirdly, service will be perfected, without weariness and without frustration. The Biblical picture of heaven includes both perfect rest and perfect service. Under earthly conditions these are mutually exclusive. The recalcitrance of the material which here we have to use means that all work involves friction and consequent weariness. The artist is always frustrated by his medium; he can never attain to the perfect expression of his inner vision. But there, in the eternal world, since purpose and achievement correspond, effort can be made without weariness, and service can never experience frustration:

> *Ubi non praevenit rem desiderium,*
> *Nec desiderio minus est praemium.*[1]

Are these things possible? Amid the chaos of this decaying world, is it reasonable to hope for such fulfilment of imperfect earthly promise and such accomplishment of that which earth seems to deny?

Clearly, judgement on the Christian hope must depend on a prior judgement on Christ Himself. Is He really the link between time and eternity? Did His coming into the world constitute a real descent of the vertical upon the horizontal, a real entry of eternity into time?

The modern mind does not find it easy to take seriously the possibility that a particular series of events could have universal significance, and that the whole destiny of man could be determined by a single life.

The difficulty arises in part from the dominance of the

1. The hymn *O quanta qualia*, by Peter Abelard (1079–1142):
> 'Nor is the heart's possessing
> Less than the heart's desire.'
>
> (Tr. Helen Waddell.)

physical sciences in contemporary education and categories of valuation. The scientist, like the philosopher, is concerned with uniformities. He abhors the exception. If exceptions occur, new experiments are made, new hypotheses formulated, until the exception itself is included under a more accurately expressed and more comprehensive law.

Precisely the opposite is true of the historian, the artist and the theologian.

In the spheres of what the Germans call the *Geisteswissenschaften*, the sciences of the spirit, it is precisely the exceptional, the individual, the particular, which is of importance. This is so because of the peculiar character of personal life. A rabbit can be regarded just as one specimen of the species *rabbit*. A man can never be so regarded. Generalizations can be made about the human species, but these can never exhaust the truth about any single man. Each individual is what he is by virtue of participation in the race, and something more. In the perplexing phrase of Kierkegaard, every man is both himself and the race.

Paradoxically, the more individual a man is, and the less he is like his fellows, the greater is his importance, and the more universal is his significance for the race. It is the concrete which is universal, and not the generalization.

No artist is ever completely original. All stand in a succession of experience and technical achievement. But the greatest artists are those who are most themselves, whose art is most perfectly the expression of an individual personality, an individual apprehension of reality; and whose work is therefore least imitable by others. No one has ever painted portraits quite like Rembrandt, because no one else has shared both Rembrandt's peculiarly tragic experience of life, and the technical excellence of his powers of expression.

Hamlet is universal. Yet in the play there is hardly a single generalization about the nature and destiny of man. Shakespeare has poured his own profound broodings about life and death into the experience of a single young man of sensitive and imaginative temperament caught in the vice of an

L.I.F.E. College Library
1100 Glendale Blvd.
Los Angeles, Calif. 90026

intolerable situation. Here concreteness and universality are not felt to be in any way mutually contradictory.

Prof. Paul Tillich has helped us greatly by pointing out the difference between two pairs of opposites, which are often confused – the general and the particular; the universal and the concrete. A particular instance of a general *law* can have no special significance, much less a universal significance. But the concrete exemplification of a general *principle* is always significant; and there is no *a priori* reason why in certain circumstances the perfectly concrete should not also be of perfectly universal significance.

Prof. Tillich believes that Jesus of Nazareth *was* the concrete which was also of universal significance. He gives two memorable reasons for believing this to be so. The first is His complete transparency, so that at every moment He is manifesting the One whom He has come to reveal, and is able to say with perfect truthfulness, 'he that hath seen me hath seen the Father'.[1] The second is His willingness to sacrifice Himself, all personal aims and claims and possessions, to the fulfilment of His mission. 'The first point is clear in the Gospel reports about the unbreakable unity of his being with that of the ground of all being, in spite of his participation in the ambiguities of human life. The being of Jesus as the Christ is determined in every moment by God. In all his utterances, words, deeds, and sufferings, he is transparent to that which he represents as the Christ, the divine mystery.' 'The acceptance of the cross, both during his life and at the end of it, is the decisive test of his unity with God, of his complete transparency to the ground of being. . . . He not only sacrifices his life, as many martyrs and many ordinary people have done, but he also sacrifices everything in him and of him which could bring people to him as an "overwhelming personality" instead of bringing them to that in him which is greater than he and they. This is the meaning of the symbol "Son of God".'[2]

If in the life of Jesus we see the perfectly concrete which

1. John xiv: 9.
2. Paul Tillich: *Systematic Theology* (London, 1953), Vol. I, pp. 151–2.

is also universally significant, how is the uniqueness of this universally significant manifestation to be explained? What is the relationship between this manifestation of being and what Prof. Tillich calls the ground of being? In more familiar terminology, what is the relationship between Jesus and God?

Much of the theology of the last 150 years has introduced great confusion into this issue by the use of terms susceptible of a variety of meanings.

Historical criticism has restored to us a living sense of the reality of Jesus as man, and has allowed us to read the Gospels with a new sense of the power and pathos of the human story which they disclose. And so we are presented with a theology which expresses itself in such phrases as 'Jesus divinest, when thou most art man'. We are told that we should not distinguish too sharply between the divine and the human, between God and man; man is made in the image of God; God belongs to man just as man belongs to God. This view contains two profound truths, of which we must never lose sight; that no revelation is possible at all unless there is such a kinship between God and man as sin has not been able to destroy; and that, if a full revelation of God to man is ever to be made, it can be made only under the conditions of a fully and genuinely human life. But to let the matter rest there is not to exhaust the problem but to evade it.

At one time preachers were in the habit of saying that God is like Jesus. Again, the phrase has its element of truth. It is true that, in spite of the fragments of truth preserved in other religions, and in spite of the value of the Old Testament achievement, almost everything we know of God is really derived from the words and works of Jesus. But we are still left with the problem of relationships. *Why* is Jesus so much like God that it is possible to invert the equation and say that God is like Jesus?

Others have maintained that we are all in our measure sons of God, and that Jesus is called *the* Son of God, only because He achieved in a superlative degree what we all have it potentially in us to become, and what, through following His example, we can become. Full weight has been given to this argument in our section on the representative relationship of Jesus to the human race. The moment we try to press it further, it breaks down on the question of the sinlessness of Jesus. *Why* did one achieve, where all others failed? And why is it that all my efforts to be a son of God as Jesus was are frustrated through my imprisonment in isolation and sinfulness?

If the terms 'divine' and 'human' no longer suggest a radical antithesis, there yet remains one radical distinction, which no evasive language can cover up, and which sets forth in the plainest light the question which the Christian Church had to answer in the earliest centuries, and which sooner or later the individual seeker has to answer for himself. It is the distinction between the Creator and the created thing. The carpenter made the table; the table did not make the carpenter. There is no possible ingenuity of language by which the parts played by the carpenter and the wood can be inverted or confused. And this single analogy does not go nearly far enough, since all that the carpenter is doing is to make a rearrangement of already existing material. When the Scripture says, 'It is he that hath made us, and we are his; we are his people and the sheep of his pasture',[1] it indicates something far beyond the relationship between the carpenter and the table, and establishes creatureliness as the indelible character of the human race in its relationship to God. The question we are bound to ask, and sooner or later to answer, is, is Jesus the Christ a part of this created universe, or, in this radical antithesis, is He on the side of the Creator? The question may be answered in one sense or the other, but no hedging can be permitted.

This was the battle which was fought out by the early Church in the Arian controversy, and which was settled in principle at the Council of Nicaea in A.D. 325. Arius was prepared to accept the Christ, the Word of God, as the highest of created things, the chief of the powers of the created world; but beyond that he would not go. Again, to borrow the help of Prof. Tillich, 'the Church fought desperately

1. Psalm c: 3.

against the attempt of Arianism to make the Christ into one
of the cosmic powers, although the highest, depriving him
of both his absolute universality (he is less than God) and
his absolute concreteness (he is more than man)'. 'Being
created out of nothing means having to return to nothing.
The stigma of having originated out of nothing is impressed
on every creature. This is the reason why Christianity has to
reject Arius' doctrine of the Logos as the highest of the
creatures. As such, he could not have brought eternal life.'[1]

From the time of the New Testament, this is the answer
which the Church has always given; if we posit the absolute
contradiction Creator: created, Jesus of Nazareth, very man
and very God, is to be found on the side of the Creator. In
that faith the Church has always lived.

Over and over again the New Testament makes it clear
that Jesus of Nazareth is to be regarded not as a product of
natural development from within humanity but as a new
power from God, through which a wholly new beginning
was made in the history of the world. 'Ye know the grace of
our Lord Jesus Christ, that, though he was rich, yet for your
sakes he became poor, that ye through his poverty might
become rich.'[2] These words of St Paul are unintelligible, if
Jesus is regarded as no more than the highest stage yet
reached in the upward progress of man towards God.

When the earliest Christian thought had exhausted itself
in finding terms in which to express its understanding of
what Jesus had done for men – prophet, Messiah, servant of
the Lord, captain of salvation, Son of God – it ended its long
search in the adoption of the Greek word *Logos*, the Word,
to set forth its deepest apprehension of the truth. 'In the
beginning was the Word, and the Word was with God, and
the Word was God.'[3] On the one hand, the mysterious
Word of the first chapter of St John reaches back to the Old
Testament, to that 'word of the Lord' by which the heavens
were made. On the other hand, it has its roots in Greek

1. Paul Tillich: *op. cit.*, pp. 21, 209.
2. 2 Corinthians viii: 9.
3. John i: 1.

philosophy, where *Logos* also means reason and proportion – that rational element in the structure of the universe, which makes it a possible object of rational study by man; and also reason in men, the faculty by the exercise of which he is most akin to God. If one single English word is to be chosen, *revelation* seems to be that which best represents the range and flexibility of the Greek word.

'In the beginning.' We are at once taken out of the world of time and space, and are warned that we are dealing with eternal realities. 'The Word was God.' God, in His own inner being, is and remains to us an inscrutable mystery: for this reason it is said that no man hath seen God at any time. But it also belongs to the nature of God that He is a self-revealing God, and has both the power and the will to make Himself known. The verses which follow set forth four modes and stages of the divine self-disclosure.

'All things were made by him [the Logos, who was God]; and without him was not anything made that hath been made.' The visible creation is, in its degree, a manifestation of the being of God: in it, as St Paul says, are to be discerned His everlasting power and divinity.[1]

'In him was life, and the life was the light of men.' In the coming into existence of man as man, the created being became self-conscious, with that power of standing outside himself and judging himself, which is commonly called conscience; this power of self-transcendence in man marks a further stage in the operation of the *Logos* as the self-revelation of God.

'There was a man sent from God, whose name was John.' The Word became the word of God in man; John was only the last, and in some ways the greatest, of the long line of prophets, who had been so possessed by the conviction that the word of God dwelt in them that they had spoken unconditionally in the form 'Thus saith the Lord'; and the consciences of men had confirmed in experience that what had been spoken was the truth of God.

'The word became flesh and dwelt among us, and we

1. Romans i: 20.

behold his glory.' The word *flesh* signifies human nature, in its poverty, its weakness, its limitations. This is the final stage of the self-revelation of God; the everlasting *Logos* makes Himself perfectly one with the human race under the conditions of human life as it is lived by men. Beyond that perfect self-identification no further step in self-identification can ever be imagined, and this is therefore the term and crown of the self-disclosure of God to men.

To put it briefly, the *Logos*, the divine word, had come forth and found expression in four modes. The word was power. The word was light. The word was speech. The word was man. That this union of the Being of God and the being of men in Jesus Christ is an inexhaustible mystery may well be granted; but nothing less than this, and nothing other than this, is the faith by which the Church has lived.

What else is the meaning of Christmas? Does the world join to celebrate just the birth of another Jewish baby a very long time ago? Even if Jesus had been no more than this, His birth would still be the most important event in the history of the world. But the significance of Christmas for the Christian is other than this; and, as a Christian would affirm, infinitely more satisfying. What it means has never been better expressed than in the great orthodox hymns of Charles Wesley:

> Him the angels all adored,
>   Their Master and their King;
> Tidings of their humbled Lord
>   They now to mortals bring.
> Emptied of His majesty,
>   Of His dazzling glories shorn,
> Being's source begins to be
>   And God Himself is born.
>
> Let earth and heaven combine,
>   Angels and men agree,
> To praise in songs divine
>   The incarnate Deity;
> Our God contracted to a span,
>   Incomprehensibly made man.

Is this possible, and is it true?

First, we must note that the Christian affirmation concerning the Incarnation, or the deity of Jesus Christ, is not primarily an affirmation concerning a historically conditioned man named Jesus of Nazareth, who somehow or other managed to climb up to be God. It is an affirmation concerning the nature of God Himself as love.

This disposes at once of the objection that Christians have spoiled the simple story of the Gospels by overlaying it with irrelevant considerations of dogma and theology. The Gospel story is only deceptively simple; the deepest questions are there, unless we shut our eyes to them. No doubt it is possible to listen to, and to some extent to appreciate, Bach's *Passion according to St. Matthew* without any knowledge whatever of musical form. But the ignorance of one listener does not affect the fact that the form is there; and it would be generally agreed that appreciation of Bach's titanic achievement is greatly enhanced by even an elementary knowledge of fugal form and of the principles of counterpoint. No doubt it is possible to read and to love the Gospel story without attempting to face the questions that arise from it. But the indifference of one reader does not alter the fact that the problems are there, and that they must be faced by all who want to go beyond a superficial acquaintance with the New Testament text. All the New Testament books were written 'from faith to faith', by people who believed certain things about Jesus of Nazareth, and desired to produce or to strengthen like faith in their readers.

The ministry of Jesus turns on the issue of His unique and special relationship to God. Although He teaches His disciples to pray 'Our Father', He never uses the expression in His teaching, or in a context where He Himself could be included in the term 'Our'. In one passage the distinction is expressly made: 'I ascend unto my Father and your Father, and my God and your God.'[1] But the implication in the

---

1. John xx: 17. The reader is reminded that most theologians recognize in the fourth Gospel a greater amount of interpretation, and less of precise historical record, than in the other three.

constant use of the words 'My Father' is the same. He claims that He knows and does the Father's will; in the light of that claim, He demands of His followers implicit obedience and full surrender. In return, He offers Himself to be to each man that which he needs for the fulfilment of his being, and this universally; so that, though He is still the same Jesus, He is a different Jesus to Peter and to James and to John – as can be seen clearly in the differing but complementary pictures of Him given in the New Testament, and in the infinitely diverse but true apprehensions recorded by the saints in nineteen centuries.

If Jesus is able to fulfil this promise, is this sufficiency for the need of every man something that can be supplied by One who was Himself no more than man? Contrariwise, if the promise is made and is not kept, must not Jesus be written off as the great deceiver and the great deceived?

This is the point which was firmly grasped by Robert Browning, and set forth, with that poetic intensity which to many people is much more convincing than theological disquisition, in the closing lines of *A Death in the Desert*:

> If Christ, as thou affirmest, be of men
> Mere man, the first and best but nothing more –
> Account Him, for reward of what He was,
> Now and for ever, wretchedest of all.
> For see; Himself conceived of life as love,
> Conceived of love as what must enter in,
> Fill up, make one with His each soul He loved:
>
> See if, for every finger of thy hands,
> There be not found, that day the world shall end,
> Hundreds of souls, each holding by Christ's word
> That He will grow incorporate with all,
> With me as Pamphylax, with him as John,
> Groom for each bride! Can a mere man do this?
> Yet Christ saith, this He lived and died to do.
> Call Christ, then, the illimitable God,
> Or lost!

> But 't was Cerinthus that is lost.

So much from the side of Jesus. But what from the side of God? If God exists, is it possible that He should wear the robe of human frame and live as a man among men; that omnipotence should be exchanged for weakness, omnipresence for the limitations of a human body, omniscience for the limitations of a human intellect? Is it possible, is it likely, that the source of all life should elect to die?

The whole basis of our argument from the beginning has been that we must not *a priori* rule out any possibilities, unless they are seen to involve a logical contradiction. The doctrine of the Incarnation does not involve any logical contradiction, though it does involve holding together in a unity of thought categories of being – time and eternity, infinity and the finite, deity and humanity – which we do as a matter of fact find it extraordinarily hard to hold together. But to be difficult is not the same as to be impossible. If we lived in a simple, closed universe of mechanical interactions, where all effects followed upon measurably determinable causes, there would indeed, as Laplace so rightly saw and said, be no place for the hypothesis called God, and the problem of the Incarnation would therefore not arise at all. We now recognize that that simple, closed, mechanically determined universe was a nineteenth-century myth, now as out of date as crinolines and bustles and other contemporary furniture of the Victorian age. The new humility of science (though not of all scientists), and its willingness to recognize again the complexity and the mystery of existence, while it cannot create religious faith, makes faith a less difficult business for the thoughtful man than for his predecessor of seventy years ago.

It all depends on what we are prepared to consider it possible that God might do. No definition of God that is at all adequate can be devised; but that which comes nearer to practical adequacy than any other is the medieval affirmation that God is that than which nothing greater can be conceived. Religion has tried to affirm this greatness in a variety of different ways. It has magnified His power. 'Lift up your eyes on high, and see who hath created these, that bringeth out their host by number: he calleth them all by name; by the greatness of his might, and for that he is strong in power, not one faileth.'[1] And indeed, when we consider the immensity of the universe as astronomy has revealed it to us, and the power that is hidden in every one of the atoms of which the world is made, we may well agree that, if there is a Creator of all these things, He must be inconceivably great in power. Others have emphasized the mystery of the being of God. Some of the early Christian Gnostics just called Him 'Depth', the Abyss. 'Behold, I go forward, but he is not there; and backward, but I cannot perceive him; on the left hand, where he doth work, but I cannot behold him: he hideth himself on the right hand, that I cannot see him.'[2] Again we may well agree that, if we try to understand the being of God, we shall be like the little boy whom, according to the legend depicted in Botticelli's famous picture in the Uffizi Gallery in Florence, St Augustine found trying to pour all the waters of the sea into the hole which he himself had dug in the sand. But the Christian affirmation is that the inconceivable greatness of God is not to be understood in either of these ways (though neither of them is denied), but in His love for all created beings. Love is something which, though very imperfectly, we do understand from within, and we know something of the degrees of it. The theist or the unitarian believes in a God who is universal benevolence, or even love. But that love remains in the tranquil serenity of a transcendent divine existence, or does not go beyond a veiled sympathy for all the groaning and travailing of created things. Such a God may be great; the Christian believes that he knows an infinitely greater. 'For scarcely for a righteous man will one die: yet peradventure for the good man someone would even dare to die. God commendeth his own love towards us, in that, while we were yet sinners, Christ died for us.'[3]

1. Isaiah xl: 26.
2. Job xxiii: 8–9.
3. Romans v: 7–8.

There, far from fear and danger,
  Sweet Peace sits crowned with smiles,
And One born in a manger
  Commands the beauteous files.
He is thy gracious Friend;
  And – oh! my soul awake! –
Did in pure love descend
  To die here for thy sake.

If that is true, I will maintain against all comers that my God, deserted, bruised, bleeding, dying, is greater than any other that has ever been thought or imagined or worshipped by man; that this God is, in fact, that than which nothing greater can be conceived.

There are times when we are so afflicted by the suffering in the world that we are inclined to shake our fists at the sky, and blaspheme whatever God allows such things to happen in His world. If we are concerned about the hundreds of thousands of refugees, who are homeless and workless and rotting in the cheerless camps that are all that civilization has been able to provide for them, we may be inclined to say to Him, 'What is the use of telling these people about you? You know nothing of what it is really like to be a refugee, and therefore you are not in a position to help them'. To which He might well answer, 'Did you never read that it is written, the Son of Man hath not where to lay his head?' Or, watching some helpless and cruel suffering, we might resentfully say: 'Why do you permit such suffering that you do not share?' and we might not immediately catch His answer, 'Well, have you ever tried being crucified?' Or, reading the record of those horrible trials in the totalitarian countries, where men are somehow constrained to condemn themselves out of their own mouths and then to stand in court listening to their friends swearing their lives away, we might say roughly, 'Here, at least you don't understand anything about that', forgetting that He is entitled to say, 'Excuse me, but having been through it, that is precisely what I do understand'.

Is it possible? We have no right to exclude the possibility.

If there is a God who is the Creator and Ruler of all these things, and if that God is love, and if He elected to manifest His love by living as a Man among men, without safeguards and without advantage, what in the world is there to prevent Him? True, the human life of God (to use a convenient phrase of H. R. Mackintosh), being by definition unique, must needs present a to us perplexing combination of the obvious and the unusual. But, if God were to choose to live a human life, could we wish that life to be in any particular different from the life that was actually lived in Galilee and Judaea 1,900 years ago?

But is it true? There are many who find themselves held back from belief, because they have heard so much talk of wish-fulfilment, and of belief conditioned by desire. They are afraid to believe, because what they are invited to believe seems to be too good to be true. But that is the one thing which we may never say in a world, which, in spite of imperfection, suffering, and frustration, still finds a place for the song of birds, the laughter of children, and the love of friends.

In the end a point comes when intellect has done its utmost and lays down its arms. Faith is an act of the whole man, in his complex constitution of emotion, intellect, and will, of feeling, thinking, and deciding. In matters of faith, will is by far the most important of the three. Intellectual exposition can only prepare the way; in the end the issue reduces itself to a simple 'Yes' or 'No', 'I will' or 'I will not'.

The end of this long argument has been reached. We have tried to handle the material honestly, to evade no difficulty, to understate rather than to overstate conclusions, and to indicate the cumulative process of investigation, by means of which an enquirer may be helped towards an honest decision. What follows after must be left to the free choice of A and B.

In the last book of Plato's *Republic* there is a magnificent myth, in which Er the Egyptian descends into the underworld and sees the souls of men preparing to re-enter the world in a new incarnation. Each soul is free to choose its own condition in the new life; and paradoxically Odysseus, the great seafarer, is seen to choose the simple life of a countryman, far from the sea. As the souls choose the clear proclamation is made – αἰτία ἑλομένου Θεὸς ἀναίτιος – responsibility for the choice rests upon the chooser; God is not responsible. This ancient tale can easily be given a Christian application.

God brings constraint to bear on no man's will. He desires nothing but a free and voluntary offering. This is seen plainly in the life of Jesus. He calls men to His service, but His authority is exercised in freedom and without coercion. Even those who have joined Him are free to leave Him if they will. He gives Himself up unresistingly into the hands of men, and allows them to do with Him as they will. What God was in Jesus, that He is always and in Himself. It is His pleasure to treat us as free and reasonable beings. 'Come now, and let us reason together, saith the Lord'[1] is the word through the ancient prophet, and it has never been withdrawn. God submits Himself to our inspection, allows us to discuss Him at our pleasure; pleads with us, but exercises no coercion; leaves us our freedom to say 'Yes' or 'No'; in the end allows us to do with Him as we will. And, paradoxically, the judgement of God now, and at the end in what is called the judgement day, is simply the judgement that we have passed upon ourselves by our judgement upon Him.

There is a story, almost certainly apocryphal, of a visitor to a great picture gallery who, after making the round, said to the custodian, 'I don't think much of your pictures'; to which the custodian replied, 'Sir, it is not the pictures that are on trial'. The foolish critics who a generation ago decried Milton told us nothing about Milton, but told us a great deal about their foolish selves.

There was a day when all the world came together for the trial of Jesus Christ – soldiers and lawyers, townsfolk, pilgrims, strangers from abroad; Pharisees, Herodians, Scribes,

---

1. Isaiah i: 18; cf Micah vi: 2: 'for the Lord hath a controversy with his people, and he will plead with Israel'.

and all the rest. Pontius Pilate the governor sat down upon the judgement seat, arrayed in all the authority and majesty of imperial Rome, and the Son of man was brought before Him to receive His sentence. It is well that we should remember that, in reality, it was Pontius Pilate who was being judged.

SHORT BIBLIOGRAPHY

There is an immense literature on all the subjects dealt with in this book. Here only a few indications can be given; and each book listed here will give valuable indications for further study:

GENERAL

BEVAN, EDWYN. *Christianity* (Home University Library: Oxford, 1932)

CARPENTER, S. C. *Christianity* (Pelican Book: London, 1953)

LEWIS, C. S. *Mere Christianity* (London, 1952)

CHAPTER 1

BOUQUET, A. C. *Comparative Religion* (Pelican Book: London, 1942)

BUTTERFIELD, H. *Christianity and History* (London, 1949)

DAWSON, CHRISTOPHER. *Religion and Culture* (London, 1948)

DIXON, W. MCNEILE. *The Human Situation* (Gifford Lectures, 1935–7: London, 1937)

FARMER, H. H. *Revelation and Religion* (London, 1954)

CHAPTER 2

BRUNNER, EMIL. *Christianity and Civilisation* (London, 1948–9)

HEIM, KARL. *Christian Faith and Natural Science* (London, 1953)

RAVEN, C. E. *Science, Religion and the Future* (Cambridge, 1943)

CHAPTER 3

NAIRNE, A. *The Faith of the Old Testament* (London, 1914)

ROBINSON, H. WHEELER. *Redemption and Revelation* (London, 1942)

ROWLEY, H. H. *The Rediscovery of the Old Testament* (London, 1946)

CHAPTER 4

DODD, C. H. *The Apostolic Preaching and its Development* (London, 1936)

GORE, C. *Jesus of Nazareth* (Home University Library: Oxford, 1929)

HEADLAM, A. C. *The Life and Teaching of Jesus the Christ* (London, 1923)

TAYLOR, VINCENT. *The Life and Ministry of Jesus* (London, 1954)

TURNER, H. E. W. *Jesus, Master and Lord: a Study in the Historical Truth of the Gospels* (London, 1953)

SHORT BIBLIOGRAPHY

CHAPTER 5

NIEBUHR, REINHOLD. *The Nature and Destiny of Man* (Gifford Lectures: London, 1941–3)

SHERRINGTON, CHARLES. *Man on His Nature* (Cambridge, 1946; also a Pelican Book: London, 1955)

CHAPTER 6

HODGSON, LEONARD. *The Doctrine of the Atonement* (Hale Lectures, 1950: London, 1951)

MACKINTOSH, H. R. *The Christian Experience of Forgiveness* (London, 1927)

CHAPTER 7

LATOURETTE, K. S. *A History of Christianity* (London, 1953)

NEILL, S. C. *The Christian Society* (London, 1952)

NEWBIGIN, LESSLIE. *The Household of God* (Friendship Press, 1953)

WILLIAMS, CHARLES. *The Descent of the Dove* (London, 1950)

CHAPTER 8

BELL, G. K. A. *Christianity and World Order* (Penguin Books: London, 1940)

BELL, G. K. A. *The Kingship of Christ* (Penguin Books: London, 1954)

LATOURETTE, K. S. *A History of the Expansion of Christianity.* 7 volumes (London, 1938–45)

NEILL, S. C. *Christ, His Church, and His World* (London, 1948)

WARREN, M. A. C. *The Christian Mission* (London, 1951)

CHAPTER 9

BAILLIE, JOHN. *And the Life Everlasting* (London, 1934)

CREED, J. M. *The Divinity of Jesus Christ* (Hulsean Lectures, 1936: Cambridge, 1938)

MATTHEWS, W. R. *The Problem of Christ in the Twentieth Century: an Essay on the Incarnation* (Maurice Lectures, 1949: London, 1950)

TEMPLE, WILLIAM. *Christianity and Social Order* (Penguin Books: London, 1942)

TILLICH, PAUL. *Systematic Theology.* Vol. I (London, 1953)

INDEX